PREPARE TO COME ABOUT

by Christine Wallace

Maggie —
To a long-time
friend and a great ally
in business — Fair winds always

Published by
Pig Dawg Press, a division of Windline Press LLC.
100 Pine St #204
Bellingham WA 98225
windlinepress.com

Cover design by Casey Burton, Happy Chaps Media

Text: Minion Pro

ISBN 978-0-9909137-0-2

For my families, both blood and salt-water.

Prepare To Come About

(Continued)

Alice came to a fork in the road.

"Which road do I take?" she asked.

"Where do you want to go?" responded the Cheshire Cat.

"I don't know," Alice answered.

"Then," said the Cat, "it doesn't matter."

— Lewis Carroll, *Alice in Wonderland*

Chapter 1

Endo-ed

"You know, Jeffery, there are times when if I saw a pregnant woman walking toward me on the sidewalk, I would cross the street rather than acknowledge her. I swear to god I would."

The waitress carelessly slid our drinks in front of us and arched one eyebrow in reaction to my statement. Jeff raised his glass, lightly clinking it on the rim of my frosty mojito. "Well then, here's to expectant couples everywhere—may they continue to procreate until you retire a rich woman and are able to keep me in the lifestyle to which I hope to become accustomed."

The cocktail lounge of the Atlanta Peachtree Plaza was situated so that it commanded a panoramic view of the comings and goings of the lobby patrons. I whipped the muddled mint leaves into little cyclones with my straw and continued to people-watch. Elevators chirped their arrival while the hotel's giant revolving doors whooshed round and round, spilling travelers into the brightly lit chamber. The hustle and bustle all around us contrasted sharply with the dimly lit, fern encrusted lounge where we sought our repose. Piped-in Gordon Lightfoot Muzak wafted about the tables, endeavoring to mitigate the sound of commerce that encircled us.

Jeff and I stopped by the lounge only long enough to fortify ourselves for the coming afternoon of taxis, airports and shuttles. Our suitcases and shopping bags lay scattered around our feet as we grabbed a few moments of relative peace and quiet prior to the journey home.

It had been an exhausting three-day conference, packed with seminars about obstetric interventions, new trends in childbirth and talks on alternative practices. My brain was full and my ass was sore as a result of too many hours in too many stuffy boardrooms. I would have preferred to skip this year's event. I hated to leave my kids behind and I was finding it difficult to extract myself from Gracewinds. However, an offer to present at a national childbirth conference was hard to turn down. Jeff and I both realized that the exposure and credibility were benefits that were too good to pass up. As Gracewinds CEO, I simply had to show.

I managed to coerce my eldest son into returning home for the week to watch his four siblings. At 23, Trent was more than capable of handling his youngest sister Juliet. However it was Trent's ability to rein in his teenaged twin sisters that was my primary interest, coupled with the fact that his mere presence would (I hoped) squelch any designs that my rebellious son Dane had of throwing another wild party in our absence. The daily phone conversations I had with Trent lasted just long enough to reassure us that Juliet was being fed and making it to her third grade class daily—and that there had been no raging keggers held on the premises. Nevertheless, it was apparent by Trent's tone after the first day that he was ready for us to come home and resume our parental responsibilities.

Jeffery glanced at his watch and then tossed back the last of his scotch. He stood and stretched, and with a big yawn announced it was time to gather up our stuff and search out a cab. My gaze took in his long, lean frame and I flashed a wide smile. The events of the previous evening replayed briefly in my mind. It wasn't often that Jeff and I could spend romantic time alone without the interruption of children, dogs or laboring women. We made the most of our opportunity while at the conference.

"Why are you grinning?"

"No reason. Jeez, can't a girl look?"

"Well, you can look all you want to once we've made it to the airport, but if we don't hustle up, we won't get there."

I gave an exaggerated sigh as proof of my assent and rummaged through my shoulder bag to confirm the whereabouts of our airline tickets. We wheeled our bags across the expansive hotel lobby to the revolving doors and were spun, then spit-out into the oppressive Atlanta sun.

"Holy crap, it's only mid-May and it's already baking hot out here!" Jeff complained as he waved down a doorman.

At that moment, my cell phone buzzed. It was Trent calling. I stepped aside so that Jeffery could handle the luggage. Once safely out of the way, I flipped open my phone. "Hullo?"

"Hey Mom. You gotta sec?"

Now, as most parents are aware, there's this little nerve at the base of the neck that sort of tingles when any whiff of suspicion arises concerning their offspring. This was just such a case. "Uh yeah, but I'm getting in a cab here to head to the airport. What's up?"

"Yeah, OK, real quick then… Sooo, Dane and his buddy had a little trouble this morning. I just wanted to let you know."

I glanced over my shoulder as Jeffery tossed the last suitcase into the trunk right before the cab driver slammed the lid closed. I gave my husband the *hang on for a sec* gesture while continuing my conversation. Jeffery responded with the finger-pointing-at-wristwatch *we gotta go* gesture, which I pretended not to see.

"Uh, Trent, what exactly do you mean when you say 'a little trouble'?"

"Oh well, it seems they were sitting out on the front porch, sorta smoking, and this dude that Dane's friend knows drives up. Apparently he's got some beef with Dane's buddy, so he's yelling at 'em from his car. And so then Dane walks over to the curb and y'know, they both tell this guy to take off. Then I guess, Dane notices that the car's probably stolen, 'cuz there's no cover on the steering column and wires are poking out and shit, y'know, like they do."

"Huh, no. I didn't know they did that. So, where are you while all this is going on?"

"Well, I took Juliet to school and then went to play some Frisbee golf down at the range. I just got home a couple hours ago."

"OK. So, then what happened?"

"I guess the guy got really pissed off that they were yelling at him to leave and so he like, backs his car up and revs it up to kind of ram it into Dane's buddy's Jeep, right? Except that his fender gets all tangled up in the Jeep's wheel well or somethin' and then his whole car just sort of flips over."

4

Jeffery walked over to escort me into the idling cab. I brushed him off and pressed Trent for more answers. "Jesus Christ. What do you mean the car 'sort of flipped over'?"

Upon over-hearing my end of the conversation for the first time, Jeffery said. "What? Who's car flipped?!"

"Shhh!!"

"It just kind of endo-ed, y'know what I mean? ...Just kinda landed upside down on its roof."

"Who the hell are you talking to? What car?"

I waved at Jeffery to quiet down so I could hear Trent talk. The cab driver was now looking at his watch. We climbed into the back seat and I continued, with Jeff straining to hear the other side of the conversation.

Our residential street in north Seattle was extremely narrow with parking allowed on both curbs. There was barely enough room to drive one-way. I couldn't fathom how a car could "endo" without hitting another parked car. By now Jeffery was nearly apoplectic, he'd deduced that the voice on the other end of the phone was Trent's and had gathered the significance of our topic.

"Did any other cars get damaged when it flipped over?" I envisioned the General Lee from *Dukes of Hazzard* flying through the air and dramatically landing upside down on top of our neighbor's Audi Quattro. Trent hastily tried to reassure me.

"No, no, nobody else's car got hit. The kid was kinda pinned inside his car and then Sasha ran over and grabbed him by his collar and sorta drug him out of the car through the window. Dane ran inside the house and called the cops right away. But then the guy breaks free of Sasha and takes off... the cops show up and chase after him. And that's when I showed up. Yeah, that's about it. "

I sank back in the taxi's seat and gave a huge sigh. Thank god! I knew very well that Dane bore no love for the police and would certainly never have invited them to stop by, unless he had nothing to hide. The rest of Trent's story I didn't care so much about—I just didn't want yet another tete-à-tete with the SPD concerning the subject of my second-born son. I envisioned what our neighbors must be thinking by now. I could see it all: my son's pitbull puppy standing over a car thief who had just crashed a stolen vehicle in front of our house—no, not crashed, "endo-ed" it.

I managed to elicit enough information from Trent in order to reassure Jeffery that we wouldn't be returning home to any pending lawsuits and then hung up the phone. *Christ on a cracker.* I was beginning to wonder at the metric butt-load of irony pertaining to my owning a business for new families, when I could just barely manage my own.

Eventually our taxi pulled alongside the departure lane at Hartfield-Jackson International. We stepped out of the back seat and were instantly confronted with a cacophony of car horns, loudspeakers and engine exhaust. Jeffery and I shouldered our carry-ons, yanked up the handles of our wheeled luggage and queued into the labyrinth for the ticket counter. I ran my hand back and forth along the velveteen cable that cordoned off the passengers... I felt relief to be heading home. Yet there was a nagging anxiety that gradually crept back into my consciousness. It was a feeling I knew very well by now. The holes in the dike were springing even more leaks, and it appeared that I might be running out of fingers to plug them.

Chapter 2

Sanctuary

The clamor of Seattle's afternoon rush-hour sifted down through *Sugaree's* butterfly hatch. The heavy *thunk-kathunk-kathunk* of cars driving across the drawbridge grate echoed along the water below. Mingled with the sounds of traffic on the Ballard Bridge were the hollow slaps of waves against *Sugaree's* fiberglass hull. Occasional creaks from random dock-lines complemented the cadence of gentle swells. I leaned back against the settee cushion and absorbed the muffled noises. Closing my eyes, I exhaled slowly. I'd been longing for this refuge all week and now, finally onboard and shuttered from reality, my stress began to dissolve.

As the light outside began to fade, I watched the shadows play across the teak bulkheads in the salon. Kaleidoscope-like images danced around the ceiling as sunshine was reflected off the ripples in the marina. I lazily flicked a bottle cap back and forth across the galley table. Somewhere in the distance I heard a train-crossing signal. I dreamt about what life would be like once *Sugaree's* masts were rebuilt and we could finally bend on her sails. My mind skimmed through picturesque scenes of tropical beaches and blue horizons. As always in my fantasies, I stood behind the wheel smiling brightly—my red hair flying in the sea breeze.

On this particular afternoon, I sat alone in *Sugaree's* comfortable salon. It felt rather strange to be onboard without

7

Jeffery, especially since I hadn't seen much of him recently. I missed his upbeat demeanor and the sound of his voice pattering on about nautical subjects. His tales of old ships and sailing lore always fired my imagination. One of my favorite onboard pastimes involved sipping a cold beer while my husband expounded upon his grand designs for our boat and our future. Today however, I wanted some solitude.

As Gracewinds continued to expand, I found myself with very little downtime. Raising five kids while Jeff and I remodeled our house meant that there no longer existed such a thing as a 'quiet place.' In the past week, I'd worked two births, both of which lasted longer than they should have. I'd met with clients and personnel in the mornings, facilitated new-moms' groups during the afternoons and taught childbirth classes in the evenings. Gracewinds' new lactation clinic and onsite birth store had recently opened, and I'd hired five new staff members. At some point, I'd managed to keep an appointment with Dane's counselor and finish hemming the girls' poodle skirts for Friday's sock-hop. A late-night trip to Home Depot for plumbing parts and two episodes of *Deadwood* with my husband rounded out the week. My days were full up.

The agitated buzz of a cell phone startled me from my contemplation. I checked the number. It was home.

"Hey there, what's up?"

"Mom? Are you making dinner tonight or is Jeff?" It took me a few seconds to determine which of my identical twin daughters was speaking. Their voices were so similar that I managed to mix them up half the time.

"…'Cuz if it's Jeff, would you please remind him for like the hundredth time that I am a vegetarian now. He always forgets and it is so lame."

It was Justine. "Alright, no worries. I'm teaching a childbirth class tonight so I'll ask him to pick up a cheese pizza for you and pepperoni for the other kids. Good enough?"

"Yeah, thanks Mom. See you tonight—or probably in the morning if you're late."

"Yup. Love you. And do your homework before TV."

"OK, whatever."

I clicked the cell phone shut and tossed it across the settee. I resented my electronic leash and disliked having to take it with me everywhere, even to the bathroom—lest I miss a call from a client in labor. And now it appeared as if even in my own little hideaway of *Sugaree,* I was still at the beck and call of kids.

As a sanctuary, our 36' sailboat served her purpose well. Without her two masts, *Sugaree* was an odd-looking vessel, hardly worthy of the term "sailboat." She bobbed up and down in her slip like a cork without the weight of her heavy sticks. Jeff was anxious to get her rigged, but it didn't matter to me that our little boat was hobbled to the dock. I had not yet acquired the status of a full-fledged sailor, so my needs were more immediate. I just wanted an escape, a place to dream and reflect.

Jeff and I had purchased the boat three years ago. She'd been neglected for decades and languished at her dock in Seattle's industrial area. Her decks had been covered in a thick layer of cement dust and the sail covers had rotted away. We'd moved her over to her current berth at Fisherman's Terminal and begun an aggressive restoration project that few would have endeavored. Gradually we brought her back to life. The boat's Norwegian name at the time, *Havørn,* translated into "Sea Bird." That moniker didn't resonate with either of us, so we rechristened her *Sugaree*--one of my favorite Grateful Dead songs. Jeff researched the process and uncovered the traditional method to rename a vessel. It called for a ceremony involving the consumption of several shots of good rum and emptying the rest of the bottle into the ocean for Poseidon. At the time, it seemed a tad wasteful and superstitious to me, but when faced with the potential for storms at sea, Jeffery had claimed "It's a gesture that's worth making to the gods."

The clock on *Sugaree's* bulkhead read 5:45 pm. I searched around for my bag and car keys, climbed the steps and slid the hatch open to peek outside. What remained of Seattle's dwindling commercial fishing fleet surrounded our little dock. I paused long enough to look at the mammoth crab-boats moored across the marina from us. They seemed impervious to the swells that caused the lithe *Sugaree* to dance up and down. I longed to remain here for the rest of the evening. "OK woman, time to get your ass moving," I said aloud to myself. "I can order the pizza on my way to Gracewinds and still swing by the hospital to check on clients before class." I slid the wooden hatch closed and locked up the boat. "Oh balls!" I'd forgotten the phone again.

Chapter 3

Town Hall

We were running behind schedule as I ran into our bedroom to grab my necklace. Jeffery scrawled a map and directions onto a paper towel for my parents while Juliet tugged at his trousers, pleading to be allowed to meet the mayor with us. As I fastened my necklace, I overheard my mother beseeching the twins to consider wearing more conservative outfits—some "nice clothes"—instead of the emo-Harajuku ensembles they were currently wearing. "Look, girls, this is a big night for your mom. You might end up meeting the mayor, so let's dress more appropriately, alright?"

"Grandma, those dresses are for old people and nerds!" Justine complained.

I shook my head as I passed by the negotiations and rushed downstairs. My dad sat in the middle of the sofa, his arms spread across the cushion-backs, one leg crossed over the other as Trent described a recent skateboarding misadventure. I instantly recognized the look on Dad's face: the one-eyebrow-up, one-eyebrow-practically-buried-into-his-eye socket look. The one that meant, I am tolerating but not appreciating this conversation. Trent continued to prattle on with his story, unfazed by his grandfather's expression.

I looked around the living room as Dane and our gangly Labrador, Porter, tore past me, chasing one another for a tennis ball. I could just make out the shadow of his pitbull Sasha, behind the kitchen door lying in wait. I had serious doubts that my parents possessed the tolerance needed to handle my eclectic brood for the few hours that Jeffery and I would be at the mayor's reception; I also doubted we would see them on time at the awards ceremony. Ultimately I gave in to the inevitable and closed the door behind me.

The poster on the door of Seattle's Town Hall read *The 2006 Mayor's Small Business Awards* and in smaller print, three lines below, was *Gracewinds Perinatal Services, Inc.* I wondered if anyone would notice if I peeled the poster off of the door; I could take it home as a souvenir. Eventually I thought better of it.

We barely arrived in time for the award recipients' cocktail hour with Mayor Nichols. Jeffery dropped me off at the entrance and went in search of a parking space. I glanced at my phone; the event started in six minutes. The real ceremony didn't start for another hour, but we *lucky* few had been invited to sip wine from plastic cups with the mayor beforehand.

I glimpsed my reflection in the glass door. My black pantsuit fitted me well and was thankfully, free of dog hair. I scrunched my bangs and adjusted my collar, hoping nobody would catch me primping in the doorway. Jeffery finally came bounding up the front steps. With relief I smiled at him. He looked good in his wool bomber jacket and brown pants, what I called Seattle formal attire.

"Are you all set?" he asked as he reached to open the door for me. "Then let's go get 'em."

We entered the spacious lobby and took in our surroundings. The décor was retro '60s, meaning that the city had not invested any money into the building for over forty years. Well-appointed individuals mingled with one another around the main floor, sipping drinks and surveying the photographs on display. Several long tables were arranged in the center of the room.

I spotted a young woman who balanced a clipboard atop her hip; we walked up to her and exchanged greetings. She handed us badges and directed us to the staircase leading to the reception. As we turned to leave, she said, "Excuse me. I see that you have eight guests registered for the ceremony. Are you expecting them *all* this evening?"

We nodded an affirmative as we made our way up the grand staircase. "I guess they aren't accustomed to having such large families attend these functions, huh?" I whispered to Jeffery and then added, "Hey, are you positive that you gave my folks the directions? They don't have much experience with Seattle traffic you know."

"Yes my dear… I told you I did. I handed directions to your dad and showed him the exit on the map. Besides, they'll have Trent along."

"I'm not sure that Trent will be much help, he's never been here. County Courthouse? Yes. District Courthouse? Yes. Town Hall? I seriously doubt it."

At the top of the staircase, we wandered into the brightly lit chamber for the reception. I scanned the room as we entered: several women chatting near the bar were all nattily attired in tailored skirts and cocktail dresses. I felt very out of place in my pantsuit, looking somewhat like a blackjack dealer—or so I imagined. The other men at the reception wore sport coats and sweaters, Jeffery blended right in. I spotted the politicians in the room quickly, their charcoal suits had that all-purpose appearance. Those suits had probably been to at least three or four other functions since coming off their hangers that morning. A couple of caterers replenished appetizers and patrolled the room, offering drinks.

"Can I get you something to drink?" Jeff asked.

"Dear god, yes please. Red wine—thanks." I gave Jeffery my most confident smile, then looked around for an empty chair. Setting my jacket and clutch on a vacant seat, I walked over to a nearby window and looked out, feeling very awkward in this congregation of business people. It seemed so surrealistic to be here.

"Hello. I take it you're the owner of Gracewinds?" A slender young woman addressed me. I offered my hand and said, "Uh, yes I'm the owner—and you are?"

"My name is Melanie; I'm with the mayor's office. Congratulations. We were so impressed with your organization," she said. "One of our co-workers is pregnant with her first baby. She is so excited to meet you."

"That's great," I automatically replied. My workday consisted of offering congratulations to many expectant parents, so that response was easy, however it took a little more effort to add as genuinely as possible, "I certainly hope that I'll be able to meet her this evening."

Jeffery joined us and handed me the glass of wine. I introduced him to Melanie and we chatted about babies for a short time until we were interrupted by an anxious-looking gentleman wearing thick glasses and a clip-on tie. "Excuse me everyone, if I could ask the ten award recipients to join me over here, we would like to introduce you all personally to Mayor Nichols."

I lined up next to the other business owners—restaurateurs, publicists, retailers, entrepreneurs and scholars. We stood together like obedient school children waiting for the assembly bell. I smiled inwardly at the formality of the process and mused whether we were expected to bow or curtsy when introduced. The double doors at the back of the chamber opened, and Mayor Nichols and his entourage sauntered into the room. Networkers, guests and staff stood to applaud. Our column was urged to move forward and it was then that I discovered my position. *Holy shit, Sherlock.* I was first in line.

I didn't have a chance to think about protocols or even what I might say because the anxious-looking, bespectacled gentleman motioned for me to come forward. "Ms. Wallace, if you would be so kind as to step right over here. That's it. I'd like to present you to Mayor Nichols."

As the mayor extended his hand to me, I marveled at what a bear of a man he was—not overweight as much as impressively sized. His photographs and television images did not do him justice. His suit differed from the attire of the minor politicos in the room: it clearly had an expensive one-function-only look. I shook his hand as confidently as I could and he smiled warmly, congratulating me on my award. We posed beside each other, his hand resting familiarly yet formally on my back much the way I'd expect all politicians are careful to do. Cameras flashed in my face and then very quickly, the greeting was over. I shook the Mayor's hand hastily again and was escorted to the end of the room where Jeffery and the other bystanders were still sipping their cocktails.

I sat down and let out a big breath. My pulse was racing.

"Well, was it everything you thought it would be?" Jeffery smiled.

"It was OK—and best of all, it was brief." I raised my glass in a silent cheer.

Jeff leaned in close and whispered, "You are without a doubt the sexiest CEO in the room." I smiled and sipped my wine.

With the other award recipients still meeting Mayor Nichols, Jeffery and I ducked out of the chamber to head back down to the main lobby in search of my parents, hoping they'd been able to corral all of the kids and find the building. The crowded room buzzed with guests and media, but I soon spied my twin daughters near the hors d'oeuvres. They had yielded to their grandmother and were garbed in subdued outfits, yet their displeasure with such conformist apparel was evident in their postures.

"Hey there. You two look really nice. Thanks for putting on something dressy for this."

Megan rolled her eyes. "Grandma didn't give us much of a choice. How did you ever grow up with all of her fashion rules?"

I ignored the question and asked where their grandparents were. Justine pointed toward the back of the lobby. "That was the only table left when we got here."

Waving to Jeffery, I negotiated my way through the crowd. My father sat next to one of the nurses from the hospital's childbirth center. A pair of Gracewinds' parents chatted with my mother as she held their two-month-old baby. I was pleased to see that quite a few of my staff and tenants had shown up as well. I was touched by the large group of friends and supporters around me.

At that point soft chimes broadcast over the speakers, announcing it was time to wind up the social hour and move into the auditorium. We joined the mass of people entering the Town Hall Theater and made our way up to the front row reserved for the award winners. I was relieved to find an empty section where we could all sit together.

"Dane! Stop it!" Juliet hissed loudly as she punched her brother.

"OK. Enough of that," Jeff interjected, quickly rearranging the seating. "Juliet, come sit by me. Dane, knock it off!"

"What? I didn't do anything!" Dane said.

"Go sit next to Grandma, Dane," I whispered.

Just then, the lights dimmed and the large screen on stage blazed with the *City of Seattle Mayor's Small Business Awards* logo. Music piped in from the speakers and the audience quieted down. I sensed Trent slide in behind my seat. "Made it!" he said. I could smell the tobacco lingering on his breath.

The program began with a representative from the Office of Economic Development welcoming everyone and then proceeding to spout off figures related to Seattle's record-breaking small business growth over the last several decades. Next up was someone from the mayor's office describing the auspiciousness of the evening's awards and naming past winners who'd gone forth to achieve national stardom, like Starbucks Coffee and Dilettante Chocolates.

Eventually the first of the recipients was announced—a company named BizXchange—and applause filled the auditorium. A short three-minute video about the company played before their CEO went up to the podium to accept his award.

My stomach began to churn as I waited for the Gracewinds name to be called. I concentrated on calming my nerves but to no avail. It suddenly dawned on me that I needed to pee, but it was too late to remedy that issue.

Soon, I heard the speaker announce, "Our next award winner, from Seattle's Ballard neighborhood—Gracewinds Perinatal Services owner and CEO, Christine Wallace!" Applause erupted, especially from immediately around me, and Megan gave an un-ladylike hoot. I smiled broadly until the clapping slowly died down and the video began to play. I watched from my seat as our logo appeared on the big screen. I wasn't present the day the film crew came to shoot the footage, and had no idea what would be on the video. But I knew they had interviewed staff members and clients as well as captured scenes of various programs in action.

The camera followed a group of new mothers in an infant massage class, the instructor demonstrating the proper techniques for soothing their newborns. One of my nurses related how she loved working for us because she was allowed to spend as much time as she needed with each client—her job in the hospital did not allow her such freedom. A couple who'd taken my childbirth class spoke about the network of other new parents and healthcare practitioners whom they'd become familiar with at Gracewinds. The video panned across our back patio with its flower beds and hanging baskets, then to the inviting lobby. It lingered on the yoga studio with its red oak floors that Jeffery had installed. Finally, the camera captured the image of a new father cradling his infant. The narrator proceeded to read our mission statement, which concluded with "providing a community of support under one roof."

The audience applauded loudly, and continued to do so as I walked up to the podium. I stood behind the lectern and when the clapping stopped, took a deep breath and stared out at the crowd. I nodded my appreciation and eked out a "Thank you, very much." I paused again. I had a long list of acknowledgements, but I wanted to—needed to give credit to my family before anyone else.

I looked into the audience and saw my kids and Jeffery sitting together. Trent had moved forward to sit next to his sisters. They all watched me with expectation and expressions of obvious pride. I began my speech. "There are a great many people who have helped make Gracewinds a reality and who've contributed to the successful business that it has become. Foremost however, are my children, and I want to say a very sincere *Thank You* to my kids: Trenton, Dane, Justine, Megan and Juliet for their willingness to do without their *own* mother so often, in order for her to help *others* become one."

I had no more than got that one out, when tears filled my eyes and I choked up. I couldn't go any further. I thought of my kids who bore the brunt of my seventy, sometimes eighty-hour workweeks, and my husband who carried the financial strain of supporting our growing business. The audience waited in silent anticipation, allowing me time to regain my composure. I stood at the podium staring back into their faces. I noticed that my mom had removed her glasses to wipe away tears. I still needed to thank the lenders, the consultants, the midwives and doctors as well as my staff and clients. I looked toward Jeffery. He rose and climbed the steps onto the stage, walked up to the microphone, and eloquently finished my acceptance speech, acknowledging all of the appropriate people. I stepped back toward the dignitaries, grateful to let him take over. When Jeffery concluded, the audience stood and cheered, clapping loudly for a long time.

As I stood on stage, feeling very foolish for tearing up over a silly speech, Mayor Nichols moved next to me. He leaned over and whispered, "You have a right to be proud of yourself and your family. You've created something really special in our city."

I looked up at him and managed a smile. I sniffed and said, "Thank you, sir."

Chapter 4

Room 204

"Take a deep breath. Good. Now, out through your mouth slowly." Her eyes fixed on me as she exhaled a measured but shaky amount of air from between her lips.

I stood close, careful to keep eye contact. Her composure hinged upon the thread of confidence and empathy that stretched between our gazes.

"Good job, Sara, that's the way. Now, breathe deeply…through your nose. C'mon, we'll do it together."

Her grasp on my hand tightened, cutting off the circulation, as her pain built. I moved closer to her face. "Sara. Ride the wave. It's almost over and you are in control. Relax your hands for me. Let the tension out."

Her furrowed brow conveyed the struggle and fear that welled near the surface of her emotions. I could feel her tenuous control begin to erode. Taking a washcloth from the small basin next to her bed, I slowly wrung it out. Once the contraction ebbed, I wiped the sweat from her forehead. I encouraged her once again to take a cleansing breath and exhale.

Sara pursed her chapped lips and gently blew out a long sigh, watching my face all the while.

"Excellent work. Hey now, that's one contraction you'll never have to deal with again. You're doing very well."

She whimpered and offered me a weak smile before laying her head back onto the pillow. I glanced up at her husband, Charles, as he rested next to her shoulders. His hair was disheveled and his eyes were bloodshot. He looked every bit as worn out as she did.

"You doin' OK?" I asked him quietly.

"I'll manage."

I handed him the washcloth and motioned to the water basin. He moistened the cloth and squeezed the excess warm water back into the stainless steel bowl. Before he could lay the cloth on Sara's brow, the next wave hit. The contraction washed over her with such intensity that she convulsed and cried out in pain. Charles massaged her shoulders as I leaned near enough for her to hear me say, "Breathe over the top of it, Sara. I'll help you. Slowly now, rise above it, ride the wave, that's the way... You're on the crest, feel it come down now. Breathe it away as it ebbs. You did it. Well done."

She stared up at us imploringly. "I can't do it anymore. I can't. I just can*not*."

I smiled at her and said, "But you *are* doing it! You are doing excellently and you're almost there."

The heavy hospital door opened and the midwife quietly re-entered the room. She raised her eyebrows at me inquisitively and I smiled, giving her a quick thumbs-up. Sara was progressing nicely into the next stage of her labor.

"How are you feeling, Sara?" her midwife asked.

Sara smiled and nodded, but the next contraction struck her with great force and she gasped, arching against the mattress. The three of us coaxed her through its duration and praised her efforts. The spasm subsided and she puffed out an exhausted sigh as she fell back onto the bed.

The surges continued on, occurring more frequently, at barely a minute interval. They built with a ferocity that took the young mother by surprise and withered her resolve. Charles and I knelt in front of her and looked up into her face. "We're so close, Sara." I whispered.

She nodded as she panted, tears welling in her eyes. The next wave of contractions brought on a guttural moaning as she caught her breath. I looked up at the midwife with a satisfied grin. This sound was what we had been waiting for. The baby had descended lower in the birth canal, triggering Sara to instinctively bear down with her contractions. It was time to push.

The midwife leaned down to be near Sara's head. "Hey there Sunshine, it's time to bring your baby down now. You think you're ready?"

Sara shut her eyes and licked her parched lips. "Ice" was all she said.

I looked over at Charles and watched as the anxiety on his face changed to an expression of timid relief. He looked at me and asked, "This is good, yes? We're almost through?"

I chuckled. "Yeah, Charles, this is very good."

Sara was too exhausted to feel relief. Her labor had extended over the course of fifty-two hours. She had spent the first day at her home, coping with her early labor. By mid-morning of the second day, they had called me in to provide support through the increasingly difficult waves of her contractions. Later that afternoon I had sat with them in their hot tub—the heat turned down to a manageable temperature for the unborn baby—coaxing Sara to breathe through the tougher spasms and letting her doze between the surges of her labor. Shortly after midnight on the second day, the midwife had given Sara a morphine injection to allow both her and Charles a chance to sleep and encourage her labor to start anew. Several hours later, we finally checked into Swedish Ballard's childbirth center with solid, effective contractions. We were all dog-tired and ready to see a baby arrive.

Sara reclined in her bed and let Charles smooth the hair away from her eyes with his fingers. She opened her mouth so that he could spoon-feed her portions of crushed ice from a small paper cup. The brief respite between her transition phase and the oncoming pushing stage gave us all a much-needed chance to recharge.

I stretched my arms above my shoulders and rolled my head slowly back and forth, appreciating the burning in my neck muscles. I yawned and observed as the nurses bustled about the birth room, rearranging items for the imminent delivery. Their oft-reenacted choreography made for effortless preparation. Stainless steel instruments, meticulously placed on a draped cart, were wheeled into the room. The dusty-rose colored walls that resembled a bedroom only minutes before suddenly assumed a clinical look as cabinets were opened to reveal their contents. Oxygen tanks, heat lamps, baby scale and operating lights were rolled into the suite on cue. The busy nurses moved around the room without disturbing the placement of a single object.

I glanced toward the windows on the west wall. The levered blinds were partially shuttered, allowing a sliver of pale light to accentuate the furnishings and participants in the space. The light settled on Sara as she lay curled on her side, underscoring her role as the centerpiece of our small drama. A purplish-grey pigeon stood on the windowsill outside, cooing as it tilted its head from side to side.

Our reprieve was interrupted by a sharp cry and panting grimaces—Sara's contractions had resumed. This time however, the surging pressure of her spasms compelled her to push downward with each gulping breath.

Without a word, we returned to our all-too-familiar duties. I showed Charles how to support Sara's legs as she pushed with the strength of each contraction. Our soothing reassurances shifted to encouraging prompts as we cajoled her to bear down with all of her strength.

"Atta girl! Way to go, Sara! Push! Push! You can do it!" To unsuspecting ears we could have sounded like a rowing team's coxswain maintaining stroke rhythm in a shell.

For well over two-and-a-half hours, Sara pushed. The baby's head would descend and we'd get a glimpse of the wet, curly hair of its crown, then, just as suddenly, the contraction would subside and the baby would recede back into the birth canal. At last, the baby's head remained at the opening and did not disappear even when the strong surge of Sara's contraction ended.

I nudged Rose, the delivery nurse at my side, and we winked at each other, certain that very soon Sara would have her new baby in her arms. Rose possessed a limitless supply of optimism and tenacious energy. We had often worked together for the past seven years, and she had been present with me when my youngest was born. I enjoyed having her in the delivery room.

Sarah's baby crowned at the next contraction; the widest part of her head had been born. I laughed and looked over at

Charles to make sure he was able to witness the birth of his child. But instead of watching the baby, Charles was looking at Sara's face with a puzzled expression.

Sara's eyes had rolled back and only the whites were visible. Her back arched dramatically as the baby arrived. I nudged Rose and tilted my head toward Sara's face. Rose did a double-take and then quickly reached behind my back to slam her fist on the red button situated on the wall. I saw the button read "CODE" and my heart stopped for a moment.

We called to the midwife, who was so preoccupied with the birthing baby that she had not noticed the unnatural arching and could not see Sara's face. She looked up as we pointed to the events transpiring at the head of the delivery bed.

"Call a crash team!" she shouted.

"We just did," Rose replied.

Within seconds the door slammed open and the emergency team burst into the formerly tranquil birthing suite. Orders were barked out, and tables and equipment were shoved out of the way.

One nurse carried the newborn from the delivery bed to the warming table on the far wall. Away from the chaos, I squeezed next to the nurse to watch her suction the baby girl's little nose, and I helped her wrap a blanket around the infant.

"Here Chris, get the baby into the next room. It's not safe to have her in here right now."

Without waiting for my response, the nurse placed the newborn in my arms and firmly pushed us out the door. I looked over my shoulder to locate Rose in the midst of the crowd around Sara's bed. I could only make out the back of her head. My eyes picked out Charles who was pinned into the corner of the room.

He stared mutely at the scene that unfolded in front of him, helpless and panic-stricken.

I held the baby close to my chest as the door shut behind me. I looked toward the nurse's station in the axis of the circular childbirth center, relieved to see three nurses rise from their work as they registered my shell-shocked appearance. They immediately rushed to my side.

"Here, let's get you both in this room, it's empty and quiet," said one of them.

I allowed them to usher me, baby in arms, through the door and help me lay the newborn on the basinet. One of the nurses switched on the warming light and checked the baby's vitals. She turned to me and said, "You alright with staying here for a while? I'm going to find the father and get him in here as well."

I took a long breath and forced a smile of reassurance. "Sure, we'll be OK."

The nurse handed me another warm blanket and patted my shoulder. "I'm so glad it's you as the doula," she said and smiled at me before she left.

I straightened my back and shook my head, looking down at the tiny, pink baby squirming on the table. Her miniscule fists opened and closed and she turned her head around to make sense of the colors and sounds about her. "Hey, little one. Can you cry? Hang in there... make some noises for me. We'll get your mommy back to you soon."

I briskly massaged the baby with the warm towel, hoping to bring circulation into her limbs. Her tiny arms and legs flailed. At last a timorous whimper escaped her lips, shortly followed by more forceful wailing. The bluish tinge disappeared from her extremities as she cried. Her lungs were working hard, and I heaved an audible sigh of relief knowing I'd done the job right.

Having participated in hundreds of births, I could handle almost every scenario when it came to delivering babies. I understood the nuances of labor and was adept at solving the emotional and physical challenges that came with the job. My prior occupation as a family practice medical assistant gave me more clinical experience than other doulas, and I enjoyed the familiarity and confidence of the nursing staff as a result. The techniques of coping with labor were innate in my skillset.

Yet the events occurring all around me were completely alien, and I felt lost as to how to proceed. By this stage in the birthing progression, the mother and partner should be together, blissfully oblivious to anything but the sight and sounds of their new baby. My duties as a doula should have been winding down, as I subtly withdrew and allowed them to bond as a new family. I felt unprepared and out of my element as I stood in the dimly lit, empty birthing suite, alone except for the new little human who was my sudden, sole charge.

My brain teemed with unanswerable questions: How would I explain this to their family members waiting in the lobby? Who would help Charles take care of this baby if Sara didn't pull though?

I looked down at the infant in front of me. She had quieted once again and calmly surveyed the intense new world in front of her. Because of the urgent events unfolding at her birth, the customary antibacterial ointment had not been dabbed into her eyes, so she was free to focus as best as she could on the contrasting shapes in front of her. She looked up at me and stared into my eyes.

"All right there, little peanut, I'm right here with you," I whispered.

The door pushed open and Charles—his face a wreck of emotions— stepped into the room, a nurse alongside him. She placed a hand on his shoulder and said, "Stay here with Chris and your baby. We'll take care of Sara. I'll keep you posted, I promise." With a quick squeeze, she patted him and brushed back out of the room.

Charles stared at me. "What am I supposed to do?" he said, just above a whisper.

I swallowed hard and managed to say, "Charles, here is your daughter. Right now your job is to take care of her. Let the doctors care for Sara."

I lifted the baby from the bassinet-warmer and placed her in his arms. Then I sat down next to them both and we just waited.

Helplessness was not something I was accustomed to feeling. I searched my brain for any tactics or tricks I'd gleaned from my years of experience. Finally, I resolved that being grounded and calm for the father and baby was all I could provide at this moment. So I was.

After a long and emotional evening, Sara was reunited with her husband and newborn daughter. The hospital staff and her midwife had worked together to stabilize her. And finally my role as the doula evolved into where it should be after a birth— that of a bystander. I snapped family photos with Charles' camera and fetched dinner for the couple at the hospital cafeteria. When I returned to the birthing suite I couldn't help but smile at the tranquil scene before me: Charles' head rested on the bed next to

Sara's; their baby comfortably tucked in her mother's arms. They all lay soundly asleep.

I tiptoed out of the room and closed the door behind me.

Chapter 5

Missing Person

I didn't really have time to meet with the sheriff that March afternoon in 2007. On the other hand, I didn't really have time to track down my teenage son, either. I checked my calendar, it showed client appointments all afternoon and a "New Moms" group starting in forty-five minutes.

Dane's behavior had been spiraling downward over the last eighteen months. Jeffery and I watched in bewilderment as my good-natured son devolved into a brooding, reckless thug. Not the bored, angst-ridden *Catcher in the Rye* sort of teen, but a mean and angry teen. It worried me to no end, since I'd already parented one son who, aside from a few "minor-in-possessions" and the occasional report card forgery, had developed into a functional member of society. I reckoned I'd handed my firstborn into the world fairly unscathed, all things considered.

Dane's rebellious journey into adulthood appeared to be ramping up in defiance before he blew out the candles on his sixteenth birthday cake. Dissension and conflict reigned, our house-rules apparently no longer applied to him. Heated fights broke out all hours of the day and night, usually ending with slammed doors and Dane leaving for a prolonged absence.

Desperate questions whirled in my mind: Should I be around more for him? Can we afford one of those special sorts of camps for at-risk youth? *(No, probably not)...* The idea of

31

dropping everything I'd accomplished so far with Gracewinds wasn't really feasible, considering all and everyone I was responsible for there. But the guilt just wouldn't abate. I wrestled with the decision of whether to focus on family and not on work: if I made myself more available, kept track of his efforts at school, or maybe tried again to involve him in a new hobby—maybe found an activity we could do together—things might just calm down. I desperately wanted the tension at home to subside.

"What if I hired a manager to run things at work? I could still keep Gracewinds going, but be around more for *all* the kids then," I asked Jeffery as we lay in bed one evening.

He rested his book on his chest and looked over at me. "You don't have enough money to hire anybody to manage the place, first of all," he replied. "Secondly, you were home a lot before opening Gracewinds and he didn't respond to that very well either, I recall."

I frowned and reluctantly nodded in agreement. He had a point. Dane hadn't exactly welcomed our efforts to draw him into the family, nor had he focused on any hobbies or sports that we'd invested in at the first glimmer interest: drumming, track, skateboarding, camping trips, even a family outing to Mount Bachelor and the promise of a snowboarding pass for good grades. None of it made a dent in his attitude.

We tried counseling sessions for months, showing up once a week and sitting in a pastel-colored counselor's office as a family. Jeffery and I answered questions, shared our concerns and waited, always waited, for Dane to respond. Nothing. The sessions he spent alone with the counselors generated the same results.

If Dane's behavior saddened and angered me, it fell even harder on his younger sisters. They missed the affable kid who would play Beanie Babies with them for hours, inventing preposterous scenarios and fantastical plots for all of their characters. Nowadays, Dane's interactions with them consisted of apathetic, rambling conversations that never lasted very long.

Jeffery and Dane were a volatile mix. The slightest comment or minor rule enforcement from his stepfather could send Dane spinning into a fury and a bitter fight would ensue—at times so loudly that I feared the neighbors would call in a complaint. If Dane's attitude was particularly nasty or if he talked back to me, Jeffery would tear into him verbally.

"Goddammit, Dane! I'm so sick of the way you talk to your mother. She deserves better than that from you."

"Whatever. Fuck you," Dane would say and walk out of the room.

The clincher happened one evening when what began as a discussion between Dane and Jeffery about a progress report erupted into a screaming match that sent the twins running for their rooms; hands covering their ears. I stepped in to mediate and found myself pulled into the battle, fending off the abusive words that Dane hurled my way. Finally Dane grabbed his coat and headed toward the door.

"Get back in here!" I hollered and followed him onto the front porch. "We're not finished yet!"

He spun around, cursing at me. Steam rose from his breath in the frigid air. We squared off facing one another with Sasha standing between us, her ears pointed forward. She looked up at us and her gaze implored us to stop the screaming. All that her pitbull sensibilities could decipher was that the two alphas in her life wanted to rip into each other

As our argument escalated, Dane shoved me back toward the door. I held my ground, but Sasha jumped as if startled. She backed away from Dane, moving toward me until her chest was even with my legs. She'd chosen which alpha to protect. Her ears lay back against her skull. She lowered her head and looked directly at him. Then a throaty, challenging growl emanated from between her clenched teeth.

Silence.

Dane looked down at his dog, I looked down at his dog, and then we looked back at each other.

"I'm outta here. You all suck!"

He ran down the steps and into the darkness as Sasha and I watched, matching expressions of confusion and dismay on our faces.

Three days went by, then four. We began regularly driving past Dane's old haunts. The friends he'd had in middle school had completely lost track of him; they could offer no suggestions as to where he might be. Dane's new friends—the ones we knew about at least—seemed to have disappeared. I knew enough about the habits of drug dealers to realize that once our car was spotted, all doors would be locked and curtains drawn. No amount of pounding on front doors would bring anyone around to answer.

Four days. Five. Then a full week and not a word from Dane. Amid the worry, guilt and sorrow, I felt a small amount of relief. I loved my son dearly, and missed his presence, but there were times when I had come close to hating him, and I was grateful to not feel that damaging emotion. Plus, without the war zone his presence created, the house became relaxed and peaceful and positive once more. The girls smiled and laughed again. We could enjoy family stories and games. Jeffery and I were husband and wife again. Things returned, in a weird sense, to *normal*.

Yet nothing was really normal. Every morning I went downstairs and looked in Dane's room, hoping to see him buried underneath his blankets and dirty clothes—home. Occasionally Sasha would spend the night curled up on his comforter, as if she regretted choosing the other side. She would look up at me when I passed by as if to acknowledge that she missed him too.

I began leaving Dane's blanket and some leftovers on the front porch each night on the chance he might stop by when we were either asleep or gone.

For all my ability as a mentor to new mothers, I was at a complete loss about my own son. After several more days had passed, a friend from work advised me to call the police.

"It'll go a lot easier on you, should he get arrested for something, if you list him as a missing child," she confided.

I shuddered. This very act seemed like a public admission of defeat.

During the past eighteen months, we had endured the parental retribution of King County's juvenile court, with its uncomfortable plastic molded chairs lining the antechambers and the eternally-late public defender who couldn't find our child's case number in his overstuffed briefcase. Furthermore, we underwent the demoralizing experience of visiting a child housed in the county's juvenile detention center. We filed through metal detectors and slid our identification into the stainless steel drawer that was the only connection to the face behind the counter. We left the girls to observe through the bulletproof glass as their brother shuffled into the common room to meet with us— wearing pale grey coveralls and plastic slippers, his face expressionless.

My first encounter with the juvenile justice system was over a year ago. A meeting with Dane's social worker informed me that Dane claimed I'd pushed him down our basement stairs. I was almost stunned into silence and disbelief, but told her she'd better check her facts. The following week when we met again, she said, "I spoke with your son's teachers and several of his schoolmates. Finally, I interviewed Dane at length …," she trailed off, tapping her fingers on his manila file folder. "Let's just say that our department will not be pursuing this claim any further. We see no validity whatsoever in his statement. However, I'd like to say that we very much appreciate your cooperation in the investigation."

She smiled at me expectantly. I managed a polite smile and wished her a good afternoon. I ought to have felt relief, but the only emotion that I could summon on that day was a deep sadness at the whole system. Somewhere, there was now a manila file folder with *my* name on it.

With the memories of those previous years in my mind, I sat in the rocking chair in Gracewinds' waiting room, glancing nervously at the clock on the wall as I waited for the sheriff. The water that trickled from my Zen fountain grated at my nerves.

As if in response, the little bells on the lobby door sounded. In stepped a middle-aged, portly man dressed in a brown sheriff's uniform.

After we introduced ourselves, the officer warmed up with some polite small talk. "My granddaughter had a midwife for her baby, y'know." He glanced around my lobby. "Yep, good experience I hear. She delivered her baby naturally."

"Oh awesome, how wonderful for her," I replied, hoping that I sounded as interested as I would have under normal circumstances.

He cleared his throat and twitched his head, in a sort of a nervous tic kind of way, and was all business from that point. I explained about Dane running off nine days prior, about his dropout and drug-dealing friends, about searching for him to no avail. At the end of my account, the officer cleared his throat and said, "Well Ms. Wallace, I have everything that I need to file our report. From here on out your son's going to be considered a 'missing child'."

I swallowed hard, and my mouth felt dry as he continued to explain what that meant and what looking for Dane might entail—including his so-called 'friends' turning him out when they learned the police were looking for him. Dane would find himself, the officer said, "Pretty short on safe havens."

I nodded, somewhat in a daze from the combination of anti-anxiety meds in my system, my worry, and from all the various situations the officer pointed out that were currently running through my head. I signed all of the necessary paperwork and shook his hand, smiling stiffly as he rambled on again about his great-grandbaby and what a really nice place I had.

Out front in the yoga studio, I could hear the new mothers arriving for their group—cheerful greetings mixed with the sounds of fussy newborns. I could just make out the *thump* of yoga mats hitting the hardwood floor and the *click, click* as each baby car-seat buckle was unfastened. The Gracewinds New Moms group was about to begin and I was their facilitator—I had to pull myself together.

I stepped into the hallway restroom and closed the door behind me. I turned on the cold-water tap and placed my wrists underneath its forceful stream. Bowing my head toward the basin, I willed the lingering fears and guilt out of my head. I felt the nausea subside just a little.

"Breathe, one, two, three. Breathe, one, two..." I counted my slow, intentional inhales as if in a birthing class. "Breathe. That's it."

At last, I turned off the tap and raised my face to the mirror—dark circles around my eyes, deep wrinkles all over my face—I looked dead tired. I *was* dead tired. I grabbed a couple of paper towels and dried my hands, heaved one last sigh, and opened the door. As I walked down the hallway toward the yoga studio, I squared my shoulders. At the entrance to the room I managed a smile and said brightly, "Hey, you guys! How's everybody doing today?"

The fourteen or so women—their newborns either in their laps or on the mat in front of them—sat in a large circle. They were there to share their joys and triumphs, their woes and hurdles of new motherhood. These stories were visceral and heartfelt. I made a huge effort to compose my facial expression into that of empathy and compassion. I sat like a statue on my pillow and let the stories and conversations wash over me. A frazzled mother said, "I'm so tired. She wakes up every hour to nurse and I can't pump enough to let my husband give her a bottle. I just feel like I've been awake for days."

Another confided tearfully, "My baby is five weeks old today. He used to be such a pleasant baby and slept all the time. Now he's colicky and fussy and never seems to stop wailing. It doesn't seem to matter what I do, nothing makes him happy. I am so tired and burned out."

One after another, often through tears, the new mothers expressed their frustration and feelings that the weariness, the pain and the worries would never end. It helped them to hear from other women that they were not alone. The comforting comments and promises that "it eventually gets better" were why they came every week. I made sure to nod at the perfect time or to furrow my brow with concern when appropriate.

Within, I was screaming silently. *You all have absolutely no idea!*

Chapter 6

A Lifeline

Weeks went by with only occasional "Dane sightings." Jeffery would come home from work and report that he'd spotted Dane walking down Aurora Avenue with some buddies, or the girls would relay some second- or third-hand news about him that they'd heard through their network of friends at school.

Late one morning in March while I worked in my office at home, I heard our dogs barking. I briefly considered checking on them—their barks were the *we're so happy to see* you quality as opposed to the *stranger at the door* tone—and I was curious, but the stack of paperwork in front of me kept me at my desk, and the barking eventually died down. I finished my task and snapped the laptop closed. As I gathered up my papers, Sasha padded into the room and plopped down in front of my feet. I recognized the expressive look in her eyes.

"What's the matter, Sasha?"

In response, she spun around in a couple of tight circles, dashed toward the door, and looked back over her shoulder, imploring me to follow.

"OK," I answered. "Here I come."

She raced down the stairs at her typical breakneck speed and was sitting impatiently at the door by the time I reached the living room. Her tail whipped back and forth and her muscles quivered underneath her sleek coat. I scratched her head and looked out the glass of the front door.

"Nobody's out there, Sash…" I looked down at her. "Who'd ya see?"

She used her thick head to brush past my legs and position herself at the door. She pressed her nose to the glass and stared out intently. Finally, she gave a quick *snort* into the window, fogging it up. Clearly antsy, she walked back to the center of the living room and continued to look at me expectantly, encouraging me to solve the riddle.

"Oh, Pig-Dog,"

In all likelihood, I figured, the family of fat raccoons that homesteaded in our big cedar tree had probably just trekked across the front yard. "I suppose you're pissed off at Mama Raccoon again, aren'tcha?" I asked her. She snorted in reply.

Oh, Christ. I could tell the damn dog wouldn't be appeased, and even though I needed to be at Gracewinds by noon I said, "Alright then. Let's go see what's out there!"

I snapped the leash onto her collar and she surged ahead of me, nearly yanking me off my feet. Sasha paced to and fro on the front porch with her face down and her tail erect. Her nose pressed against the floorboards, her sniffing punctuated by noisy snorts every three or four breaths.

"Whatever was here is long gone, girl."

I allowed her to continue her scrupulous investigation for a few more minutes and then decided it was high time for me to get to work. "OK, Sash, you've already had your walk this morning. No fair trying to get one more out of me!"

I gave her leash a quick jerk to let her know I was serious and turned back toward the door. That's when the tiger caught my eye.

"What the hell is that?"

Propped against the door jamb was a stuffed tiger. Its garish orange fur and plastic, bug-eyed expression had that cheap, carnival-toy look to it. The stuffed animal leaned over in a tipsy, drunken-sailor pose. One of its ears had that damp-and-dingy look, as if a puppy or toddler had chewed on it. I turned around and looked out at the street. Perhaps one of the neighbors found it and assumed our kids lost it.

As I stepped over to examine it, Sasha's tail wagged animatedly, her eyes lit up and she gave me her goofy grin. I held the tiger up and examined it closer but could see nothing of note. Then Sasha jumped and put her paws on my stomach—something she only did when extremely happy.

"Off, girl!" I said, and shoved my knee into her chest to force her off. "Bad girl, Sasha."

I frowned. I was curious, but knew this was a mystery I didn't have time to solve right then. Sasha obediently followed as I walked back into the house and set the toy on the dining room table. She sat quietly while I unfastened her leash and then ran off to join Porter who was sunbathing in the middle of the library floor.

I'd made myself over ten minutes late for work. Grabbing my keys and gear, I muttered, "Damn dog," and left the house.

When I returned home later that evening, Juliet met me with the stuffed tiger in her arms. "Mom! Look what Dane left!"

"Dane?!" I echoed. "How do you know it was Dane who left it for you, honey?"

"He won it for me at the Puyallup Fair!" She hugged the natty thing and planted a big kiss on its befuddled looking face. "I left it at his girlfriend's house, and he said he'd bring it back for me someday." She galloped toward the kitchen then turned around to say, matter-of-factly, "It's 'cuz he misses me I'm pretty sure."

I stood with my hand on the front door-handle, stunned. "Don't run in the house," I called after her, not knowing what else to say. I wondered if this could be some sort of peace offering.

My first reaction was to hop into the car and go search for Dane. If this was a white flag or some sort of attempt to reach out to us, I wanted to pursue it while he still might be in the neighborhood. I thought better about that plan because I knew that if I pushed it too fast, he would just pull back like he always did. It was better if I let him come back to us on his own time. I simply needed to be patient a little bit longer.

The microwave oven beeped several times, bringing me back to events at hand. I carried my briefcase and groceries into the kitchen and came upon the twins engrossed in some sort of cooking project. They jumped when they noticed me in the doorway. I could tell by the guilty looks on their faces and the open bag of Jet-Puffed Marshmallows on the countertop that they were microwaving them—against prior orders.

"Clean up that mess, you two. I have to get dinner ready," I said absentmindedly.

I ignored the glances they exchanged but noticed the relief wash over their faces as I set my bags on the counter and didn't say anymore. I went upstairs to change my clothes. I needed to focus on how to proceed regarding my son. As I slid into my sweatpants I heard the front door close and the excited greetings of the girls and the dogs. I heard Jeffery teasing Porter and Sasha, then the scratching of claws on the hardwood floor as they peeled out in pursuit of whatever toy he'd tossed for them.

I slipped on my house shoes and went downstairs, anxious to tell Jeffery about Sasha's morning discovery. As we prepared dinner, we discussed our options for reaching out to Dane. We went back and forth, covering every conceivable scenario.

Finally, Jeffery offered a solution. "Why don't you call Trent and get him to come up here. He may be able to get through to Dane where we can't."

I stopped peeling the carrots and pondered his suggestion. "Y'know… that could work."

My oldest son lived in Oregon these days, but I knew he'd make the drive north if I explained the situation to him. I phoned Trent the next morning right after breakfast.

"Hullo?" a sleepy voice grumbled into the phone.

"Hey there. It's me."

"Hey, Mama. What's shakin? Why the hell are you calling me so early?"

"Well, since it's about nine o'clock, I took a gamble that you might be awake like most normal people in the world. I guess I was wrong—my bad."

"Yeah, yeah, yeah. Advance the subject or hang up the phone."

I told him about the problems with Dane, that he'd been gone for almost two weeks, that he was an official "missing child," that no one knew where he was. Then I told him about the stuffed animal and my hesitations about attempting to approach him if

44

he wasn't ready to talk to us. "Can you please come up and help find him…maybe talk with him?" I finished.

Trent was quiet on the phone for a short while. At last he spoke. "Well, Mom, I've actually talked with him on the phone awhile back. He's going through some stuff."

"Yeah, no doubt," I replied. "I didn't exactly think he was doing this for extra credit in school. But really—you spoke with him?"

"Yeah, I did." He yawned loudly and then said, "OK, I'll come up and talk some sense into the little shit in person, but if he doesn't want to talk to anybody, he just plain won't do it. You understand that, don't you?"

"Yeah, I get it. Well, if you can't get him to figure it out, then I give up." I knew my voice sounded strained.

"All right, Mama. I'll come up."

"Thank you, Trent. I'll try and find out where he is so you don't have—"

"Mom. I know where he is. I'll see you on Friday."

I hesitated, wanting to ask where Dane was, but instead just got out, "Love you…" I heard the phone cut off mid-way.

Chapter 7

A Lamb to the Wolves

I sat cross-legged on the hotel carpet, totaling up our receipts for the weekend. The little Hewlett-Packard adding machine whirred away as I punched in the numbers. I pushed "sum" and the bold numerals appeared on the register tape. I blinked, amazed at what it read. "Whoa. It really pays to pimp out my husband every now and then."

"I'm yours. Use me as you will," Jeff replied and looked over my shoulder at our sales. "Holy crap!" he said. "We made all that in the last forty-eight hours?"

I nodded. "Well worth the trip I'd say."

"I think I'm gonna ask the boss for a raise," he said and finished packing up the last box.

Attending the 2007 Childbirth and Post-Partum Association's annual conference in Los Angeles was a last-minute decision on our part. Earlier in the month the organizers had called me, requesting that Jeffery present his "Foundations for Fatherhood" program. The growing popularity of his classes had not escaped their notice.

Jeff initially balked at the prospect when I suggested that he should present at the conference. The prospect of standing in front of a room full of women, "Like I'm some kind of an expert," did not excite him. He had joked that it would be akin to getting thrown to the wolves.

I argued that a bunch of women must get awfully tired of hearing themselves speak about the same old things year after year. I imagined this fact alone would make him a welcome diversion, and then reminded him that we'd have a chance to be alone in the evenings. Eventually, I'd worn down his resistance.

With the decision to attend and our reservations made, I arranged coverage at the office and found a substitute for my childbirth classes. Our close friends invited Juliet over for the weekend, promising rides at the Seattle Center. Justine and Megan opted to stay with their dad and stepmother. My prodigal son Dane had recently moved into a basement apartment a few blocks from the house, and offered to come over and feed the dogs. Pleased that my son wanted to be part of the family again, I took him up on it. After leaving him with a four-page list of instructions and phone numbers, we headed to the airport.

The conference was in full swing and the afternoon sessions had just started. Copies of my book, *The Pocket Doula,* along with some of our most popular merchandise from Gracewinds' retail store were on display at our booth. We'd learned from the previous year, that the only way to make these conferences affordable was to peddle our wares. I tidied up our table—the last wave of shoppers having made a real mess of it. I rearranged the books so that passers-by could easily peruse them and displayed the other merchandise for browsers to see from a distance.

I let Jeffery interact with the women who stopped by our booth. He had such a natural way of charming them and could discuss everything from baby-wearing options to which crèmes were recommended for stretch marks. He always pulled off a sale of some sort. It didn't hurt that he was incredibly handsome. Schmoozing was definitely not my forte—I proved most effective in short, one-on-one interactions, or when presenting in front of a group or classroom. I preferred to step in only when Jeffery needed me to answer questions about my book or Gracewinds. We made a pretty effective sales team that way.

After the bell rang signaling attendees to adjourn to educational sessions, I exhaled a sigh of relief. I desperately wanted to go stretch my legs.

Jeffery suggested we catch the Disneyland shuttle in front of the hotel. "Let's do a few rides this evening."

"Oh man, I'm not sure I have enough energy left to deal with the 'Happiest Place on Earth' tonight."

"Come on—when have you and I ever had a chance to knock around Disneyland without all of the kids? We could make-out inside The Haunted Mansion…"

Despite serious doubts about the potential for romance in the middle of a graveyard amusement park ride, I submitted. Besides, I remembered that there was a new pub on the California Adventure side of the theme park. The promise of cold beer to counteract the sugar-coating of Disneyland made it easier for me to consent. We hopped on the shuttle and went off to meet the Mouse.

By the end of the night, Jeffery's mouseketeer ears were slightly askew and my Jack Skellington tank top was·dripping wet. The warm, spring evenings of southern California made it irresistible to sit outside under the stars and swill cold, over-priced ales. We repeatedly splashed down the Grizzly River Rapids plume-rides after establishing a routine of drying off at the pub and taking plastic to-go cups of beer with us to drink in the line for our next turn. The end result was a good buzz that we capped off in the cocktail lounge of our hotel lobby.

The shrill wake-up call the next morning seemed to come far earlier than what we'd set up. Jeffery slammed the receiver back onto its cradle without lifting his head from the pillow. I lay flat on my back and stared at the ceiling, waiting for clarity to arrive. Eventually, I acknowledged that the alarm was indeed correct and I nudged my husband, "You better get movin' buddy. You're their first speaker today." There was no response from his side of the bed, so I kicked him a little harder. "You—into the shower!"

"Hrmmphhh…" was his muffled response.

With a good deal of difficulty I rousted him from the covers and pointed him toward the shower. After re-reading the conference agenda I yelled toward the bathroom, "Holy crap— Hurry up, Jeff! We're only going to have enough time to grab a quick cuppa coffee before you need to be down there."

Jeff walked out of the shower with a bath towel wrapped around his narrow waist, his gaze still sleepy. Drops of water sat on his chest and shoulders. I pulled on my tights and watched him start to dress. He was in fine form for a man of forty years. His climber's frame was still muscular and lean; his long arms were very well defined. "Hmmm, I wish I'd taken you up on that Haunted Mansion idea last night." I slid my toes into my boots.

Jeffery turned to face me. "Hell, there's no time like the present." I could see he was prepared to follow through on his original proposition.

"Knock it off!" I laughed. "You have a couple hundred anxious ladies downstairs waiting to hang on your every word!"

"Raincheck then," he said and briskly rubbed the towel over his head to dry off his shaggy blonde hair.

The elevator door opened and we stepped into the lobby. Jeffery detoured into the Tully's kiosk to grab us each a coffee and we hustled down the escalator. The lower-level conference rooms were already teeming with women. Soon enough, I spotted the two event organizers. They enthusiastically waved at us as we approached. "Well, there ya go Sport—those are your wolves," I said as we headed in their direction. "The blonde is April and the other one's Tracy. Now go get 'em!"

The room filled rapidly and I slid into a seat near the back door. Women of all ages took their places, and I marveled at how many attendees were making it to the early session—typically the least favorite time slot of each day. I scanned the conference hall and watched the ladies file though the door, feeling a little smug at being able to detect the occupation of many. The short, low-maintenance hair styles of some women shouted 'labor and delivery nurse' from across the room. Crocheted ponchos, cotton blouses and Birkenstock sandals were a dead giveaway for the 'natural-birth doulas' and midwives. The rest of the contingent was harder to pigeon-hole, so I simply lumped them all into the 'general administrative and physician' category. With the exception of some convention staff and one or two technicians, Jeffery was the only male in the room.

Tracy stepped up to the podium and twisted on the microphone, it made the typical screechy-feedback noise that signals the beginning of a speech. She patiently waited for the stragglers to settle into their chairs, and when the noise had died down, she began her introduction. "Well, mornin' ya'll!" she drawled in her thick Alabama accent. "I'm glad to see so many people here for our mornin' session! And you know, I'm thinkin' it must have somethin' to do with our first speaker today!" She turned to smile at Jeffery, who was sitting behind her on the small platform. "This morning, we have a gentleman presenter—all the way from the Pacific Northwest. He's a father *and* a stepfather— he also happens to be the creator of the Gracewinds' 'Foundations for Fatherhood' program. So, here to speak about the importance of the partner's role in early childhood development is Mr. Jeff Carson."

Jeffery rose as the applause started and with little hesitation launched into his presentation. I smiled from my vantage point in the rear of the hall, sipped my latte, and observed the general reaction to his speech. He'd practiced it with me several times back home and he knew the material very well. His audience was genuinely spellbound by the anecdotes, punctuated by figures and facts on the graphs projected behind. I watched their rapt attention to his emotional tale about what it was like to hold his newborn daughter when she was only seconds old—it was as if they'd never heard a father speak about a baby before. The frantic scribbling that emanated from his oration on "Global Parental Leave" statistics further indicated their fascination with the subject matter. I admit to feeling a twinge of jealousy as I observed the captivated audience. I'd never had this kind of reaction when I spoke at these things.

Photographs of beaming fathers with their babes in arms flickered across the giant screen as he concluded his lecture. Applause erupted in the big hall and as he folded up his notes and prepared to leave the podium, hands shot up like wild grass. As Jeffery continued to answer question after question, I weaved my way through the late-arrivals near the door and headed over to the tradeshow floor to prepare our booth for the day.

The second day of every convention always tended to be a bit slower than the first day, and I was glad for the pre-opening quiet in the exhibit hall after the excitement of Jeffery's talk. The response from the conference attendees was more than either of us had expected—I was proud of him.

Eventually, a conference worker opened the heavy doors and women poured into the hall. They were in pairs or bands of four or five, and with our booth situated so close to the entrance, I could hear much of what they were saying—their conversations were animated.

"He was simply wonderful! I swear I got all choked up when he spoke about holding his little baby and watching her pink-up in his arms!" said one.

"I'm going straight back to my boss at the hospital and get this class added to our programs," said another. "Do you suppose I could get him as part of the deal?" she added, giggling.

"Oh hey—there's his booth!"

A horde of women streamed to our table and I stood up to greet them. They jostled around each other to grab copies of *The Pocket Doula* and paw through the other titles we had on display. I answered rapid-fire questions about Jeffery's program, my book, Gracewinds and the other classes we offered. At the same time I tried to add up merchandise totals in my head while opening another case of books and keeping up the rapport as best I could. "…Thanks so much. I'm sure you'll really enjoy using the book in your class … Uhm, yes we do have wholesale prices available ... What was that? Oh, yes we can ship to hospitals ... Here's your credit card back…." I needed some help at our table, and fast.

At long last, I spotted Jeffery at the entrance to the tradeshow hall. He was surrounded by about twenty women, his head and shoulders visible above their smaller frames. He was smiling from one to the next as they demanded his attention, but I could tell he was overwhelmed. I beckoned to him, but couldn't catch his eye. "So what's this now? You signing autographs, for Chrissake?" I muttered.

He finally managed to make his way over to our crowded booth, his gaggle of admiring fans tagging along. As he extracted himself to slide in behind the table, I fought to get a word in edgewise. "Help!"

The buying frenzy continued well past the bell that announced the next session. A few women lagged behind in hopes for some one-on-one with Jeffery. I squeezed around behind him and patted him on the butt as I walked away. "I need to pee—I'm pretty sure you can handle it on your own for a bit." He managed a quick nod while in mid-sentence so I headed toward the exit. "My husband, the rock star." I muttered.

When I returned to our ransacked little table, Jeffery was all alone. He'd pushed his chair toward the back of the booth and was slumped back with a dazed and exhausted look on his face. "Well, that was really somethin'," I said and slid a plate with sandwiches and some chips in front of him. "Are you planning on taking this show on the road anytime soon?"

He tore into the roast beef hoagie and offered his take on the experience between mouthfuls. "Man, there is a *big* need out there for classes like ours," he said. "I bet we could start an instructor's training program if you wanted to."

"It's definitely worth looking into," I replied and sat down next to him. I rubbed his neck while absentmindedly picking through his potato chips. "So, how many books do you think we sold?"

"Easy." He looked under the draped table. "All of 'em."

"Wow. Nice." I scanned the table. It looked as if a Walmart's Black Friday sale had just occurred. "Why don't you take a break? This is something I can handle on my own now. We've got a few hours before they're released again."

He yawned. "Alright. I think I'll go upstairs and take a nap. The Grizzly River Rapids seems to have caught up with me."

The day ended on a mellow note. The atmosphere was subdued compared to the fervor of the morning break. It may have been tempered somewhat by the afternoon session's topic. 'Obstetrical Emergencies' apparently did little to instill a post-lecture buying frenzy amongst the conference attendees.

Shortly before dinner time, I tiptoed into our room. Jeffery was splayed across the bed lying on his stomach, his head dangling off the side. There was drool marks on his pillow. He hadn't even bothered to kick off his shoes.

"Pssst. Wake up."

"Huh? What time is it?"

"Oh, about time for dinner—you slept all afternoon."

"Wow." He sat upright, rubbing his eyes. "Did you have to break down the table all by yourself?"

I chuckled. "Not a problem. There wasn't much left to put away—thanks to you."

"Well then." He pressed his fists into his temples and squinted, shaking his head. He yawned. "OK. I'm awake now. So, what should we do for dinner?"

"Well, we've been invited to dine with the organizers—Tracy, April and their husbands," I answered. "Apparently they want to talk with us about a certification program for Foundations instructors." I stood up, balancing on one foot while I kicked my boot off of the other. "Or…"

"Or what?" he asked.

"We could pretend we were back on The Haunted Mansion ride…"

Chapter 8

From A to Z

It was a stunning weekend morning, and I had nothing on my agenda for the entire day. As usual, I awoke earlier than the rest of my family. The fine autumn weather beckoned, so instead of brewing a French press pot at home, I walked Sasha down to the corner coffee shop.

A disarranged Sunday Seattle Times at one of the tables caught my eye as I made my way toward the barista. The "NW Weekend" section lay on top and there was a color photograph of two tall ships under sail. I paused to examine the page more closely.

The ships, named *Adventuress* and *Zodiac,* were in Lake Union for the weekend, offering free tours. The article was entitled, "Sailing from A to Z." I didn't really have any keen interest in old-fashioned boats myself, but I knew that Jeffery loved this kind of thing. So I devised a way to surprise my husband: I could deliver him coffee, hustle him out of the house—and keep the whole thing a secret until we arrived at the ships. My enthusiasm built as I waited for my latte. Sasha attempted to keep up as I raced back to set my plan in action.

A short time later, our car eased into the gravel lot on Westlake Avenue. Juliet came with us; the only one of the kids who'd shown any interest in seeing the historic boats. I looked out my window toward Lake Union and marveled at how the towering masts of the two ships broke the waterfront skyline. The wooden structures seemed out of place on the modern lakeside, yet they held their own amongst the hustle and bustle. They bobbed and swayed in a genteel manner with the rhythm of the wakes from the seaplanes nearby.

"Wow! How'd you find out about this?" Jeffery asked.

"I have my methods."

We lined up to board the vessels and were shepherded into the line for the *Zodiac* first. This suited Juliet fine, as it was the larger of the two ships by at least twenty feet. The freeboard of the ship's hull was so high that even standing on the dock, Jeffery's six-foot-two- inch frame barely reached the caprails.

We stepped up the boarding ramp and onto *Zodiac's* deck. Juliet at once broke free of my hand and tore off for the bow. She wanted to investigate the chains that supported the massive anchor; so big that it was visible from the parking lot. Jeff and I strolled along the deck and examined the helm station toward the back of the ship. The immense wheel, some five feet in diameter, was made entirely of wood and very traditional looking, right down to the fancy knot tied around the center spoke. "That's called the kingspoke," Jeffery said.

The mahogany gearbox directly behind the wheel, housed the screw that connected the wheel to the rudder, it was so… *elegant*. Both Jeffery and I wanted to touch everything. Book-ending the wheel stood two large brass items that I couldn't identify. Jeff explained that the one to the right was called the "telegraph," or "throttle" in a modern ship, and the one to the left was called a "peloris," designed to take sightings off of land— "bearings" he called it. I was impressed by my husband's knowledge of all of these foreign, nautical objects. Five years of owning *Sugaree* had not familiarized me with a very workable maritime vocabulary.

We heard Juliet calling us—or rather, we made out the unmistakable "Mom!" and "Dad!" amidst all the noise on the boat's deck. She had climbed onto the deckhouse roof, midway down the ship. I ran to pull her off of the ornate mahogany structure, afraid she would scratch something.

"Oh, she's fine up there," I heard someone say. "We climb up there to furl the foresail all the time."

I looked around and saw a balding gentleman with a denim shirt that had 'Zodiac 1924' embroidered on the front pocket. Juliet ignored my look of disapproval and scooted around the deckhouse on her bum as she stared up at the rigging. I followed the crewmember below into the charthouse.

Rich mahogany trim contrasted with the white enamel of the ship's bulkheads. Everywhere I turned there was bronze or gleaming brass. From the exquisite workmanship, I could tell that the shipwrights had taken great pains to restore it to the original period style. A sloped worktable, littered with charts and instruments, stood in the corner of the deckhouse. The only visible nod to modernism was a radar and GPS unit that hung above the table. Portlights situated around the room allowed ample sunlight and air movement through the cozy space. Along one side of the little deckhouse ran a settee and a lattice work coffee table that held magazines like *Classic Boat* and *Blue Water Cruising*.

The three of us spent nearly an hour poking our head into windows and around scuttles, deck boxes and the like. It was a wonderland of nautical sights, sounds, and even smells.

Eventually, we made our way across the dock to the other schooner called the *Adventuress*, which we heard referred to as *Zodiac*'s 'sister ship'. We were appreciative of her lines and many details, but after our tour of *Zodiac*, the *Adventuress* seemed almost a miniature of the other vessel and somehow didn't garner as much of our esteem. Perhaps one could blame it on 'love at first sight'.

It was getting close to lunchtime. "Well," I looked to my two companions, "have we seen enough?"

"I expect we have," Jeffery replied. I could tell that he was reluctant to leave.

"OK, c'mon then." Even though it was a Sunday, I had, in fact, many small errands to run, including some last-minute chores at Gracewinds. We started to walk toward the parking lot when Juliet grabbed my arm.

"Look, Mom! They're going on a sail this afternoon! She pointed to a sandwich board in front of the *Zodiac*. "Can we go, please? *Pleeease?*"

Jeffery didn't utter a sound, but he didn't have to. His face said it all. I stopped and heaved an exaggerated sigh. Juliet and Jeff could see which way I was leaning. They stood silently waiting for my decision. After a brief discussion with Jeff about our budget, we signed up for the day sail.

There was only an hour and a half before we had to re-board the boat, so we dashed back home to have lunch and then stopped by work so I could finish my chores. But my tasks took longer than I expected, and we had less than ten minutes remaining once we got back into the car. As Jeff parked the VW, we could see that passengers were already onboard the *Zodiac*. It appeared as though we might be too late.

"Come on!" shouted Juliet, and she tore ahead.

"You guys take off. I'll grab the coats and be right behind you," Jeff said.

We barreled across the parking lot, down the gravel path that led to the Naval Armory, and raced onto the dock. To our dismay, we saw the lines had been cast off and the big ship was pulling away from the dock.

"OK—everybody jump!" Jeffery hollered from behind me.

We clumsily ran up the boarding steps and leapt across the widening gap to the gangway—almost knocking over a crewmember who looked at us with astonishment as he prepared to fasten the life-line across our path.

"We made it!" I said, suddenly aware of the thirty or more surprised faces staring at our ungainly appearance on deck. We recovered our dignity, then identified ourselves to the crewmember whom I'd met earlier that day. He smiled, shaking his head, checked our names off the manifest, and welcomed us aboard. The *Zodiac* motored out into Lake Union.

With barely enough time for us to stow our bags, a booming male voice shouted, "All hands! Prepare to raise sails!"

Crewmembers dashed about us everywhere, they threw coils on the deck and began to grab onto one thing then pull on another. Several deckhands yanked on some long straps which were wrapped around the sails above us. A stout, short-haired woman in a crew shirt tapped my arm and asked if I'd like to help with the foresail sheet. "Yeah sure, why not?" I said.

I joined her near the mast. Juliet jumped in as reinforcement. The woman introduced herself as Laura and began to show us what to do. She demonstrated 'belaying', which means wrapping the line (they're not called 'ropes' on a boat), or in this case 'sheet,' around a thing called the 'pin' in a figure-eight pattern. Then she showed us a locking hitch to 'make it fast.' We learned to 'ease out the sail' and to 'sheet in the boom.' She concluded by saying we were to watch and listen and she would tell us what to do and when to do it.

Moments later the same commanding male voice bellowed, "All hands to the main!" We hustled back where a long, thickly fibered line lay down the length of the deck. We were told to split up on either side of the ship and to pick up the line with both hands—and not to let go until we were told. I thought that was rather ominous sounding. The crew began to sound like ringleaders—or maybe it was more like Viking oar-masters—as they called out, "Pull when your down-haul pulls. All together now!"

I glanced around for what a 'down-haul' might be and spied two strapping guys at the main mast, one on my side and one opposite. The young man on my side held on to the line with one hand about chest-high, while the other rested on the tree-sized mast. He looked poised and ready to go. On command, both men jumped up and heaved down with both hands again and again. The rest of us pulled on the line in synch, and a kind of rhythm developed as we slowly made the boom that carried the expanding sail rise up horizontally toward the sky.

"Everybody—pull together! Get smart or get strong!" the crewmember hollered.

I started to wheeze a little between tugs. This was more cardio exercise than I'd done for months (with the exception of my dash to the boat earlier in the day). I could hear the gasps coming heavier from others around me as well, and felt a little better.

At long last, the heavy gaff boom was raised to its peak. We were told: "One, two, three—drop it!" and so we did. I collapsed on the nearest deck box to catch my breath.

"Next sail is the fore—everybody up. Let's GO!" yelled that same crewmember.

I began to develop a mild irritation for this guy with each new 'motivational' command. "Who is he kidding?" I rasped. Staggering to my feet, I followed the others on my side forward and we all picked up another line similar to the one before. Off we went, all together, in one wincing, sweating chorus line of grunts.

"Heave, Heave, Heave!"

I panted and glared toward the guy calling out commands. But he remained nonplussed by anyone's expressions of exhaustion and continued to bark out orders. He reminded me of my high school swim coach: a mustachioed sadist with a drill sergeant's temperament.

Once the sails were all up and filled with wind, our boisterous leader adopted a more cajoling and upbeat tone to his commands. He also congratulated us for hauling up the largest mainsail on the west coast and urged us to be quick about "making up those lines."

Laura waved to me impatiently, so I heaved a big gulp of air and made my way over to what she had referred to as my 'sailing station'. It was time to trim our sail, she told me. At her guidance, I let the sheet run through my hands, with the continuous patter of Juliet's editorializing and corrections in the background.

"Too fast, Mommy!" and "Don't let it out so far!" and "Hey—Mom, she's telling you to belay it!"

I put the locking hitch on the figure-eight as I'd practiced before and let Juliet take charge of coiling up the line. Taking a step back, I looked up: the sails were all set and the ship was under full sail. It was a magnificent sight to behold.

I wandered over to Jeffery's station and he showed me how they controlled the topping lifts to keep the boom from dropping during a tack. He went on with so much enthusiasm that I knew I'd done the right thing when I'd hatched my plan to visit the *Zodiac*. What a wonderful thing for my husband—to be on such a ship for the day. I realized then that I was feeling like a changed person as well.

All too soon we were ordered to lower sail. With much care and choreography, the huge sails were brought down. We all helped to furl as neatly as possible, and then wrapped the canvas to the booms with the long black gaskets so they would be contained at dock.

With our tasks completed, Jeffery and I leaned against the charthouse, watching the activity on deck while we sipped on our water bottles. My gaze wandered aft, down the length of the deck. At the wheel stood a handsome, middle-aged man. I assumed that he must be the captain. He was simply dressed in a white tee shirt and light-khaki pants; a striking contrast to his dark tan. He had salt-and-pepper grey hair—the kind that conveyed a distinguished rather than elderly look. And although his eyes were hidden behind polarized sunglasses, I could tell by the set of his brow that he was a serious sort of guy. His economical smile never seemed to interrupt his concentration at the wheel. On occasion, he would engage in conversation with others around the quarterdeck; chuckling or nodding, but always he returned his attention to the course ahead. I nudged Jeffery and pointed toward the helm. "How in the hell do you suppose one ever gets to know somebody like that?"

"I dunno," Jeffery shrugged. "Certainly not by running in the circles that we do."

I nodded in agreement and then, tilting my head sideways, I squinted back at the captain. It didn't occur to me to walk up and introduce myself, or even to try and get a closer look. I imagined that we, the passengers, were relegated to a different realm—sort of like steerage on the *Titanic*. The helm station seemed to be sort of a VIP lounge; one could gaze upon the occupants from afar but there was no admittance for the 'talking cargo.'

Jeffery had lost interest in the power-hitters on the quarterdeck and was engaged in conversation with a female sailor sporting heavy dreadlocks. He was living the dream, being on board. It was like *Horatio Hornblower, Master and Commander* and *Captains Courageous* all rolled together in one afternoon.

I left Jeffery with the salty deck wench, and went in search of Juliet. It didn't take long to find her in the galley, munching on a peanut butter cookie and jawing with the ship's cook. She barely acknowledged my presence as I walked through. I stepped into the main salon and saw twelve berths neatly aligned; curtains open to reveal the bunks. Inside one of the lower berths slept an old tabby cat. I stroked his neck but his interest in human company was not such that he could even be bothered to purr. I took the hint and left him alone.

Since my family members had made themselves at home onboard, I decided to try and do the same. I ventured back up into the charthouse and took a seat next to an elderly deckhand. In less than fifteen minutes, I learned that his name was Rocky, that he was as old as the *Zodiac* (85 years), that he had a ten-year-old granddaughter who lived with him and his wife, and that he'd been a *Zodiac* volunteer on and off for almost twenty years. He confided that the other crew called him "Yoda." He did have a very Yoda-like quality about him—minus the green skin. He then told me all about how my husband could become a volunteer onboard.

"He's a good sailor, that one," he commented. "I saw him haulin' on those lines." Rocky finished our conversation with a randy compliment about my derriere, which I chose to overlook due to his advanced age and occupation, but his comments about volunteering on the ship stayed with me.

By the time *Zodiac* pulled up to the dock, we'd fallen completely in love with her. The sun had lost its warmth, so we zipped up our sweaters, put on our coats and prepared to disembark. I held back, reluctant to leave for some reason I couldn't quite explain. Jeffery lagged behind as well, trading contact information with the volunteer coordinator. Then we made the descent and caught up with the other passengers as they strolled down the dock. Jeffery's eyes beamed as he and Juliet fired off stories of their separate experiences on board, each trying to talk over the other.

As we neared the end of the dock, I took a fleeting look back at the *Zodiac* and caught a glimpse of the captain sitting near the fantail, a coffee cup in his hand. He watched our group depart until all the passengers were safely ashore, he then gave a brief nod in our general direction and disappeared below.

Juliet summed it up as she happily proclaimed, "I'm sure glad we didn't miss that boat!"

Chapter 9

About the Money

"Test, one-two. Test, one-two. OK, you're live now." The sound man folded my lapel over the tiny microphone and brushed my collar flat. I sat very still at the table while the cameramen and technicians adjusted their angles and positioned the light screen. Behind me, hovering in the doorway, were several Gracewinds staff members and my new office manager. I couldn't quite see them from my seat at the table, but I could hear their whispers and giggles as they commented on the extraordinary procedures unfolding in our lobby.

The production crew parted to allow the TV host to enter the room. Christine Chen was a petite, attractive woman in her mid-thirties. She'd been an anchorwoman on Seattle's Q-13 Fox News. Her current role was host for "About the Money," a weekly financial interest show. This is what brought her into my business on a sunny fall afternoon in 2007.

I'd been introduced to Christine over a year ago when she'd been the keynote speaker at the Small Business Administration's Awards celebration. She'd presented me with the SBA award for Western Region's "Women in Business Champion." Now, with the recent news that Gracewinds had just received the National Association of Women Business Owners "Trailblazer" award, with a check for $5,000, she'd requested a feature about me for her "CEO Spotlight" segment.

By now, I'd grown accustomed to giving speeches and had been interviewed in the paper and on radio numerous times. However, I didn't exactly feel at home in front of the camera. I fidgeted with my shirt collar and squirmed in my chair. Christine reached across the table and patted my arm, "Just pretend they aren't even in the room."

I nodded and returned her smile, opting not to voice my skepticism. Christine clipped her microphone onto her silk blouse and tossed her head, her glossy brunette hair swinging behind her shoulder. I assessed her appearance and appreciated her perfect manicure and professional make-up. She had the effortless "put-together" look that pointed toward a long career in front of the camera.

I clung to my informal dress code and sported a brown suede blazer over a linen tank top. My corduroy trousers and suede Tevas were a glaring contrast positioned across from her patent leather high heels and shimmery hosiery.

"Alright. Are you about ready to begin?" She asked.

"I believe so. Is there anything in particular that you want me to say?"

"Don't worry about coming up with any topics; I'll sort of feed you the questions one at a time. We'll stick to your awards and Gracewinds' success story. Maybe you could speak a little about how it all began." She instructed. "I won't leave you hanging, don't worry. And remember this isn't live, so we can stop and maybe frame your story as we go."

I nodded and heaved a big sigh, hoping that my inner feelings would not be conveyed on film. Sure, I didn't mind talking about the business—it was always good exposure. I'd recited our success stories so often that I could do it in my sleep:

This award, that award, expansion, growth, books, babies, blah blah blah… I felt like an actor playing a part: the character of an entrepreneur and birth guru—the networking "Doula-mama" and mentor to women business owners nationwide. The trouble was, I didn't exactly feel that part right now.

For the past few months, family life weighed heavily on me once again. We'd finally managed to stabilize Dane's chaotic lifestyle, and figured the hard part was over. Jeff and I grew almost complacent. Then Megan and Justine hit 'sweet' sixteen. The household was rocked once more against the jagged shores of teenage hormones. Only this time, with the girls, it manifested as tears and inner rage and bouts of seething silence. The situation reached a grim climax several days before when I stumbled upon a box of razors in the girls' bedroom. While they were at their dad's house for the weekend, I'd gone in to gather their dirty clothes. Poking out from underneath their sofa was a tattered *My Little Pony* jewelry box. I reached down to pick it up—I'd never noticed that particular box before. My heart nearly stopped when I saw the contents inside the box. Several razors blades mingled with unwrapped Winnie the Pooh Band-Aids.

Since that discovery, Jeffery and I sat in bed nearly every night, wracking our brains for a tactful way to discuss our concerns with the girls. Once I'd explained the practice, Jeff had a string of questions: "Is cutting like what… a suicide attempt?" "Are they trying to punish us?" "Is this some sort of new trend at school?" "Jesus Christ, Chris, I'm way out of my depth here—I've never even heard of this kind of crazy thing!" We would whisper back and forth until the early hours. Then, in the morning we'd head off to work—Jeff to his contracting job and me to Gracewinds, internally distressed and searching for answers. It made for some very long days.

"OK. Everybody ready? Let's roll."

As the tape began to roll, Christine switched into 'anchorwoman' mode and guided me through the introduction and initial questions. We covered the past recognitions and press that Gracewinds had received and then segued into the upcoming award.

"So, this award has a prize of $5,000 attached to it. Congratulations on winning that. Seriously!" She said. "Do you have any big plans on what to do with that money?"

I slipped back into my CEO-role and answered. "As a matter of fact I do. We've just formed a nonprofit and have established a mother-baby center in southern Kenya. You see, the rate of HIV infection in this region is one of the highest in the world—so we've implemented a perinatal center there to educate pregnant women about the need to breastfeed their babies. We're so thrilled that this money will cover the construction of our mother-baby center. The Swahili word for it is *chakula bora*—it means a gathering place… somewhat like what we have created here in Seattle."

"Oh, wow!" Christine appeared truly fascinated. "So, in addition to the Gracewinds' facility here, you'll be opening a similar center in Africa? That's remarkable! Tell me Christine, how are you able to keep all of the balls in the air? Doesn't it get a little, you know, overwhelming at times?"

I chuckled and leaned back in my chair. "It can be a bit… challenging." I replied. However, I have a really strong support group around me. I think the key to my success—well, Gracewinds' success to be sure, is my luck in finding top-notch individuals, many of whom are experts in their field. Basically, I make sure that they've got the freedom to practice the way they want to—something that they can't always do in larger organizations. They've really grown to love it here. The result is that we inspire each other—really we do. And great things come from working like that."

Christine simply nodded in agreement as I spoke. I paused for a moment and thought about what I'd just said. I'd never spoken it aloud exactly like that, but I was quite smitten with my last sentiment. It was true, these women inspired me daily and I, apparently, was an inspiration to them.

Christine glanced over at the director and nodded. She let down her on-camera persona and turned back to me. "That was excellent. Thank you for sharing that last little bit. Now, what I'd like to do before we wrap it up is touch on the beginnings of Gracewinds and then end with your thoughts about the future. Sound good to you?"

The interview continued for fifteen or twenty more minutes. As she wrapped up the segment, she asked the one question I'd been dreading. "How does your family manage with you so busy? Do you have any challenges with life at home?"

I reached for the glass of water in front of me and took a measured drink. Swallowing hard, I managed a smile and said, "Well, it's definitely a one-day-at-a-time thing, Christine. I can tell you though, honestly, that it's the joy and the love—and sometimes even the pain—that I get from my own kids that keeps me motivated to do this work, you know, helping other parents get their start—I couldn't do it without my own family. And I really mean that."

"I imagine." Christine agreed, "Well, I am so grateful that you sat down to talk with us today about your business. Congratulations and best wishes for the continued success of this invaluable organization."

"Thank you, it was a pleasure."

And with that, the film crew shut down their lights and began to pack away equipment. Christine reached across the table to shake my hand and said, "This is a really wonderful story, Chris. It's so nice to do a feature that's not just about finance or software!"

I escorted her to the door. As I waved goodbye and turned back toward the lobby, I met with a smattering of applause from my staff members who were still crowded in the lobby doorway. I responded with an exaggerated bow. "*Thank* you, thank you—all of you little people who helped make this day possible."

After the disruption of our workday, everyone got back to their jobs and I pulled out my cell phone. I located the number in my contacts list of the counselor we'd visited years ago for Dane and dialed the number. "Hello? Yes hi there, my name is Chris Wallace. Mmm, mmm, right. Well, I'd like to make a family appointment for my twin daughters. OK, sure I can hold."

Chapter 10

Tall Ships

We stood at the end of Port Townsend's public pier in in the blistering heat. I felt the skin on the back of my neck sting, warning me I was in for a good sunburn. However I didn't mind, I had an entire week of freedom from my job and the chaos of the city. Jeffery and Juliet were with me, and soon enough we'd be onboard the *Zodiac* for a trip through Puget Sound. The ship was due at any moment and I could feel my excitement build as I waited for her arrival. I hovered at the railing and watched for her masts.

Port Townsend's waterfront bustled with tourists, and I found myself being jostled about as onlookers crowded onto the pier for better views of the water. Small Beetle Cats skittered about near the shore and farther out several sailboats raced an imaginary course through the deeper water.

We chatted with others on the dock as we waited for the *Zodiac.* Jeffery met a couple from Colorado and traded climbing stories with them. Juliet held the attention of several onlookers as she spoke about the *Zodiac* and our upcoming trip to the Tacoma Tall Ship Festival. "We're going to go to this big show with tons of tall ships just like the *Zodiac!*" she exclaimed.

"What kind of a boat is the *Zodiac*?" asked one of the tourists. "The only Zodiac that I've heard of is a rubber dinghy."

"No, no, this one's a *schooner,*" Juliet informed him.

"Is that like one of those old-fashioned pirate ships?" asked an elderly lady.

"Actually, a pirate ship is kind of a *square*-rigger," Juliet explained. "Schooners have two masts—sometimes even more. But the main mast is the tallest one... that's the mast that's farthest back." She added, "But *Zodiac* just has two masts."

I smiled as I watched my youngest child hold court. She had absorbed so much in the last year while volunteering on the big boat. Her knowledge of classic sailing vessels and maritime history had surpassed mine months ago.

"What about that little one out there with two masts?" a younger woman inquired.

"Oh, um, I'm pretty sure that one's a *ketch*. We have a ketch too, her name's *Sugaree*."

"A ketch—" continued the woman, "what makes it a ketch instead of a schooner?"

Juliet pointed toward the boat. "See her little mast in the back? That's the mizzen mast and it's shorter, so she's a ketch. If the little mast was behind her wheel—well, then it would be called a yawl."

"And that one out there—the one with the red sails?" a boy about Juliet's age interrupted. "What's that kind of boat called?"

"A sloop," she said instantly. "Oh, wait, no, it's actually a *cutter*. See, if they've got just one mast they're either a cutter or a sloop. It depends on whether they have two stays for their headsails."

"My goodness, how does a young lady such as you know so much about boats? How old are you?" All Juliet's listeners nodded in questioning agreement.

"My dad taught me, and I'm eight years old," she answered. "Also I learned on the *Zodiac*. Captain Tim knows a lot about all the boats—he even knows the different kinds of square-riggers. I only know about the *Lady Washington* and she is called a brig—she starred in *Pirates of the Caribbean!*"

A bearded gentleman with binoculars was scanning the various boats on the horizon as Juliet gave her impromptu tutorial. He spotted a ship in the distance and set the glasses down long enough to turn and asked Juliet what he was seeing. "Hey, is that your ship, little sailor?"

Juliet stood on her tip-toes and squinted. I followed the direction of their gazes and saw a gaff-rigged schooner far out in the distance.

"Oh yeah! That's her! That's the *Zodiac*!" Juliet yelled, "Mom! Hey, Dad! The Z's here!"

The crowd of tourists watched and waited for the tall ship to come closer. Gradually the great schooner rounded Point Wilson and everyone got a closer look at her. There were a number of gasps and comments of awe. I saw with pride that she flew all four of her sails and was making way nicely as she headed toward the shore of Port Townsend.

Juliet jumped up and down at the rail, barely able to contain her excitement at watching the ship arrive. My heart skipped a beat as well. *Zodiac* was a sight that never ceased to amaze and delight me and I couldn't wait to get back aboard.

Jeffery edged up next to me and put his chin on my shoulder, saying, "She'll do in a pinch, huh?"

The sightseers were awestruck. *Zodiac* gracefully paraded past the town, slowing in her course as her sails were lowered one by one. Her white hull stood in brilliant contrast with the cerulean blue of the bay. The reflection that she cast ghosted before us in the rippling water. By the time she had reached the end of the buildings downtown, her sails were doused and she pointed her prow to create a great sweeping arc. We watched as the crew lowered her tender over the leeward side.

"Amazing!" said the woman next to us. "You all get to go on *that* boat?"

"How old is she?"

"How big did you say she was?"

"Where is she from?" The tourists fired questions at us.

Juliet, however, was no longer interested in answering their questions; her mind was bent on one purpose—to get onboard the *Zodiac*. "Come on, Mom and Dad! I don't want them to leave without us!"

We gave our farewells to the group of onlookers and made our way down to the lower dock. The *Zodiac*'s inflatable tender motored up to where we stood. A young man whom we didn't recognize drove the boat. He gave us a perfunctory smile and looked past us toward town. Jeffery strode forward and offered his hand. "Hi there, we're your cargo, I believe."

The young crewman gave Jeff a puzzled look and shook his head. "Uh, I was told to come here to pick up Jeff and Christine. I'm not sure who you guys are."

Jeff gave me a quizzical look and turned back to the young man. "Well, my name is Jeff and this is my wife, Chris."

Juliet piped in with, "And me—Juliet! Did they tell you about me?"

The young man smiled and shook his head. "Well, darn. Sorry. I didn't realize we had *two* pairs of Jeff and Chris's on the roster these days!"

"What's he talking about, Mom?" Juliet whispered.

"I dunno. But let's just get our things in the boat."

As we piled our bags into the tender, I handed him my French press pot. He smirked. "You know, we do have coffee on the ship, right?"

"Yeah, I've tasted it."

"Ah."

He threw us each a large puffy orange life jacket. "Here, you'll need to fasten these up before I can let you in the tender." Before he engaged the engine he said, "Well, welcome aboard you guys, it's nice to meet you. My name's ET; I'm the first mate on *Zodiac*."

"ET? You mean like *ET phone home?*" Juliet asked.

"Yeah, no…" he answered.

"So, you're not the captain's son then?" I asked. "I heard that he was onboard during the sailing season." I was really curious to know what Captain Mehrer's son was going to be like. I doubted he could possibly be as taciturn as his father.

"Hah! Nope, I'm *definitely* not Calen," ET said with a grin. "But yeah, he's on board. You'll meet him soon enough. We've gotta really full ship for this transit down to Tacoma. I put you guys in a cabin, though."

We spent the rest of the brief ride to the big ship in silence. My nerves started to get the best of me. There were so many new crewmembers that we hadn't met during the winter refit period. ET seemed like a pretty likable kid, though. *Kid—shit, he's barely older than my twins and he's a first mate.* I felt my insecurities rise and hoped we'd fit in, and that I wouldn't make any lubberly mistakes.

The tender came alongside *Zodiac* as she idled with the current. A ladder had been placed over the side and we climbed onboard. Everything felt so familiar—just like she was last winter when we'd sanded and varnished her for weekends on end. But with her running-rig back in place, her sails bent-on and her crew back on deck, she had a much more essential air about her. *Zodiac* became her working self once more. We looked about the decks quickly and received waves from some familiar faces as well as neutral nods and casual salutes from many strange new ones. Intimidated, I snatched my belongings and went for the passageway below-decks.

Once we located our stateroom and laid claim to our bunks, we climbed upstairs to join the rest of the crew on deck. By now, *Zodiac* had throttled up to cruising speed and Port Townsend looked like a hazy wisp on the shoreline. The wind had increased, prompting me to send Juliet in search of our jackets. After some time, I located Jeffery aloft in the rig.

"Hey!" I called. "That didn't take you long! What are you doing?"

"There's a twist in the boat falls here. I'm just trying to trace it down so we can work it out." Jeffery climbed down from the ratlines and landed on the deck with a thump. He gave my shoulders a squeeze. "How *'bout* this?!"

"Yup. How 'bout it. It feels really good to be back."

For the next several hours we relaxed on deck. The other crewmembers introduced themselves throughout the afternoon. We learned that we were 'the *other* Jeff and Christine,' the second married couple with those names to work on the *Zodiac*. I hoped we'd measure up to our doppelgangers.

Jeffery fell in with the foredeck crew immediately. He soon had his needles and palm out and set about whipping the ends of the new jib sheets. It occurred to me that Jeff and the other sailors who were busily stitching, resembled my grandma's Kiwanis sewing circle. I searched around for a project but found I had little to offer in the way of skills for such ship details.

Eventually, I found a sunny spot on the salon roof and lay down to read. Soon enough, my daughter's piercing voice cut into my reverie. "*Caaaaay-len!*" she screamed. I sat up and searched the deck, partially out of motherly concern, but mostly out of curiosity. I wanted to identify who this Calen kid was.

I spied my daughter, rolled up in a deck cushion like a burrito. She had been wrapped and tied, attached to the gantline and lifted several feet above the deck. ET stood with his arms crossed, laughing while another teenaged boy hauled her up on the line. "Enough! Calen! That's high enough!" Juliet yelled.

"You kept teasing me. You wanted to go up higher," challenged the teen.

"OK, OK. No more teasing. I promise," Juliet whined.

ET looked over at me, "Whaddaya think, Juliet's-mom? *Will* she stop teasing?"

"Well, historically speaking, not a chance. You'd best get a written agreement before you bring her down."

"How 'bout this, Juliet," ET suggested, "we'll let you come down, but if you tease Calen or me any more… just once more—you're goin' overboard. Have we got a deal?"

"Yeah, yeah, yeah, I promise!"

Calen eased Juliet down to the deck and she wriggled out of her confines. She got to her feet and whacked Calen on his arm. "You're *so* dead!" she called and ran below. Calen rolled his eyes and knelt down to untie the deck cushion. He looked to be about seventeen or eighteen years old and had that thick-neck, heavy-shoulders look of a high school wrestler. His face was tanned and friendly. I liked him immediately.

"So, I take it you've gotten to know my daughter."

He looked up at me and grinned. "Yeah, well she's *kinda* hard to ignore."

That evening, the *Zodiac* dropped anchor south of Appletree Cove. Everyone enjoyed dinner on deck and watched the sun set behind the Olympics. We sat together in a circle on the quarterdeck, trading stories and allowing the darkening sky to settle upon us. I felt my stress melt away as I soaked up the thick blackness of the night, absent of all the ambient city lights. Our voices were the only noises in the bay. We talked and laughed and then just sat together for a time without speaking. The tranquility all around became almost tactile, as if I could reach out into the night and touch the stillness. And then, one by one, we said our good nights and went below to our bunks.

That next day, we set our course for Quartermaster Harbor off of Vashon Island. We were to meet up with the entire fleet of tall ships and anchor there for the evening. "The Vashon Island Yacht Club is throwing a BBQ for the crews of all the ships tonight," ET told us. "Make sure you've got your crew shirts—and make sure that they're clean." To drive home his point, he looked directly at a few of the saltier crewmembers.

"Mom, do I get to go to the BBQ too?" Juliet asked.

"Well, since you're a deckhand as well, I don't see why not. I just hope ET thinks your shirt is clean enough to pass." I resisted a laugh as she tore down to our stateroom to examine the condition of her outfit.

We sailed for most of the day and arrived at the entrance to the harbor around two o'clock. The captain ordered the sails dropped and the headsail crew to put in their "harbor furls."

"What's a harbor furl for?" I asked Jeffery.

"It means we take extra time and pleat the sails like an accordion," he answered. "It looks really nice from the shore but it's kind of a pain in the ass to do."

"Ah hah…" I had so much to learn.

Later that day, *Zodiac* motored slowly toward her anchorage. The wide bay of Quartermaster Harbor opened for us, the green banks genuflected to the water, encircling us in a rolling arc of tree-line. I stood with Juliet at bow-watch and gazed at the scenery surrounding us. Birds of differing sizes swam nearby, diving and bobbing for the small fish at the surface.

The shallow depth of the harbor made it necessary for the *Zodiac* to anchor in its center, and since she had the deepest draft of the fleet, the other vessels were assigned spots that encircled her, nearer the shores. By the time our anchor sunk to the bottom, other ships began to arrive at the mouth of the inlet.

Juliet and I climbed atop the staysail boom and from our perch we watched the impressive vessels appear. The first to pull in was the *Nina*, dark-hulled and compact—she was the replica of the 15th century caravel that Columbus sailed to the Americas. As she dropped her anchor abeam of the *Zodiac*, we marveled at how small she was (for a tall ship). It seemed impossible that Columbus and his crew could have sailed over 25,000 miles in that vessel. She measured no more than sixty-five feet on deck with only five feet of freeboard above the water line. "How could they have all fit?" I wondered aloud.

Juliet replied, "They slept up on the decks—except for Christopher Columbus."

"How the heck do you know this?"

"I studied the *Nina*, the *Pinta* and the *Santa Maria* in fourth grade, Mom."

"Good for you." Being the least informed onboard was beginning to wear a bit thin for me.

"Oooh, look, Mom! It's the *Lady Washington* with her sails still up!"

I peered toward the mouth of the bay and, sure enough, the *Lady* and her sister ship, the *Hawaiian Chieftain* came drifting into our sights, square sails billowing and pendants fluttering. The *Lady* took the lead position, her bright yellow hull contrasting nicely against the pines on shore in the background. Closely on her heels came the *Chieftain*, her cannon still visible on deck—no doubt from a recent sea-battle with her sister. The two square-riggers, neither requiring as much draft as the *Zodiac*, motored to the docks as they lowered their canvas.

Jeffery and ET joined us at the bow. Jeff handed me a glass of red wine. "Here, this is what you're missing."

"*Gracias, mi amor.*"

"Hey, ET! What's the name of that big ship?" asked Juliet, pointing beyond the sisters.

ET squinted into the horizon and called out, "The *Lynx*, Juliet. Check out her raked masts. Aren't those cool?"

I waited until she drew near our beam and looked up at her tall masts, slanted gracefully backwards. The rake made her appear as if she was going much faster than her two knots through the crowded harbor. "I bet when she has her sails up and has a good wind, she looks awesome!"

For the rest of the afternoon, we sipped wine and watched the various tall ships gather. By dinnertime, there were nearly forty vessels at-rest in the serene little bay. Portlights glowed in the fading summer evening as each ship lit their decks from below. The time to go ashore for our BBQ had arrived, and we lined up to board the tender.

Our trip across the bay took much longer than it needed to as we tendered from vessel to vessel, circling each ship to get a fish-eye view and called out greetings to those who were still on board. We arrived at the dock to find that the access to shore was blocked by the two square- riggers.

"Permission to come aboard to get to the dock?" yelled ET.

"Aye, climb aboard, *Zodiac* hands!" came the response from a costumed *Chieftain* deckhand.

"Pssst, Mom, he looks like a pirate!" Juliet whispered.

"Yeah, I see," I whispered back. "They dress up like old-fashioned sailors on these two boats."

"Wow. Wouldn't that be hilarious if Captain Tim dressed up like a pirate?" Juliet cackled at her notion. The image of our captain in a tricorn buccaneer's hat made me smile.

We scrambled across the decks of the *Chieftain* and the *Lady*, then onto the wooden dock that led us to land. Jeffery and I walked together, hand in hand, up the hill toward the music emanating from the yacht club. We stopped at the peak and looked down across the bay. Soaring masts rose above the still water like reeds in a marsh.

"Hey, check it out." Jeffrey pointed. "The *Zodiac* has the tallest sticks in the bay."

"Well, it just goes to show—size does matter!"

"Really? I thought it was what you did with them that mattered most?"

"Well, either way, *Zodiac* comes out on top."

With our animated mood in place, we spent the evening enjoying burgers and cold beer. We listened to live music under the canopy and spat watermelon seeds into the grass. I met tall ship sailors from all over the world as well as from local ports. On the lawn, children from the other vessels played tag with Juliet as parents and friends sprawled out on blankets and chatted. ET and Calen sat next to me and entertained us with stories of the different ships. "We pranked the *Adventuress* on our way to Port Angeles last week… got 'em good. You better keep an eye out for them during your night watch—they'll be out for revenge!" Calen warned.

84

"Just don't prank the HMS *Bounty*, whatever we do," added ET. "The last ship that tried to get away with it paid pretty dearly. It's like the *Flying Dutchman* crossed with *Black Pearl*, so I hear."

Dusk set upon the islands. Someone lit a fire in the giant pit and cedar sparks raced each other to the heavens. I leaned back into Jeffery's lap and looked around the group of my new shipmates, watching the orange light play upon their features and expressions, people of different ages and backgrounds, bound together by love of old ships and maritime traditions. The worries and obligations of my so-called *real life* had disappeared. I existed now in a world of sailors, camaraderie and yarns of mythical ships. When it was time to return to the *Zodiac*, I strolled back to the dock in the moonlight with Jeffery and Juliet, thinking to myself about what an exceptional life this was.

The morning of the Tacoma Tall Ships Festival dawned bright and warm. Before we finished breakfast the temperature had climbed to the mid-seventies. We brought out the soft rags and Brasso and set about polishing all of the bronze and brass on deck until it glistened. The fir decks were hosed down and swabbed, and several crewmembers launched the inflatable tender to paddle around *Zodiac*'s hull with a brush and sea water, scrubbing down her white topsides. The captain ordered that all covers be taken off of the mahogany superstructures, so we carefully pulled the heavy green fabric away from the charthouse, gear box and scuttles fore and aft. Captain Tim gave the large *Zodiac* pendant to Juliet and asked her to run it up the main gantline. She skipped over to me, her face flushed. "The captain gave me a job!" She exclaimed in a voice just above a whisper.

I helped her snap the clips onto the line and run it up to the spreaders. The breeze took hold of the pendant and it unfurled in a flourish of green and gold. *Zodiac* gleamed in the sun, ready for her arrival into Commencement Bay.

The next step was to gussy up her crew, so we went below to don our best attire. Our dress code for festivals consisted of khaki pants, navy blue *Zodiac* shirts and deck shoes or topsiders. With our hair brushed, hands scrubbed free of grime, and sporting clean, hemmed trousers we looked like we actually belonged to our magnificent ship.

The other tall ships were getting their makeovers as well, and shouts could be heard across the water as busy deckhands set about their tasks.

ET called all hands to midship for a brief meeting. We assembled at the main fife rail and waited for our instructions. "Alright everybody, Cap'n just got the line-up for the Parade of Sails. Looks like we are in position number eleven, following the *Chieftain* and in front of the *Bounty*." Excited murmurs buzzed around me as the deckhands offered their collective opinions about our position.

"Listen up!" ET interrupted the hubbub. "We're gonna be under full sail but we'll be using our engine as well. There's gonna be a thousand gapers out there in their little power boats trying to get a good look at these ships." He pointed toward the mouth of the bay. "We'll need three bow-watches and everyone on the lookout at all times wherever they're stationed. The escort boats can be just as bad as these crazy knuckleheads. They'll cut right in front of us without thinking. Oh yeah, and crab pots. It's crabbing season, so they'll be littered all over the place…. Just keep a sharp eye is all I'm saying."

Captain Tim walked up to the group and said, "The *Lady* and *Chieftain* will likely pick the worst time to stage one of their sea battles, guys. It'll hold up the entire procession and if we don't space ourselves adequately, we'll end up with *Bounty*'s bowsprit stuck in our transom. Be alert and keep the helm informed."

The ship's bell rang six times meaning it was time to weigh anchor and move forward to our place in the line-up. As each ship left Quartermaster Harbor, they were paired with an escort boat, a small motor-yacht which would guide them through the route in Commencement Bay. The Parade of Sails was to circumnavigate the expansive bay, resulting in a grand arrival at the Tacoma waterfront. Thousands of spectators were expected on land as well as the literally hundreds of vessels packed into the bay.

The *Zodiac* throttled up and left the mouth of the harbor. I stood on bow-watch as one of the lookouts. Miles of water stretched out in front of me, swarming with crafts of all sizes and types. Everywhere I scanned there were little motor boats zipping to and fro. Coast Guard patrols ripped across the bay, chasing down errant vessels, their blue lights flashing. The entire area had taken on a carnival-esque atmosphere.

"Hullo up there!" someone called.

I looked down and waved. A power boat came alongside and its skipper leaned out of the cockpit. "Ahoy, *Zodiac*! Welcome to Tall Ships Tacoma! We're your escort. I'll be monitoring channel six-eight. Give a shout if you need me!" He pulled ahead, crossing our bow with little room to spare.

I shook my head. There was so much going on all at once. Suddenly I noticed two bright orange buoys bobbing ahead of us. "Uhh… crab pots—right off our starboard bow!"

Jeffery raced back to the speaking tube and lifted the brass plug. He leaned in and spoke. "Helm. Crab pots. Thirty feet ahead. One point off starboard."

I felt the *Zodiac*'s helmsman shift her heading slightly to port and watched as the crab pots slipped by our starboard side. "Balls! So close."

"This is going to be a helluva lot of fun!" yelled Calen as he came forward to reconnoiter the course.

I nodded and kept up my watch.

For two hours the *Zodiac* paced herself through the maze of tall ships. Captain Tim throttled the engine up and down accordingly, to maintain the proper distance from the *Chieftain*. Balanced on the bowsprit, I looked forward as well as took quick glances back over our decks. I thrilled at the spectacle of all the enormous ships under full sail. The swaying column of schooners, brigs, barques and windjammers twined around the bay in breathtaking pageantry. Behind our helm, I noticed the HMS *Bounty* gaining on us; she appeared menacing, as if in hot pursuit.

"This is so amazing!" Jeffery said, his eyes glistening. I smiled and nodded.

KABOOM!

I jumped in surprise. Smoke and powder rose from the port-side deck of the *Hawaiian Chieftain*.

KABOOM! *Lady Washington* answered. The two ships had slowed to a near standstill to stage their battle. I felt *Zodiac*'s engine grind to a halt and could hear the gears reverse into astern propulsion. *Bounty* drew closer to our transom. By the way her prow was nosing toward port, I assumed she was taking action to prevent colliding with our stern. And from my vantage point on the bowsprit, I could look straight into the transom portlights of the *Chieftain*. It was unnerving to be so close to two other big ships while underway, and I marveled at Captain Tim's ability to keep *Zodiac* under control in such a tight situation.

We spent several tense moments yawing back and forth until the mock sea-battle concluded. At last, engines revved and the parade commenced. My bow-watch replacement tapped me on the shoulder and I hopped down from my perch inboard of the breastworks. Jeffery and Juliet sat behind me trading quotes from *Master and Commander*.

"What? Did I kill a brother of his in battle—a son perhaps?"

"We must run like smoke and oakum!"

"Nerds," I quipped as I walked past them.

The entrance into Foss Waterway lay dead ahead. The ships filed into the narrow channel and were escorted to their respective docks. The *Zodiac* maneuvered carefully into her space in front of the Foss Museum. Groups of spectators called out and waved at us as we sidled into our moorage. Directly ahead of us was the *Nina*, our neighbor from the previous evening. We leaned out over the rail to get a look at the ships in front of her.

"Oh boy! The *Bounty* is next! Let's go see the *Bounty*!" Juliet exclaimed.

"Hang on there, kiddo!" Jeffery said. "We have to get our ship ready for the tourists before you can run off to see the others. Remember, you're a *Zodiac* crewmember. You need to pitch in just like everyone else." Juliet sulked for a moment, then just as quickly cheered up.

"Holy smokes! What is that?" I asked. A massive ship had arrived in Commencement Bay, escorted by at least a dozen vessels. She had two giant masts as well as a mizzen, plus countless sails of various shapes filling her rig, at least four headsails protruded to the tip of her bowsprit. The colossal hull must have stretched for over 300 feet. News station helicopters hovered nearby as she slowly made her way into the narrow inlet.

"Oh! *Hell* yes! That's the *Eagle!*" exclaimed Jeffery. "Excellent!"

I raised my eyebrows as I heard him speak. I'd never, in all my life, heard such excitement in his voice before. He appeared as jubilant as his daughter. Pointing toward the ship he told her all about the *Eagle.*

"That right there, Juliet, is the Coast Guard's sail-training ship!" he explained. "She's called a barque. The United States won her as a prize of war from the Germans after the Second World War." He set Juliet onto the caprail and held her waist. "She has a triple helm—that means that it takes three wheels, bigger than *Zodiac*'s, to move her!"

"Wow! Dad, can we go onboard to look at her?"

"Oh, most definitely!" he promised.

The rest of the day blew by. We raised the *Zodiac*'s dress flags from the deck to the top of our masts. Jeffery and several deckhands constructed a boarding platform on the dock and affixed it to the gangway. Crowds of tourists lined the piers, waiting to board the vessels and walk our decks. Families with small children gazed up at the ship with awe, pointing to the giant blocks and towering masts. I looked down the line of sightseers and smiled. I remembered the thrill as we queued up to board Zodiac for the first time.

The crew spent hours standing on deck answering the multitude of questions about *Zodiac* and the history of the American fishing schooners. I placed myself on the foredeck, near the windlass and the speaking tube, showing youngsters how to blow into the brass pipe so that the helm could hear the whistle and message that followed. "This here is the original wireless!" exclaimed an elderly gentleman.

"Things were so simple back then!" said one parent.

By eight o'clock that evening, we'd welcomed over a thousand tourists onto our decks. The entire crew was worn out, but not Juliet. "Time to go look around!" she decreed.

Jeffery and I followed her off the ship and spent the next few hours walking the docks and visiting the other boats. Several vessels had "dressed ship" with strands of small white lights rigged to their stays and shrouds. It gave the docks a magical quality—Disney would have been jealous. The boats rested on their moorings, and appeared as tired by the day's events as their crews. I ran my hand alongside *Zodiac*'s hull as we returned to our ship—she was still the finest of them all to my eyes. Just before midnight we crawled into our bunks and passed out for the night. Tomorrow would be another busy day.

By the end of the week, Jeff and Juliet had managed to tour every single vessel at the show, and before departing they were on a first-name basis with many of the other captains. By the end of the festival we were all sunburnt, exhausted and sore, but I wouldn't have traded those days for anything in the world. Living—even for just a week—among the historic ships and their crews was enchanting. I didn't want it to end, but I knew all too well that it had to—for now.

Chapter 11

The Summit

The time spent during the cab ride from Dulles International airport into the heart of Washington, DC, was all that was required to erode the side effects of the Alprazolam I'd been prescribed. Somewhere along the way into adulthood, I'd evolved into one of those white-knuckled flyers I used to mock in my younger days.

As the medication slowly wore off, my excitement began to build. We pressed our faces to the windows of the taxi, staring at the images through the rivulets of rain that trickled down the glass. Every squeal of recognition that escaped my daughter's lips as we passed another recognizable monument only served to escalate my own anticipation and thrill.

Finalists from across the seven regions of the nation were assembled in DC for the 2008 US Chamber of Commerce Small Business Awards and Summit. Also assembled were hundreds of other business owners, lobbyists, investors, financiers and politicians to hustle, pontificate and commemorate the winners. And here I was, with my little business all about babies, preparing to rub elbows with the movers and shakers of the corporate world—it was a staggering and amusing thought at the same time.

The driver announced our arrival at the Renaissance Hotel with a laconic drawl. As he piled our assortment of unmatched luggage on the curb, we unfolded ourselves from the back seat of the taxi. Jeffery paid the driver, and Juliet and I picked up our bags and stepped through the revolving door.

The Renaissance Hotel lobby was grandiose. Tropical flowers in the centerpiece erupted into colorful patterns atop translucent glass balls in the main fountain. Crystal chandeliers hung throughout the first-floor lobby. Juliet stood stock-still in the large room, mouth agape and eyes sparkling, unable to give voice to her usual opinions for the first time. It was truly a sight to behold.

When we checked in at the front desk, the clerk congratulated me for being an award finalist and presented me with an oversized fruit basket and a bouquet of flowers. I enjoyed a slight smugness as I toted my bounty across the lobby and up the elevator. Juliet was, of course, completely recovered from her stunned silence and was not nearly so subtle. She made sure to inquire whenever we were in range of bystanders, "Mommy, does everybody get the flowers or is it just the winners?"

"Shhh, Juliet!" I replied each time. In truth, I felt lucky to have her along with us at that moment, if only to allow me to feign modesty for the sake of appearances.

We explored our fancy hotel suite and unpacked our bags. I arranged our belongings in the various bureaus while Jeffery reconnoitered the honor bar. It took some convincing to wrest the window-side bed away from Juliet and her multitude of stuffed animals (smuggled into her luggage in lieu of clothing), but we eventually got everything settled and headed out the door for a walk around town.

The hotel was only a few blocks from the White House, and even though it was nearing dark, we aimed for there first. As we walked along the narrow sidewalks, I noticed that the cherry blossoms had started to bloom in the mild April weather. Before we knew it, we'd arrived in front of 1600 Pennsylvania Avenue. The white-washed mansion stood in the middle of a painstakingly manicured lawn. It appeared aloof and yet somehow inviting of the attention. We gazed for some time in quiet awe, each of us pondering the decisions and events that had occurred inside those alabaster walls. I envisioned John and Bobby Kennedy bowing their heads over the great desk in the oval office, or 'Tricky Dick,' slumped in his armchair, ice clinking in his glass as he came to terms with the desperate situation of his presidency.

A light in one of the lonely office windows came on and brought me out of my reverie. I imagined it belonged to one of the current administration's speech writers, burning the midnight oil to concoct a plausible spin for the nation's threatening economic woes. With that revelation—and what it might mean for my business—the magic of the moment left me and the White House became just another McMansion with high security fencing. We continued our walk toward the National Mall.

It was nearing midnight when we reached the most outlying of the monuments. Our feet were sore and aching. Juliet had moved well beyond the whining stage and into the demanding-a-piggy-back-ride stage. It was at this point in our cross-continent expedition that we discovered DC city cabs, unlike their west coast counterparts, did not accept credit cards. We staggered back to the hotel—fourteen long city blocks filled with restaurants and retail stores but no ATMs. I swore to myself that I would never, ever, wear shoes with heels again, or travel without some cash.

The next three days were a blur of eye-opening experiences for me. I had anticipated high-energy meetings with entrepreneurs and 'idea guys' like myself. I pictured rooms abuzz with networking and strategies for participants to apply at home. So I was unprepared for the corporate Armani-suit-and-tie and Manolo-Blahnik-high-heeled atmosphere. Instead of something productive, the seminar conversations revolved around the looming corporate tax-rebates, or which lobbyists were most productive on Capitol Hill. I began to feel like a flannel-clad fish out of water in a very big pond. I wondered whether any of *them* were going without paychecks that month just to make their payroll.

The night of the awards banquet arrived. The social hour preceding the event occurred in the foyer of the ballroom. The opulence and pizzazz of this function made the awards reception hosted by the Seattle mayor's office back in 2006 look rather quaint. Jeffery and I found ourselves in a sort of shell-shocked comfort zone of our own creation, seated alone at a table. We made idle conversation about the kids or whether the side-yard gate had been locked before we left, but the silence between these topics seemed easier to endure. Jeffery radiated discomfort in his pressed trousers and starched collar, while I fidgeted with nylons that kept adhering to my dress. The other attendees and invited guests mingled and socialized with ease, conversing blithely about gross profits and employee benefits packages that cost them their collective appendages.

Eventually an attractive middle-aged couple sat down next to us. They were also award finalists, winners from the New England region. After several minutes of polite conversation, we learned that they were in the process of expanding their manufacturing business. Their gross profit contained so many decimal places above what Gracewinds had managed to earn that year (or any year), that we struggled in vain for some relative ground to continue our discussion. I started to wonder what qualified a company as a *small* business these days. After sharing a few more cocktails, we discovered they had not had a vacation together for over ten years, either because he couldn't leave the operations or because they were borrowing money to fund their growth.

Jeffery leaned over to me and quietly whispered, "So, thirty million or three hundred thousand—some basic things just never change, do they?"

The award banquet was pleasant and (thankfully) adherent to the doctrine of brevity. The presentations were well-organized and diplomatic. It was clear to me from the start, somewhat cynically, that Gracewinds had been included in the line-up as the "sentimental entry." We were there to tug at the collective corporate heartstrings, to create a warm and wistful feeling about what small business in America could do toward the betterment of our world. Perhaps I was being unfair, but such were my thoughts as the presentations continued. The grand prize went to a Minnesota manufacturer of hydraulic parts, jockeying for government defense contracts. Jeffery and I tipped back the last of our champagne and congratulated ourselves on being finalists, then savored the chocolate torte before we headed back to our room.

As we stepped out of the elevator, Jeffery's arm was around my shoulder. He let his hand run down the back of my dress, resting on the curve of my spine. "You look beautiful tonight, Ms. CEO. You can wear this dress again you know, any time you like."

We walked down the hotel chuckling softly—much more in our element, just the two of us. After several failed attempts, Jeffery slid the card key into the lock and pushed the door open slowly so as not to disturb Juliet. We stepped into the suite and saw that she lay curled in a ball, snoring lightly. Then we saw the blinking light of the hotel phone. I gave Jeffery a puzzled look and set my award on the nightstand. "Who do you suppose would be calling the room?" I whispered and walked over to the desk phone to retrieve the message.

The kids and neighbors all had our cell phone numbers. I knew for certain that if there had been an emergency at work, my manager would have texted me. "It's just probably an investor, wanting to offer us millions for Gracewinds now that we are celebrated award winners," Jeffery offered. He tossed his suit jacket on the bed and went to get a beer.

"Shhh. You'll wake up Juliet."

I dialed the automated system and retrieved the message. The recording said it was left at 11:47 eastern standard time. "Huh, it's only about ten minutes old."

Jeffery sat on the foot of the bed, sipping his beer as I listened to the recording. My expression must have conveyed the nature of the news because he suddenly got up and walked toward me.

"What is it?" he asked.

"It's from a fireman, uh, you know…an EMT." I looked at the notepad where I'd written down a number. "He asked me to call."

I punched in the digits and waited. A man's voice answered.

"Hello, you left me a message to call this number." I sat motionless, quietly listening.

"What? What's going on?" Jeff asked.

I covered the receiver with one hand and mouthed, "Megan's in the emergency room."

"The hospital? What in the hell happened?" Jeff's voice had risen in his alarm and Juliet stirred.

"Dad? What are you guys talking about?" she asked.

I spent several more minutes listening to the officer and responding to his questions. Finally I asked a few of my own. "Were you able to get hold of her father? She's supposed to be staying with him." I listened. "Hmmm. No, I don't know how to reach her stepmother. Megan should have her number."

Eventually, I hung up the phone and turned to Jeffery (and by this time, an increasingly anxious Juliet). "OK, here's what they were able to tell me." I took a deep breath. "Apparently Megan took too much cold medication, and then she called the ambulance."

"She took too much on purpose?" Jeff asked.

"Well, the medic wasn't sure. He said that she was alone in the house and they couldn't reach anyone else, so they found out where we were staying from Megan."

"Oh Mommy, I'm scared for Megan. I wanna go home and see her."

"Don't worry. The man said she was OK. They need her to stay overnight to do some tests. She's gonna be just fine." *Though what do I know?*

I looked at Jeff and nodded my head toward the bathroom. He took the hint. "Hey, Bug. Listen, it's OK. Grab your animals and curl back down under the covers again. I'm going to chat with Mom for a minute and then I'll come lie down next to you for a little bit. OK?"

She nodded and wiped her eyes. Jeffery joined me in the bathroom.

"So, he said they had to do some blood work to ensure there was no long-term liver damage." The concern on my face registered with Jeff.

"Jeez, how much did she take? What the hell was she thinking?" he said.

"I don't have a clue—both girls have been pretty stable and happy for the past few months. The counselor just told me on our last visit that she felt really pleased with all the progress they were making. I know Megan broke up with that Eric kid about a week or so ago, but I got the impression that it wasn't that big a deal for her though. I dunno. Maybe I was wrong."

"Can you talk to her? Is her dad on his way over there?"

"You're asking me things about which I have no idea," I snapped, but then softened. "She didn't have a hospital room yet, so I couldn't talk with her. I'm betting that they've already pumped her stomach, probably given her some activated charcoal."

My medical knowledge of procedures in circumstances like this poured back into my brain. However at this moment, I would have preferred not to know all the minute details of what was likely transpiring.

"Well, holy crap." Jeff shook his head. "What do you want to do?"

"Wait, I guess." Then I added, "Maybe we'll get a call from her dad."

My cell phone rang as if in answer. It was the twins' dad; he had arrived at the hospital and was with her. I couldn't recall ever being so happy to hear from my ex-husband. I quizzed him about all of our concerns, and then asked him the question we were afraid to voice. "Troy, did she do this on purpose? Was this an overdose?" *Christ almighty, please let it be no.*

Troy answered that, no, she claimed it wasn't an overdose (at least not an intentional one). She had a bad cold and was just taking more and more of it until she read the back of the box and scared herself. Troy said she was sorry and frightened—and that she wanted to talk to me. I felt instant relief at hearing this news, however my mother-instinct wasn't completely buying it.

"Wait a sec—I'll give her the phone."

Megan's voice came through, shaky and weak. "Mommy?"

"Megan—sweetie! Hey! I'm so glad you're OK! Wow, you gave us a real scare!"

"I'm sorry, really. It wasn't on purpose, I promise. I love you… I'm really sorry. Please don't be mad."

"It's OK, nobody's mad at you. We're all just really concerned, that's all, and super glad that you're being taken care of. I'm just so thankful, that you called somebody."

We talked for a short while longer. I put Juliet on the phone to quiet her down, and then Jeffery got on the line to say he loved her. Finally, we told her we'd call and check on things in the morning.

I hung up the phone and gave a heavy sigh. I walked to the bed and bent over Juliet to offer her a big kiss. "Did you get your trophy, Mommy?" she asked.

101

"Yep. It's right there by the phone," I answered. "Why don't you get to sleep now? It's really late and I'll show it to you in the morning." She snuggled next to Jeffery and closed her eyes. I pulled off my little black dress and donned one of Jeff's tee shirts for bed. As I pulled the cover down, I looked across to Jeffery who was propped against his sleepy daughter in the next bed and gave him an ironic smile.

"Pssst… hey, you. I love you," he whispered.

"I love you."

Separate beds and wracked nerves had definitely not been the way I'd envisioned our night of celebration would end, but I figured we'd recover somehow. We always did.

Chapter 12

The Speech

The next morning was the final day of the Summit. Sleepily, I reached over toward the center of the bed where I expected Jeffery to be. My hand rummaged around the pillow but came in contact with nothing except sheets and comforter. His absence reminded me of the events of the night before. I rolled over to find him asleep next to Juliet, his arm draped over her shoulders. She'd kicked most of her stuffed animals off the bed in her sleep and they lay scattered around the floor near the nightstand.

Quietly, so as not to disturb the two of them, I tiptoed into the bathroom to check on Megan. I dialed the hospital and spoke with her nurse. She reassured me that it had been a quiet night and that Megan was doing well. "She's sound asleep right now though—exciting night and all y'know."

I suddenly realized that given the time zone difference, I must have called them in the wee hours of the morning. I quickly apologized for my timing. The nurse assured me that Megan could call us later and that she'd probably even be released by mid-afternoon. I thanked her and hung up. My morning just got a little brighter.

As I padded back to find my suitcase, I noticed a crisp, photocopied notice entitled "Secret Service Protocols" on the floor by our door. I pictured one of the polyester-vested bell boys spending his graveyard shift slipping notes under each guestroom door. I stooped over to examine the information, *"When you speak with a Secret Service Agent…"* I changed into my conference outfit and pondered the connotations of that particular set of instructions.

President George W. Bush was to be the keynote speaker for the morning session of the U.S. Chamber of Commerce Awards Summit and the anticipation of his impending arrival was generally becoming contagious. By the time I returned to our suite from my brief errand to the lobby gift shop, my pulse had quickened to a triple-Americano status. I had just brushed up against x-ray machines, conveyor belts and metal detectors, been diverted around velvet-roped barricades and pipe and draped vestibules. The plush lobby was definitely taking on a very "security checkpoint" kind of atmosphere.

The hotel's spit and polish brigade was in full swing as well. Everywhere I glanced, a plump ethnic woman in a ruffled apron was polishing a doorknob, light fixture or tabletop to within an inch of its life. I had no clue that a five-star establishment could apparently languish in such shoddy condition until a dignitary of this caliber deigned to make an appearance. Even the fountain appeared to trickle and gurgle in a sprightlier manner on this morning.

I had chosen to wear my casual linen pants and cotton blouse with my comfortable leather sandals as I knew we were going to be walking through airport terminals all afternoon. Jeffery sprawled across the bed, and I asked what his intentions were for the early part of the day.

"You have a reservation for this breakfast as well, you know," I reminded him.

Juliet interrupted with an emphatic, "Daddy is taking me to the Washington Zoo. We're going to see the panda bears!"

Jeff lazily rolled over and said in his best deadpan, "I believe I would rather spend my morning staring at a panda's ass than to sit around listening to a horse's ass." He paused, waiting for my reaction. "Besides, as soon as he starts in about the state of the economy, I'd likely stand up and say something that would get me hauled away... Tax rebates my ass!"

Nonplussed, I nodded in agreement and walked into the bathroom to brush my hair.

I arrived late to the Presidential Breakfast; most all of the other participants were already seated in the giant conference hall. I peered past the big double doors, blinded suddenly by the glare of television lights and followspots warming up. The Secret Service agents were friendly and conversant as they checked the contents of my purse and pockets, and I confess to being a tad disappointed by their behavior. I was hoping for stern and austere personalities, *a la* Clint Eastwood. Instead, they politely cleared my registration and returned my handbag. I noticed my little Obama "Hope" button on the strap of my Guatemalan bag. I chuckled and shrugged it off as a good token to bring into a political breakfast. Besides, I was tardy enough that I was sure to be shuffled to a place in the back of the room, indiscernible in the mass of attendees.

The doormen greeted me as I stepped into the entry. They were tall and good-looking in their uniformed suits and ties, plasticized brass nametags positioned identically on their chest pockets. One of them raised his brow in recognition of something on my badge, glanced down at his clipboard and said, "Ah, Ms.

Wallace, so glad that you are here. Will Mr. Carson be joining you for breakfast?"

I replied courteously that no, he would not, but refrained from sharing Jeffery's reasons as to why.

"I'm sorry to hear that," he replied, with utmost formality and respect.

"This way please," said the taller of the two, and I followed him into the great hall.

We walked further in and still deeper through the densely situated tables, all packed to capacity with attendees. The room itself was dark, lit only sporadically with media bulbs and follow spots waiting for their cues to light up. I didn't know anyone seated in the room, but everywhere I turned, I could smell the money. It was like walking through Nordstrom's blindfolded, the aroma emanated from the gentlemen in suits as much as the well-heeled ladies. In a moment of *deja vu*, I found myself wishing that I'd chosen a dressier outfit instead of my comfortable traveling clothes. It occurred to me then that I had planned on sitting in the *back* of the room.

My lanky young guide led me to the front of the room where the velvet ropes separated the plebeians from the elevated dais that the heads of state would occupy. Two vacant chairs awaited me, positioned directly in front of the stage platform and the presidential podium. An officious young man busily affixed the presidential seal to the front of the faux wooden stand as I took my seat. My thoughts were racing. *Surely not here... I don't even vote Republican.* The quizzical look on my face must have registered with the doorman.

"These tables are reserved for the award winners," he explained.

I nodded, sitting down, and reached for the napkin on my plate, smiling at the seven others around the table. I hoped that they would assume my tardiness was due to fashion rather than lack of organization. Then I tried to enjoy my breakfast and appear nonchalant about the whole situation.

Not long after I finished my first cup of coffee, I was drawn into the intriguing floor show of the Secret Service routine. The energy in the noisy, bustling hall became frenetic as the crisply suited, well-built men with their formally trimmed haircuts and polarized aviator sunglasses appeared in the room. Several of them posted themselves at the dais, arms down and hands clasped at the front of their charcoal suits, scanning the audience. Others walked back and forth, like sleek, alert Dobermans patrolling the yard.

The conference attendees continued their polite conversations, but all eyes were glued on the agents, who were completely beyond caring that they were the center of attention, while pretending to be unrecognizable. These were the Secret Service agents I'd been waiting for—down to the little microphone coils peeking out of their starched white collars that disappeared into their ears. They even touched two fingers to their temples and bowed their heads as they mumbled back and forth to each other.

I briefly contemplated pushing back my chair and making a run for the ladies' room, just to see how many of them would tackle me. I found the whole performance more entertaining than a Broadway show. But the wee bit of maturity in me won out and I kept to my seat.

There was no need to announce the arrival of the Commander-in-Chief. The agents stiffened as one, the press corps went into a frenzy, and like wild animals that can sense a foreign presence, we knew when President George W. Bush had entered the hall. We could not yet see him behind the pipe and drapes, but everything told us it was so— and suddenly he sauntered onto the stage.

The spotlights snapped on in brilliant synchronicity and the room erupted with applause, mine included, though I had no particular fondness for the man. Yet I stood in unison with the others to shower adulation on one of the most powerful leaders of the world. I watched around me as men leaned into one another sharing their opinions about the moment, and women stared at him radiantly, smiling widely.

I turned my gaze back to the podium and continued to clap, applauding for the office, if not its inhabitant. My concentration was broken, however, by the arrival of a new table member.

Since Jeffery had elected to visit the panda bears, I had been left with an empty adjacent seat. And who was I so lucky to share breakfast with this Sunday morning? None other than Bush's former Chief of Staff, Andrew Card, the man who had played a major part in 'rolling out the Iraq war.' This was to be my breakfast partner. We both took a cursory glance at each other and scooted our respective chairs in opposing directions. There would be no breaching of any barriers at this summit breakfast.

All would have been well that morning if not for one particularly unnerving habit of President Bush. Apparently, when speaking in public or in front of the camera, Mr. Bush liked to search out a familiar and sympathetic face to direct his oratory.

108

This focus, coupled with the tendency to pepper his remarks with knowing winks and half smirks, made him appear to be a more approachable and friendly leader. But it could also create some very uncomfortable moments for any unwitting recipient of those gestures. For this morning's breakfast speech, Mr. Bush directed his beam straight at his longtime buddy, Andrew Card. Because of my unfortunate position within this firing range, I landed on the receiving end of the President's chummy and far-too-familiar winks and smirks. My consternation grew every time he punctuated a remark and shot a gesture zinging over my left shoulder. I felt an obligation to smile supportively or give a courtesy laugh every time he paused with a jerk of his head, eyes twinkling with mirth. It created a most unique and uncomfortable breakfast experience.

Several hours later, conference adjourned, I stood with my family outside the hotel and breathed a deep sigh of relief, glad to be putting the trip behind me. The cab pulled up to the curb and we loaded the luggage. I plopped into the backseat next to Jeffery and Juliet. Throughout the entire ride to Dulles International, Jeffery pestered me for details of the banquet. I filled him in on the highlights—and the lowlights. Afterward, during the six-hour flight back to Seattle, I replayed the president's speech in my mind. Mr. Bush's upbeat sound-bites for a rebound in the economy didn't ring true to me. The slump in my business that started back in January showed no sign of abating. For the first time since opening our doors in 2002, I was experiencing a decline in profits. It seemed pretty obvious to me that his much-ballyhooed rebate wasn't going to stimulate Gracewinds significantly. I hoped to hell I was wrong about that.

Chapter 13

Shoaling

"**M**om! They've got Jelly Bellies in the bar fridge! Can we eat 'em—please?"

"What? Yeah, yeah, go ahead. They probably cost eighteen bucks a bag, but what the hell." I replied. My attention wasn't on the honor bar right then. The silver-paneled, completely round suite of the downtown Westin Towers fascinated me. I stood in the center of our hotel room and tried to figure out how they managed any right angles when they built it. Normally I would've turned to Jeffery for his expertise, but he and Juliet were at the Cinerama. *It'd have to be designed like a pizza slice or something emanating from the center… but why aren't there any little wedge-shaped portions?*

The twins plopped onto their queen-sized bed and fought for the remote. They clicked through all of the channels and argued about what to watch. I walked past them into the bathroom and started the hot water for a shower. The theme song for SpongeBob SquarePants wafted into the bathroom and I shut the door. *Jeez! They're sixteen—aren't they a little old for that stupid cartoon?*

"…If nautical nonsense be something you wish… SpongeBob SquarePants… Then drop on the deck and flop like a fish… SpongeBob SquarePants!"

"*Arrgh!* That frigging song is going to stay in my head all night now!" I yelled to no one in particular. I pulled off my sweater and stepped out of my jeans and climbed into the shower, allowing the jets of hot water to hit my back. "This is very nice." I muttered, standing with my back toward the jets until my skin felt like it might burn off my body. Working the expensive-smelling shampoo into my hair, I watched the foam trickle down my shoulders and breasts in curving rivulets, puddling around my feet to be washed away. The shower was roomy and well made. Jeff and I could have both fit in here quite comfortably. I began to regret our decision to split up the kids for the weekend and give them each their own parent. Had I known how swanky the room would be, I'd have petitioned much differently.

My thoughts were interrupted by a rap at the bathroom door. "Hey Mom, can we do room service? I want a hamburger and Megan wants some cheesecake."

"OK. But that's pretty much it. We still have to go shopping tomorrow for your present and you don't want to blow it all on candy and room service."

"Yep, thanks Mom—you're the best! Hey, do you want to order anything?"

"Nope, I'm good hon'—thanks though."

I turned off the shower and reached around for one of the plush towels that hung nearby. As I dried off in front of the steam-covered mirror, I pondered our extravagance. The lavish digs, my *laissez-faire* attitude toward add-on expenses and the holiday shopping spree really weren't my *modus operandi*—in fact, given our last six months, I could barely afford the shampoo I just used. *Screw it.*

The preceding months had been brutal on our family. We began to feel the pinch as early as May. In spite of President

Bush's promises to stimulate the economy with his tax rebates, the Seattle real estate bubble deflated and the local software companies were hurting. Since Gracewinds' customer base consisted largely of Microsoft and Amazon techies as well as mortgage brokers, the "economic bumps in the road" filtered right down to our level.

Jeff had added a second job in mid-summer to keep the creditors at bay and I no longer received any salary in order to pay my staff. We'd long since maxed out the line of credit we had borrowed two years ago for Gracewinds' expansion. Our sailboat *Sugaree,* was on the loan as collateral; her new masts and rig increased her value enough to secure our debt. The house remodel took a back seat to the business when it came to financing, so we lived in our partially finished house and hung sheets over unfinished doorways when necessary. There was no money left to finish them.

By the end of summer, we could tell things were not improving. Customers who would normally not have batted an eye at $90 baby carriers or plopped down $300 for a breast-pump now opted to borrow them from friends instead. The shelves in our little baby boutique were sparse. I found myself appropriating capital from one Gracewinds' program to pay off another. I knew this was dangerous, but I had no choice.

Shortly after school began, Regence announced that they would no longer cover outpatient lactation consults. The other insurance providers followed suit immediately. It made no sense. Gracewinds' clinic went from being the busiest privately run lactation clinic in the city to a row of empty rooms. Women couldn't afford the $200 visits out-of-pocket. I had to let several of my nurses go by the end of the month. It saddened me to think of the countless babies forced onto a bottle because their mothers couldn't afford to see a nurse.

The morning of September 15th brought news that Lehman Brothers had collapsed and AIG teetered on bankruptcy. We stood frozen in front of our television set for hours as the collapse of Wall Street and the global financial system was broadcast from every news channel. There was a sickening knot in my stomach that wouldn't go away.

By the end of September, I'd started to receive vacate notices from several of my long-term tenants: massage therapists, naturopath pediatricians and a psychotherapist. Their practices had dwindled to the point where they couldn't afford rent payments.

The ominous note from our lender arrived a month later. Gracewinds was two months behind on our expansion loan: *Sugaree* was in danger of being repossessed—before we'd had the opportunity to sail her. Jeffery made the wrenching decision to sell his 1949 Chevy long-bed truck to pay the overdue loan installments. The afternoon the new owners drove away with Jeffery's beloved truck was one that I would never forget—that same day, the government bailout for AIG reached 150 billion dollars.

Our quality of life at home took a nosedive. Jeffery and I spoke very little; we found it easier to keep the growing concerns bottled up inside rather than discuss them. We squabbled about inconsequential things and lost our patience with the kids frequently. We could no longer hide the money problems from the girls—they saw the bright red *past-due* stamps on the utility bills turn up with increasing frequency. When the water stopped running because our payments lapsed, they didn't ask why.

Eventually, the twins requested that they be allowed to stay at their dad's house for extra weeks. I cringed inside as I agreed, realizing that at least, our food bill would not be as high. With the twins increasingly absent and Dane now living in his own apartment, Juliet suffered through a very lonely autumn.

One rainy Tuesday night before Thanksgiving, I heard Jeff pull up to the house. It was already dark outside, but I could make out Justine and Megan chatting with him at the curb. It was our turn to have them for the holiday. The girls carried two grocery bags in their arms. Thinking nothing of it, I went back to the kitchen and unloaded the dishwasher. Suddenly, loud voices emanated from the street and the front door opened, then slammed shut. The twins ran upstairs without a word. "What the hell—hey! What's with the door slamming? Hullo... *any*body?" I pushed the door of the dishwasher closed and walked to the bottom of the stairs. "Would somebody please tell me what's going on—why did you guys slam the door so hard?"

Juliet appeared at the top of the stairs. She held her Breyer horse by the tail. "They're in their room crying, Mom."

"Do you know why?"

"No. They told me to go away." She turned and walked back into her room. The sounds of "Philadelphia Chickens" could be heard from her bedroom as she opened her door.

I sighed and hung my head. *No drama, not today please.* Climbing the stairs, I strategized ways to bring my moody 16-year-olds back to a relative norm before we sat down to dinner. I tapped on their door. "Hey, it's Mom. May I please come in?"

A muffled "OK" could be heard from the other side of the door.

"So, what happened?"

"Jeff is such a douchebag." Justine replied. Megan had her face buried in the pillow next to her sister, but I could make out a rumble of agreement emanating from her side of the couch.

"Well, when it comes to douche-baggery, you're going to have to be a bit more specific. What exactly did he do?"

"We went to the food bank with Patty and Amelia on our way home today," Justine said. "We picked up some cans of stuff and they had French bread and bags of stuffing, too. We grabbed enough for the family and brought it home. When we showed it to Jeff, he exploded and got all mad about it. He said we were taking poor people's food."

Megan sat up and sniffled. "I told him that *we* were poor people right now and he yelled at us to go inside. We were just trying to help." She buried her face back in her pillow.

"I hate him so much right now!" Justine said.

I blinked back a tear before it could roll down my cheek and cleared my throat. "Guys, you were doing what you thought was right. It's real sweet, what you did—I mean, I would never have thought about doing that when I was your age. You've got to understand though, that yeah, even though we're really tight on money right now, we can somehow make it through Thanksgiving—I promise."

"Mom! That's what food banks are for! Jeff's just being a snob!" Justine replied.

"No, he's not. He's stressed out and worried. He probably got a little defensive because… well, in his mind he feels he should be providing for our family I suppose. The way things are right now—I think the bags of free food probably made him feel guilty or ashamed. It makes me feel a little guilty, so imagine what he must be going through. Can you try?"

The twins didn't say anything, but the sniffles had dried up. I tried another tack, hoping to resolve the issue before Jeffery came upstairs. "We appreciate what you guys did, and you did it for the right reason. Let's just try and have a good evening and a happy Thanksgiving. You know, the pilgrims were really poor when they had their first Thanksgiving. We're better off than they were, right?"

Justine nodded and Megan took her head out of the pillow to acknowledge my comment. "I love you guys."

"Yeah, love you too, Mom." They said in unison.

I stepped outside into the hallway and shut the door behind me. Juliet opened her door a smidge. "You hungry Miss Bug?" I asked.

"Yes."

"Well, come help me set the table then."

Later that night as we lay in bed reading, Jeff finally spoke about the evening's events. "I apologize for snapping at the girls. It was just sort of the last straw—seeing them carrying those groceries from a food bank. I shouldn't have reacted that way. Maybe... I dunno, maybe we should all go down to a food kitchen on Thanksgiving and volunteer for a few hours. That way they can get a handle on what it means to be really poor."

He didn't just try to stretch a turkey dinner for six people out of a twenty dollar bill at the QFC this afternoon. I didn't have anything constructive to add, so I listened.

Jeff propped himself against the headboard with his magazine in his lap. There was a prolonged silence in the bedroom, interrupted occasionally by Sasha's snores. Finally he said, "I worry about the holidays, Chris—hell I'm worried about beyond the holidays. I… I just… "

I reached across the bedspread and placed my hand on his forearm. "I know."

On December 1st, the talking heads at CNN announced that the National Bureau of Economic Research had officially declared we'd entered into a recession a full year earlier—in 2007.

"Well, no fucking *DUH!*" I shouted at the screen.

The reporter continued… something about the S&P 500 falling 80 points and the Dow closing with a drop of 679 points. They mentioned that the General Accounting Office had released a report claiming the oversight of the Troubled Asset Relief Program required additional actions to ensure "integrity, accountability, and transparency."

"Yeah, good luck with that," I said aloud. "Those qualities do not exist on Wall Street."

The news anchor droned on with various other depressing statistics while I half-listened, scratching Sasha's belly. The kids were already in school and Jeff had piled his tools in the car over ninety minutes ago and zoomed off to work. I sat on the hardwood floor in my robe—I didn't need to get dressed, we'd closed the store three days prior. I'd recently let go all but one of my nurses and had scaled the manager down to part-time. The education program and doula services were currently the only things operating—although I'd borrowed so much money from the class enrollment to pay off the store's inventory that I wouldn't be able to cover my instructors' salaries at the end of the week. *I am the CEO of nothingness right now.*

Sasha's damp nose pressed against my calf, seeking more belly rubs. I'd apparently zoned out once again, a tendency that occurred too often these days. I did not sleep; the sounds of Jeff's or Sasha's snores would wake me every night between 1AM and 3AM. Eventually I'd walk downstairs, sit in front of the computer and scroll through websites devoted to the current economic meltdown or sites that covered warning signs of suicide. By about 5 AM, I'd plod back upstairs and climb into bed just before the household began to stir. During the day I functioned like a zombie.

Gracewinds limped along, yet neither Jeffery nor I had the nerve to pull the plug, even as the death throes worsened. This was something akin to family members watching a loved one agonize through a terminal illness, unable to turn off the life support. We just couldn't make that call. The implications for everyone were too dreadful; the chain of events which would occur once it happened intimidated me too much to even think about it.

The tinny rattle of our mailbox alerted Sasha and she leapt across the living room to bark at the mailman. I got up and walked toward the door. It no longer concerned me whether the neighbors saw me in my house robe. I opened the door and went out to gather the mail. Sasha bounded after me, giving a couple gruff barks toward the taillights of the mail truck for good measure. Porter stood at the threshold, his breath visible in the frosty air. "C'mon, back inside, everybody!"

Sasha brushed past me as I thumbed through the bills. I kicked the door shut behind me and continued to inspect the post. A letter from one of the local hospitals caught my eye and I tossed the rest of the pile onto the dining room table. I tore open the envelope and read the numbers on the check: *one-thousand-two-hundred-dollars.* I'd completely forgotten about the half-case of books I'd sold them over two months ago. The hospital's accounting department had taken a few extra weeks to process it, but here it sat. *Wow, money.*

I left the check on the mantle and went back to the television.

By early evening, Jeff had arrived home from his other job in time for dinner. I gave him the check and asked for his advice on which bill we should put it toward. He held the paper in his hand and stared at it for several minutes. I walked back toward the library—I didn't really care which bill we paid, there were so many of them. The way I saw it, the money would just get absorbed into the mountain of debt and that would be it. Bye-bye twelve hundred dollars.

"Chris, come here a minute, will ya?"

I turned back to the living room and stood next to my husband. "What?"

"I've been thinking all afternoon. As a matter of fact, right about the time that NPR announced Bernie Madoff's arrest and then upon hearing that we lost over 250,000 jobs nationwide last month… I've just been doing a lot of thinking." He placed the check in my hands. "Here's what I say. Fuck it. You are going to take this check to the bank tomorrow and you are going to cash it. Take it to their bank, not ours—our bank account's overdrawn. You're going to cash this here check and then we're going to take our kids for a fun weekend—whatever they want to do. God knows, there is no bill that I can completely pay off with this amount. And god knows that once we get back home, we'll be facing the worst week of our adult lives. Gracewinds has got to go—we can't save it. So, what I say is let's give our kids a Christmas weekend with some good memories. After that... well, I guess we'll deal with what comes next."

His voice cracked as he finished his statement. He sighed and sat down. I noticed he was still wearing his work coveralls that were coated in sheetrock dust; I also noticed that he'd just planted himself on the white cushions of our David Smith antique chair but I didn't give a shit. I just nodded and tried to offer my best smile. I'd never seen my husband so defeated and tired looking. I mean, he'd come home plenty exhausted before from crawling underneath foundations or hauling bags of concrete, but this was a 'tired-in-the-soul' kind of look. I'd married a man six years younger than me but at this very moment he looked about seventy. *I wonder how old I must look.*

The red numbers on the alarm clock glowed: 2:41 AM. I watched the digits change to :42, :43, and then :44. *I wonder if this is our last hotel.* Justine and Megan snored lightly, tangled up in the sheets of their queen size bed. The thermostat clicked on regularly and pumped warm air into the suite. I remained in my bed and stared at the lights of downtown Seattle through the sheer curtains of our 22nd floor window. The usual luminosities of the city were augmented by scores of holiday lights. The effect, as viewed from behind the curtains, was a fuzzy mix of glowing colors. The distant noise of early morning traffic combined with the Westin's heater created an appropriate soundtrack for my middle-of-the-night anxiety attack.

I left my laptop at home so I wasn't able to fill my wakeful hours web surfing. I certainly didn't want to spend the next few hours mulling over what Jeffery and I could've been doing together in this luxurious bed. Instead, I rolled onto my side and watched the twins sleep. Megan lay on her back, mouth partially agape and snoring—a sort of low, buzzing kind of snore. Justine, closest to me, had rolled on her side with her arm and right leg dangling off the mattress. Her breathing noises were more intermittent: a small little snort that kind of startled her in her sleep and then even breathing for several minutes… then repeated snorts. The dirty plates from room service were scattered across the floor and their clothes haphazardly pitched everywhere. The light from the crescent moon seeped into the room and illuminated the cellophane Jelly Belly bag. The crinkled plastic lay on the bedside table next to Justine's bra with some of the rejected Jelly Bellies scattered all around.

I gazed at length upon that crinkled bag of candy and tried to imagine how the Westin could justify tacking an $11 room charge onto a dollar's worth of jelly beans. I finally rolled onto my back and gave up. *It really doesn't matter anyway.* I prayed that those Jelly Bellies, the SpongeBob cartoons, the room service and the time alone with their mother would be what the girls would remember about this holiday. I could somehow bear the rest.

Chapter 14

On the Rocks

The cedar trees in our front yard dropped their small branches as the wind howled past the house. Occasionally, a gust rattled the single-pane windows in the library, causing the dogs to jump in their sleep. The storm began to gather strength shortly before dinner and by the time I'd tucked Juliet in bed, gale-force winds seemed to be here to stay. I huddled under three blankets on the couch, waiting for Jeff to return from clearing out what had once been our business. The clock on my phone read twelve-thirty in the morning.

Despite chronic migraines, I left the television set on almost 24/7—tuned to CNN or MSNBC. The incessant roll call of faltering and collapsing corporations became my white noise—my umbilicus to the outside world. I'd long quit paying attention to the specifics of what any of the talking heads were saying; it just mattered that they continued saying it. *Misery loves company.*

Today's sound bite concerned the government's recent Band-Aid approach to squelch the financial hemorrhaging. A bland looking anchorwoman yammered, "In its latest effort to try and stimulate the U.S. economy, the Federal Reserve has cut its key interest rate to a range of between zero percent and 0.25%, and said it expects to keep rates near that unprecedented low level for some time to come." *Blah-dee, blah-dee, blah.*

My thoughts kept returning to what Jeff must have been going through that evening. He'd volunteered to clean out our space—the detritus of Gracewinds. I envisioned the overwhelming amount of equipment, furniture, file cabinets packed with patient information and inventory folders—a decade's worth of commerce that needed to be cleared out by morning. I pictured Jeffery packing yoga balls, barbells and infant CPR mannequins into the trunk of our car. I wondered how many trips to Goodwill he must have made by now.

He had been hard at it for over nine hours, heading over to the building straight after work. He wouldn't let me join him—wouldn't even hear about it. Apparently, my fragile emotional state was too great a concern to everyone. The fact that Jeffery was having to tackle this job by himself greatly disturbed me. This shouldn't be his responsibility. It should have fallen to me—and now amounted to just one more failure of mine: that I wasn't strong enough to participate in the final undertaking of my dead business. My constant companions, incompetence, bitterness and despair welcomed some new friends now: guilt, shame and self-loathing.

I dozed in and out of a restless sleep for another two hours, then was jolted to consciousness by the dogs as they bolted toward the door. Jeff was home at last. I could barely make him out in the darkness but I could hear his keys jingling as he reached down to pat Porter and Sasha. He whispered in an effort not to wake anyone. "Good dogs, OK… yeah, I know Porter—Sasha's just a big bully. Quiet down guys. Come here, you stupid mutt… that's a good boy—Sasha! *Down* girl!"

"It's fine, I'm awake. You don't have to be so quiet."

"Hey there. How's your head?"

"Mmm, I'll live."

Jeff walked into the library, the dogs at his heels with their tails wagging. He tossed his coat onto the chair and came over to where I lay. He bent over and gave me a kiss. "I'm glad to hear that." As he brushed by my face, I caught a faint scent of Gracewinds on his shirt—a sort of blending of massage lotion, Murphy's oil soap and rubber yoga mats. It made me smile and simultaneously tear up. *My last breath of Gracewinds.* Jeffery stood upright and arched his body, digging his fists into the muscles of his lower back. "God, I'm sore—would you mind if I grab a beer and sit with you for a while? I know it's the middle of the night and all, but I just don't think I'll be able to go to bed yet."

"Sure, of course. It's not like I'll fall asleep anytime soon." I didn't want him to leave. I missed Jeff's companionship—even in this solitary state in which I now existed.

Jeff wandered into the kitchen. I heard the sound of the fridge door open and shut and the *click click* of the dogs' nails skittering on the tiles. He popped the cap off his beer and then poured some kibble into bowls.

"Dammit." I muttered under my breath. I'd forgotten to feed the dogs again.

Jeff re-entered the room and sat down on the couch, moving my feet onto his lap. He let out a prolonged sigh. "Well, it's done."

I let him take a few sips of his beer before asking, "Did everything go all right? I'm so sorry that you had to take care of this by yourself."

"You did *not* need to be there for that, honey." He polished off his microbrew in three big gulps. I always admired how he could drink a beer like that—a very high school-ish fascination.

After a brief pause, Jeff sighed and then began. "It went pretty smoothly all in all—but that dumpster out back is overflowing now. Ralph came by around eight o'clock. Y'know, he's always been kind of a hard-ass as a landlord but I'll hand it to him, he was professional enough to know that an LLC in Chapter 11 is virtually untouchable. He was really friendly and even offered his truck if I needed it. I didn't take him up on it, but I thought he was being pretty decent all things considered."

I didn't feel as magnanimous as my husband toward my ex-landlord. "First off, his wife's an attorney remember? He wasn't being nice—they just want us out of there as fast as possible so they can get a new business lease signed."

"Well, he could've been worse is all I'm saying. I left the place kind of a mess. There just wasn't enough time to patch nail holes or vacuum… you know, that kinda thing."

"Jeffery, do you remember what that building looked like when we got it? Jeez, it was an empty warehouse space. We installed hardwood floors, clinic rooms, cabinetry, bathrooms… we painted, landscaped. Man, trust me, they came out A-OK on the deal."

"Yeah, you're right." Jeff absentmindedly massaged my feet as we talked.

"Bastards."

"Yeah, I guess they pretty much were, weren't they?"

We lapsed into silent reflection for several minutes. I pulled the blankets around my feet, covering Jeff's lap as well. He smiled and sighed. The fatigue and emotional toll of the day's events were evident not only in his features, but his posture.

I wished that I could see him smile again, but since I couldn't come up with any upbeat topics at the moment, I fell back on sarcasm. "Let's consider the bright side of this: We no longer have to deal with cheap, greedy landlords. That's got to be worth something. Hmm, *oh*—and Comcast—we will never, *ever* have to deal with those assholes again." It worked. Jeffery smiled at me. "Lemme see, who else... Merchant Services—no more sitting on hold with India, trying to process a return credit. And—oh yeah, no more miserable insurance companies, imagine that! I've heard the last of some stupid jerk telling me that I have the wrong goddamn ICD-9 code so they won't pay up. Christ, I *hated* those guys! And now that I come to think of it, I won't miss dealing with Labor and Industries, either!"

"You've filed your last quarterly B&I report!" Jeffery joined in the game.

"Word, dude."

"No more annoying sub-tenants that can't change their own light bulbs—no more cleaning restrooms twice a day!"

"You know what else? No more airplanes. I've flown to my last conference, thank god. I can flush those anxiety meds down the toilet."

"Well. I think I need another beer for that." Jeff plopped my feet back on the sofa and went to fetch another beer. He returned to his seat and planted both feet back on his lap, draping the blanket back on top. "I guess we're well out of all that, my dear. You sure are one fortunate woman, huh?"

"I s'pose." The levity began to ebb. Jeff noticed my mood sliding backwards and ran his hand along my leg. "Hey, c'mon. Don't get so down again."

"I'll be OK," I lied.

"I tell you something else you won't have to worry about—that HP printer you hated so much? Well, it no longer exists in this physical universe. I went all *Office Space* on it and beat the crap out of it."

I smiled, remembering the scene from the movie where the employees took baseball bats to a much-hated copier machine. "I always wanted to do that," I said.

"Yes, you've mentioned that before. Several times, actually. I took care of it for you. The printer now sleeps with the fishes."

"*Hah*. So what did you do with the router and all the phones?"

"You know, I let the tenants pick though most of that stuff. It saved me having to make another run to Goodwill. I gave the instructors carte blanche for the inventory and supplies and what was left of the Pocket Doula books. It sort of helped make up for not being able to pay them." He took a few pulls on his beer and then let his head fall back on the sofa cushion. "Do you wanna know what the hardest task was today?" He looked at me and continued. "Taking down the baby board. It was just about the last thing I did. The car was packed full and I went back in to scope out the last of the stuff inside. I walked down the hallway and spotted the board." He paused for another long swallow. "I just stood there for about ten minutes looking at all those photos—I could only identify like maybe, a tenth of 'em. Isabella, Maryetta, Emma, Max, Oliver, Solvieg, Amelya, Matho... All these babies and parents—hundreds of 'em on that board... There were a couple photographs from *Grace-a-palooza* –the ones of the kids getting their faces painted and that one of the band in front of the inflatable slides and jumpy castles. And it just got me going—for the life of me, I can't think of any other business that's organized a community street fair to raise money for a clinic in Africa, you know? Not a single one. Then it got me thinking of all the rest—like the bluegrass clambakes we had in the backyard when we'd have all the families over... Little kids and babies running all over the yard, dancing and stuff." Jeff stopped and turned to look at me, his eyes were watery. "Damn, Chris Wallace. You sure did a good thing."

I nodded silently because I couldn't form any words. Jeff was experiencing what my own mind had replayed continually for the past few weeks. I pitied him, because I knew it was a fruitless kind of reminiscence that only made the sorrow deepen.

Chapter 15

Flotsam and Jetsam

For weeks after the doors of Gracewinds had closed for good, I remained in my bed. The kids quietly tiptoed up and down the hallway so as not to disturb me. Occasionally one of them would venture into my bedroom to strike up a conversation. Their efforts were met with little more than a blank stare or halfhearted nod. I'd then draw the covers over my face and roll away until they gave up and left the room. Eventually they stopped trying and left me alone in my silence.

I didn't intend to shut out my family. In fact, the guilt of my inability to engage with them drove me even further into the solitary darkness. A part of me realized that I was clinically depressed—the other part couldn't have cared less.

Jeffery persisted in trying to rouse me from under the blankets for some sort of conversation. Failing that, he would sit silently on the edge of the bed and just wait. Finally, he enlisted Juliet as his agent to check on me. She'd sneak into the room and carefully lift the covers to give me a kiss. "I love you, Mommy," she would whisper, and then quietly walk out of the room, shutting the door behind her. Sasha was the only family member I allowed into my world during this period. She sensed my frame of mind and climbed up next to me, licking my face with her sandpaper-like tongue until I was forced to respond. "That's enough, you silly dog," I'd mumble and lift the blankets to allow her to crawl under. In truth, she may have been nothing more than an opportunist, seizing the chance to break our rules and sleep in the bed. But I felt deep down that she wanted to comfort me as best she knew how.

Once or twice during this dark time, the "old me" would fight her way to the surface. I'd look out the picture window of the bedroom and consider venturing outside. *Maybe I could walk around the back yard for a little while.* But almost immediately the darkness would surround me and crush any uprising of hope. *You mean the backyard that you were counting on seeing your children get married in? The same yard that you planted all those fruit trees and gardens in—that yard? It'll be somebody else's yard soon... most likely bull-dozed up and developed. Why even bother? There's no use.*

Christmas arrived and I was still buried under the blankets. The holiday lights that appeared around the neighborhood only deepened my sadness. I could see many of their colored rooftops glittering from my window, but instead of lifting my spirits, they merely heightened the contrast to our own dark household. Our home remained desperate and barren, devoid of any hint of cheer.

For holiday seasons past, Jeffery and I had decorated our three-story craftsman handsomely, like a scene from Dickens' *Christmas Carol.* We always draped swags of evergreen across the front porch and the archways indoors. Our vaulted ceilings allowed for a ten-foot Noble fir to command the corner of our living room, the rich, golden yellow of the walls complementing the deep green of the tree. The large oak mantle over the hearth became a centerpiece of the house, with cedar branches bordering the nutcrackers that my father had hand-carved for me.

Our family's usual ritual to herald the start of the Christmas season consisted of making fudge and hot spiced cider for an evening of trimming the tree. Jeffery would spend several hours wrapping each branch with strands of white pea lights. After dinner, we'd play classical music and the kids would help me divide the ornaments into equal piles for each of them. The ornate hand-blown glass ones were reserved for the "grown-ups." Each one of the girls would place their decorations on the branches with meticulous care. The inevitable squabbles would break out concerning territorial placement. "Don't get too worked up about it, you guys," Trent would advise them. "Mom always waits until you're in bed and reorganizes them anyways."

"Shhhh!" I would tell him. "They don't need to know that!"

The finishing touch occurred when Jeffery wrapped iridescent ribbon into elegant swirls around the branches. For the next few nights, the younger kids would bring their blankets into the living room and sleep underneath the big tree.

Our holiday party typically occurred shortly after the tree trimming. Baskets of cinnamon oil-soaked pine cones littered the downstairs of the house and, combined with the pungent aroma of evergreens, gave it a very yuletide fragrance. The girls spent their afternoons in the kitchen helping me bake cookies and sweet breads. Dane got his very own plate of fudge and Trent gleaned more than his fair share of the homemade peanut brittle. On the night of the party, our house would glow from within with dozens of candles and twinkling lights in all of the rooms. My kids loved bringing out the antique china dishware that belonged to their great-grandmother. We placed each piece on the long mahogany dining room table amongst tapered candles and flowers. The house would overflow with good company and music every year.

This year, our house sat empty and colorless. The gas had been shut off several days before because we couldn't pay the bill—Jeffery's paycheck went toward the electricity and water. What remained of it, he'd given to Gracewinds' manager to compensate her for the last paycheck she'd never receive. We still had a few more weeks of groceries left in the freezers and the pantry, but nothing remotely resembled a Christmas dinner.

One evening, Jeffery came in to the room and sat on the corner of the bed. "I was thinking…" he said. "Maybe we should get out of the house—do something…anything? You know, since we closed Gracewinds you haven't left the house—shit, you haven't really left this room. What if we drove down to the Seattle Center for an afternoon?" Since I didn't roll away from him, he continued. "I'm pretty sure that my old girlfriend still works at the ballet. If you want, I could give her a call and see if she'd comp us some tickets to The Nutcracker?" He waited.

"Take the girls," I said from underneath the covers and rolled over.

He sat in silence for a short time. "OK. I will." And I heard him walk away, the door latching quietly behind him.

Several days later, Jeff and the kids went to see the Pacific Northwest Ballet's production of The Nutcracker—he even got Dane a ticket. I lay next to Sasha, alone in the eerie stillness of the empty house, no sound but the ringing in my ears. I pictured my girls' faces as they watched the opulence of the performance. I wished that I'd been mentally well enough to go and share it with them. It burned me to know that this special outing came from my husband's old girlfriend, that I couldn't offer my family anything of value at this point. I knew that they missed me and worried about me. I loathed myself and what had become of all of us, and I feared for our future.

I couldn't stop the unrelenting, condemning voice in my head. The rational side understood that this situation was not my fault. The other part, the one that increasingly controlled my every thought, just kept piling the coals of accusation onto the fire of my guilt. I lay awake night and day, unflinchingly allowing the litany of blame-ash to rain down upon me.

There was so much to feel guilty about. I blamed myself for thirty-five Gracewinds' staff members without steady work, for the disappointment of my business mentors who'd supported me and believed in me, for the needs of thousands of families who had looked to my company for support and guidance. I blamed myself for the pain that Jeffery was going through—my husband, who'd sacrificed so much for me and for Gracewinds. I blamed myself for my children's confusion, and for loss of their home. *Where will we end up?* I had failed them all.

The kids and Jeff announced their arrival back from their outing with a slam of the front door and the pounding of footsteps up the stairs to my room. I figured that I owed it to them to at least pretend I was interested in what they were about to tell me.

"Momma! You should have seen it!" cried Justine.

"Hey! No fair!" screamed Juliet. "I said I got to tell her first!"

133

I sat up against the headboard and put a faint smile on my face. As long as I let them do all of the talking, it really wasn't noticeable that I didn't participate.

Eventually, the kids came back to my room more often to share stories of their day—significant and inconsequential.

One evening, when I felt able to summon the strength to get out of bed, I dressed and fastened the leash onto Sasha's collar. The realization that her master was finally able to resume our evening walks must have been almost more than she could bear—she left a trail of pee on the floor to prove it.

We walked for hours. I have no memory of where. I do remember that the biting cold froze my breath before it left my nose, and there was no sound except for the rumble of passing cars and the crunching sound my boots made on the frost-covered sidewalks.

We walked in silence, the dog going about her important business of sniffing and examining, and me immersed in contemplations of how to bring about an end to it all. I pondered how much pain I would feel on impact by simply stepping in front of one of the heavy trucks that came barreling down Holman Road. I wondered if I could do it in such a way that no other cars would be involved, I could just keep it between me and one unlucky driver…

My thoughts ran this course for quite some time, until Sasha, sensing that I was up to something, looked over her shoulder and beyond the leash. She seemed to be saying, *'If you're thinking of taking me with you, I'd prefer that we go home now.'*

"I love you, stupid ol' Pig-dog," I told her. "Come on, I'll take you back home."

134

We walked up the porch steps and looked in through the beveled glass panels of the front door. A fire was crackling away in the hearth and Jeff and the kids were eating pizza in a tight circle in front of it. For a brief while, I felt the Ghost of Christmas Past standing there with me, watching the scene unfold inside.

I took a deep breath and opened the door. I unsnapped Sasha's leash and let her dash across the room—knocking over two glasses of Coke en route.

"Hey, Mom! There you are!" the girls cried out when they saw us walk in. Jeffery stopped in mid-bite and looked deeply at me.

"So, have you guys saved any of that pizza for me?" I asked, and took a seat next to the fireplace. I reached for a plate and Megan placed a slice on it. I smiled at my family and for the first time in weeks, I really meant it.

Chapter 16

Plot a Fix

New Year's came and went. There were plenty of setbacks and wrong turns on my path to emotional stability—let alone financial concerns and existential quandaries. Still, the pain began to lessen and was replaced by numbness. I could handle that—it wasn't great, but it wasn't as debilitating. I focused only on the issues that I needed to get through each day. Jeffery coaxed me back into spending some Saturdays helping out on the *Zodiac*. In time, things started to improve. Eventually I started to put ideas into words and could participate in talks with Jeffery and the kids about what was to come next for our shaken family.

While I fought it inside, I knew we were likely going to have to sell our house—the home that we'd spent so much time and effort restoring. The home where our kids had grown up— *were* still growing up. We just didn't have the money to remain, and selling it would give us some options. Besides, Dane now lived on his own and the twins were a little over a year away from college. Trenton was long-married with kids of his own in Oregon. Juliet was basically the last little bird in our nest.

No matter when we sold our house, Jeff and I knew we'd need to find work—a worrisome endeavor in light of the economic bust that killed Gracewinds. The fact that we'd both been working on our own—as a business owner and a sole proprietor—made the prospects even gloomier. In the job market's current state, where could two independent sorts turn? Whichever angle we approached it from, our conversations invariably reverted to 'What would we do next?'

One weekday morning over coffee, Jeff and I sat in the kitchen alcove and considered the options. "I could probably find a job for a construction outfit," Jeff said. "The rate would be less than half what I make as a general contractor, but it would be steady work... if there *is* any work out there, that is." He split open a sesame bagel and spread the cream cheese sparingly over both halves. Handing me the top half, he continued, "Assuming that we sell this place—move into a smaller house, maybe outside of the city, we could start to put some money back into our savings."

I stared out the window at the bamboo and sipped my coffee. "You see how much taller that stuff has grown since last year?"

"What are you talking about?" Jeff asked.

"The bamboo. What's it called? Castellan? Maybe it's the one with the cool name—*Yashadake Kimmei*. I think... Anyway, it's like, tripled since this time last year."

He looked out the window, then back at me over the rim of his glasses. "OK. Are we talking about *plants* now, Chris?"

"Huh? Uh, no, sorry. Go ahead, I'm all ears."

"Well, I was thinking—you have all this executive experience. Maybe you could find work in upper management somewhere."

"Yeah, no. That's just not gonna happen." I got up and poured the last of the French press pot into my cup. "Do you want any more of this?"

Jeffery sighed. "Are you even listening to me?"

I sat down and added the cream, stirring my coffee. "Oh, I hear you. We gotta find jobs. I'm taking you seriously—I *totally* am. It's just… I'm just… I'm not gonna be able to play that game anymore, that's all. I'm not working for 'The Man' anymore."

"Uh, OK," he nodded slowly. "So… what do you think you *want* to do, if working for 'The Man' is out?"

I snapped my fingers to get Sasha's attention and pointed to the bagel crumbs under the table. Sasha obediently licked the tidbits from the tile and plopped down at my feet, lest any other morsels should fall from above.

"Look, honey. I played by their goddamned rules and I gave my pound of flesh—working eighty or more hours a week. My kids did without their own mother so that I could spend all my time helping *other* women become one—remember that line—and where'd it get us? How's our family doing right now— tell me that? I was a good little capitalist and did what I was supposed to do: I provided fucking jobs, I sure as shit paid my taxes and submitted all my financials and profit and loss forms… and where did I end up? 'Thank you very much, Mr. Mayor; thanks a lot, President Douchebag.' Where the hell is *our* bailout?" I walked over to the counter and set my empty cup down next to the sink. "Ya know, in only eight years we helped over 5,000 families get their start. Christ—we built a goddamned health clinic for moms and babies in Kenya! What did A.I.G. or

138

Citigroup or fucking General Motors ever do for any little babies? I say screw 'em. *Hasta la victoria siempre.*"

Jeffery pushed back his chair. "Bravo. But you're kind of preaching to the choir here, honey. We can't all just slap on a beret and join up with the guerillas now, can we?"

I chucked a section of bagel at his head. "I'm totally serious, dude."

"I know you are. You've got every right to be angry. I happen to be pissed as hell too, you know. We've just got to be realistic about how we're going to manage things—you know, before you start your little revolution. We ought to seriously think about how we can live off the grid and still earn some kind of a living—raise a family, right? Hell, I can think of all sorts of alternative ways we can go—I've got shelves of books all about it! We can come up with a plan where you won't have to kowtow to *The Man,* but we still need to find some sort of way to earn money."

I sighed and picked up my cup to wash it. How could I make my husband fully understand? He of the 'hopeless-romantic-syndrome.' Jeff had always harbored a dream that we'd end up in a treehouse or building a home out of straw bales and making our own clothes. He'd be ecstatic to find an old school bus and raise the kids out of that if I'd let him. "Off the grid" to Jeffery Carson meant freedom and a pioneering spirit. To me, "off the grid" meant turning my back completely on the American lifestyle. I had no interest in continuing to claw and scratch for our little piece of the dream—I no longer believed in the dream. I'd just witnessed too many small companies like mine close down while the major corporations prospered. Once Congress signed the bill funneling billions of dollars into Wall

Street and left small businesses to drown, I checked out. The system was rigged—the rules had finally been exposed. Game over—time to come up with new rules.

I went over to my husband and straddled his waist; sitting on his lap, I wrapped my arms around his neck. "Jeff, all I know is that I'm more than willing to admit defeat, OK? 'The Man' won— hey, good for them. So I'll pick myself up, dust off and keep going—and do all that bullshit 'contributing member of society' song-and-dance thing. But it's going to be on *my* terms, *not* theirs. *They* cheated, goddammit, and not one of *them* is getting penalized. So now, I refuse to play."

Jeffery slipped his arms around my back and pressed his lips on the side of my neck. "OK," he said. "Let's find a way to play by our own rules then."

Chapter 17

A Reach

The twins elected to spend the first week of January at their dad's, and with only Juliet in our house, life seemed very mellow—all things considered. Returning to some sort of a 'normal' routine again helped us, even if only in pretense. We'd have dinner early enough to help the youngest with her homework and even got back into a nightly routine of the "Dirty Jobs" series—Juliet and Jeffery's favorite show. Everything fell back into place, until morning came around… the time that I *should* have been heading to work.

During school hours, I had ample opportunity to contemplate how we might proceed with our plan. The driving concern for me hinged on living without obligation to banks, credit cards, home loans… anything that tied us back to the *system*. I just needed to figure out what that scenario would look like. There had to be a practical, reasonable way to accomplish this—I needed to pinpoint how to make it work for us.

One school night, I tucked Juliet into bed and wandered through the house, turning off lights as I went. The basement stairs were illuminated by the faint light of Jeffery's desk lamp. I walked into his office and reached for the switch. Sitting on the desk was a framed 5x7 photo of the three of us standing next to the giant windlass on *Zodiac's* foredeck. I picked up the picture frame and studied the photograph, smiling to myself. Memories of the Tall Ships Festival came flooding back. I wished that life could always be as unconventional and straightforward as it seemed onboard that ship.

When I reached the hallway to our bedroom, I carefully stepped over Porter, asleep just outside our doorway. Jeffery was already under the covers, reading a past issue of *Fine Woodworking*. Sasha had curled herself up on my side of the bed. I paused in the doorway and crossed my arms. Jeffery raised his head, glanced over at me, and then closed his magazine. "What?"

"Do you remember the conversation we had a few years ago—we were talking about what might have become of us if we had never met?"

"Yeah, I remember. Does this mean that you're thinking about leaving me now?" He raised his eyebrows.

"Nah, not yet… but, what was it you were saying about a boat?"

"I probably said something like I would become some pathetic old guy with a smelly dog, living on an ancient wooden boat and cruising around the world." He sat up in bed. "Why do you ask?"

"Hmmm. Find me some boats to look at," I said, and went to brush my teeth.

Within three days, Jeffery had bookmarked over twenty boats for sale in the region. I skimmed through the online photos and read the descriptions. I began culling out the ones that were either too far gone for our abilities and situation, or too far out of our price range. By the time I finished editing his compilation, we were down to fewer than half. Jeffery phoned several of the brokers and scheduled appointments to tour some of the nearest boats, and we began taking our weekends to look at vessels for sale up and down the Puget Sound. The styles of the boats we looked at were as wide-ranging as their sticker prices, and we felt like we were spinning our wheels. We needed to set some concise parameters, so out came the old HP adding machine, and we got serious.

I found Jeff at his desk after dinner one evening, surfing through yacht brokerages online. He had the calculator next to his laptop. "Hey there, how goes your number crunching?"

Jeffery paused and pulled me over to his chair. I stood beside him and browsed some of the pages. He said, "I figure that by the time I finish up the remodel and we sell the house, pay off our debts including the balances we owe our folks, and then factor in costs to modify whatever boat we buy... we oughta end up with just enough to purchase one of these middle-range vessels."

My propensity for skepticism left me feeling less enthusiastic about our prospects. I figured that Jeff's idea of a 'middle-range' vessel was a tad different than mine. I cleared my throat and replied, "We need to make sure that whatever we end up with, there's enough left to keep something in a savings account. We'll need to cover our health insurance and other stuff I'm sure we're not thinking of yet—and living 'off the grid' has no retirement plan, you know."

Jeffery changed the numbers in the search field to *under $100K*. We both gasped at the results. "Narrows down the types of boats we're lookin' at a bit, doesn't it?"

"Whoa. Nothing but fixer-uppers," I moaned. "We just spent the last ten years living in a construction zone. Please promise me we don't have to do that again."

"I know, I know. Don't give up. We'll find something out there, I'm sure of it." He gave me a sideways hug, pulling me closer to his chair.

After that revelation, it took a few days for me to work up the enthusiasm to look at any more of Jeff's boats. Our readjusted price range left us with few options but to shop for decrepit yachts that needed a lot of work, or fish boats and old tugs that needed complete conversions to make them livable. I could scarcely imagine going through another extensive remodel project like the one we had barely completed on our home—*and* on the water. *Christ!*

With frugalities and a loan from Jeff's mother, we were at last able to pay the overdue gas bill and by mid-January the house warmed up once more to a comfortable temperature. The snow from the past week's storm made a picturesque scene outside our living room windows. The dogs sprawled on the kitchen tiles, soaking up the radiant under-floor heat, and the kids ran around the house in tee-shirts once more. Nevertheless, I continued to spend most of my days upstairs—I didn't like to be reminded of what I'd soon have to leave.

One afternoon, I lay across the bed with my laptop propped up on pillows, searching for more boat candidates. Megan came in and sat down on the bed beside me. She watched me work and absentmindedly picked at some loose strings on the quilted comforter.

"Mom, why do you guys want to move onto a boat so badly?"

"Well, there's not a simple answer." I sat up to look at her. "We love the water y'know—especially Jeffery. We want to have the ability to travel, to get away from the craziness on land I suppose, and we want to live inexpensively. I think for me, it's because I just want to disconnect. Does that make sense? Why do you ask?"

"Well, I just don't want to move onto a stinky old boat, that's all. It's not fair." Megan pouted just a bit.

"But you like *Sugaree*."

"That's different. Why don't you guys just live on *Sugaree*?"

I chuckled. "Could you see all of us trying to fit inside *Sugaree* and live year-round?"

"Yeah, I guess that wouldn't work. But no matter what boat you get, it's still going to be super cramped and we'll all probably end up stinking like diesel and fish."

"Not always—*Zodiac* and *Sugaree* don't smell too bad, do they? What if I promise you that if we even get *close* to considering a boat we can afford to buy, we'll bring you along to look at it before we decide? OK?"

"No, not really," she said matter-of-factly. "I just don't want to move onto a stupid boat." She stared at the thread she was unraveling from my quilt and then added, "I think I'm just going finish my high school year with Dad, then."

"You aren't even willing to give it a try? Even at first, or part-time?"

"Nuh-uh. But don't worry—I'll come and visit you, of course." She slid off of the bed to leave.

"Hey—wait a minute," I said. She stopped at the doorway and looked back at me. "I'm not even sure what's going to happen at this point, but one thing's for sure. We're going to find something, somehow, that will work for everybody—all right?"

"OK." She shrugged and walked out the door.

Damn. Just… damn.

Later that week we called a family meeting. Given the recent revelation from Megan, I wanted to find out what the rest of my brood *really* thought about our plan. Everybody piled into the library after lunch was over. The girls squished together on the couch and the dogs stretched out in the middle of the floor. Jeffery walked in holding a few printouts of some of the boats we'd been considering. He sat down in the big armchair and cleared his throat. "OK, gang. Mom and I want to hear what you guys think about the boat thing. I guess we assumed that everybody was good with our plans, but maybe we weren't paying attention. Does anybody want to say something?"

Juliet's hand shot up as if she was in class. "I want a boat! Can I bring all my stuffed animals with me though?"

"Well, it depends on how big your bunk is, but you'll be able to bring some of them." Jeff looked directly at the twins. "What do you both think about it?"

Megan sunk back into the cushions and folded her arms across her chest. She stared into her lap and didn't speak. I looked over at Justine, trying to read her body language. She concerned herself with the chipping nail polish on her left thumb and picked at it noncommittally.

"Justine?" Jeffery asked.

"Well, I don't really care one way or the other, you guys," she replied. "It's more your thing anyways—I mean, I'm going to cosmetology school next semester and I sort of wanted to find my own place with Patty when that happens."

I knew full well that the girls were nearing their high school graduation and that we'd once again be facing the empty nest syndrome—I'd gone through it with both of the boys with varying degrees of impediments. I just didn't wish to face the inevitable right now—especially after all the endings we'd endured lately. Justine's comment made me realize there would be another big finale to deal with soon.

"It's not like you're getting a boat and then sailing far away, right?" Justine continued. "I mean, you'll still be here, won't you?"

Jeff replied that we hoped to stay in the northwest until we found a boat that fit our requirements, but we couldn't be certain. We hadn't really moved past the 'find a boat' phase of the big plan.

"What about Porter and Sasha?" Juliet piped up. "Are they going to live on the boat too?"

Holy shit. The dogs—what about our dogs? I shot a quick sideways glance over at Jeff, hoping that he had prepared an answer to that question. I'd not yet made the leap beyond moving our children onto a boat; finding one that could also accommodate a 60 pound Labrador and a high-energy pitbull had not occurred to me—until just now. Jeff sighed and sat back in the chair before responding. "I don't think it's possible to keep both dogs on a boat. There just won't be enough room and it wouldn't be fair to them."

Megan sprang from the couch and ran upstairs. "Well, we know which dog has to go, don't we!" She cried as she left.

"Mommy! We don't have to sell Porter? Do we?" Juliet looked ready to cry.

Things weren't exactly going the way Jeff or I had anticipated. Unfortunately, I was no help to him, as the slightest trauma might catapult me back to my previous state. I blinked back my own tears regarding this latest news. Sasha definitely enjoyed most-favored dog status; I spoiled her rotten. But Porter... dufus that he was, he belonged to the girls, and they worshiped that stinky, shedding dog. I had to admit a certain fondness for him as well and really didn't want to give him up. I'd feared this type of emotional messiness would occur months ago. *And so it begins.*

Jeffery finally gave up and adjourned the meeting due to a sudden incursion of female emotions. The subject of dogs— specifically Porter— was tabled until a later date and all talks of boats was postponed. Juliet followed Justine upstairs to watch *Transformers.* I looked over at my frustrated partner and smiled. "And you thought that a lack of separate bedrooms would be the deal-breaker."

For the next few weeks, we worked at crossing items off of our *to-do* lists. I sat at my desk leafing through a distance-learning brochure one afternoon, when Megan and Justine came in and sat next to me on the floor. Sasha wriggled out from underneath my chair and began vigorously licking their faces, her tail wagging so hard it knocked Megan's glasses off her nose. They laughed and screamed at Sasha to stop, pushing her away, each toward the other. This made the dog only more excited.

Finally I put a stop to it before someone got hurt. "Sash—enough. Come here, girl—now, sit!"

"Pig-dog slobber! *Yccchhh!*" Megan wiped her cheek with the back of her sleeve. "Her breath smells like *Fritos!*"

"What are you guys up to? I could swear you were supposed to be cleaning up your room. There is no way you could be finished with that chore already—'cause I've seen the amount of crap in your room!"

"We're taking a break." Justine replied. "We've run out of trash bags."

Megan threw the tennis ball that Sasha had gummed and the pitbull dashed out of the room behind her toy. Growls and barks from the hallway led me to believe that poor Porter had been napping directly in the ball's trajectory. "Mom, we talked to Trent this morning and I asked him if he'd keep Porter when we move out. He said that he'd have to run it by Jessica, but that he probably could take him." She chewed on her cuticles while she waited for my response.

I mulled it over briefly. Porter probably wouldn't be a very good farm dog—his main talent was that of finding the warmest spot on the floor and he didn't really like to run around outside either. I didn't think for one second that Trent's wife would allow Porter inside their house…On the other hand, they did have a roomy garage and lots of wild rabbits on their property. *Who knows, maybe he'll end up being a retriever after all.* "Yeah, I think that's a good idea. Smart move."

"Hurray! Porter's staying in the family," she shouted.

The dogs crashed into the room at the sound of Megan's outburst. Both girls fell onto their beloved pet and pinned him to the floor with kisses and belly rubs. Sasha pounced on top of the pile and soon my office rang with screams and barks and snorting dog noises. I gave up trying to read in peace and left them to their own devices.

Chapter 18

Reconnoiter

The mournful music of Ray LaMontagne resonated from our living room. I hummed along with the tune as I leaned against the open kitchen door, gazing out into the darkness of the yard. Below me, I could hear the scuffling of the dogs, chasing and wrestling with each other. Somewhere out in the black void a siren pierced the evening's silence, then faded away. I whistled for the dogs, and two pairs of luminous eyes appeared out of the blackness. As they darted up the steps of our porch, I observed the sheeny gloss on Porter's coat—they'd been rolling in the wet grass. "Hold it right there, buddy!" I caught the Labrador by his collar as he tried to bolt past me. "You're getting dried off right now, pal—stand still." I grabbed the towel we kept for such occasions and scrubbed Porter while Sasha petulantly awaited her turn.

So engrossed was I with the canines, I didn't hear Jeffery come up behind us. He threw his coat on the kitchen table and it startled me, allowing Porter to duck between my legs—dashing upstairs to find the girls. Sasha took her cue from the bigger dog and raced past as well, leaving muddy paw prints across the kitchen tiles. I tossed the towel on the floor and wiped their tracks away with my foot. "Hi there—you surprised me."

"Apparently so!" he said, heading toward the fridge.

"We're out of beers—one of the repercussions of our new 'austerity policy.'"

Jeffery let out a sigh and shut the refrigerator. He peeled off his overalls and sat down at the table. "I don't think much of this 'austerity' thing—I've been dreaming about a cold beer the whole way home."

"Yeah, well get used to it. I've been dreaming about roasted coffee for the last three days. Until you get another check from your clients, we're back to the same-old-same-old."

"Well, I guess if the poor bastard at Goldman Sachs can tolerate getting his CEO bonus cut back to seven *million* dollars, I can cowboy up and do without my cold beer after work."

He kicked off his heavy steel-toed boots and tipped his chair back. "It was a long, dirty day though. A beer would be really nice about now."

I hadn't seen much of Jeffery lately; he'd spent the last two days down at the North Lake Union dock where the *Zodiac* wintered. The re-ballasting project had dragged on longer than planned and they needed his help to load the old iron and steel ballast onto pallets and weigh them. He came home each evening smelling of rust and metal and looking like a miner. "How are you guys doing down on the ship?" I asked.

"It's coming along—slowly. Captain Tim's staying onboard during the week to get this project finished in time. Oh—he'd like to talk to you while he's in town."

"Why am I supposed to talk with him?" I asked. The less-than-approachable captain still unnerved me, even after months of volunteering onboard the ship. Normally, I had no trouble warming up to people, but Tim's standoffish manner and habitually stern personality made me second guess everything that I said and did around him. Sure, I liked him—even admired him—but he intimidated the crap out of me.

Jeff replied, "He's interested in discussing some marketing projects that you might do for the ship."

"Wait a minute—how in the hell does he know that I've marketed before?"

"Well, I may have mentioned it in passing. Actually, I suggested he talk with you." Jeffery left his chair and walked over to the sink. Filling a glass with cold tap water, he gulped it down and continued. "I think I may have solved our dilemma in regard to the next few months."

"Whaddaya mean solved our *dilemma*? And what does this have to do with me and Tim exactly?" The frozen pizza that I'd placed in the oven before he arrived began to smell done. I pulled the oven door open to check it, and the aroma of pepperoni and cheese filled the kitchen.

"Well, we need a place for you guys to live while I finish up the remodel and the realtor shows the house, right?"

"Yeah."

"And Tim needs someone to help him build up his business… somebody who knows how to do PR and marketing." Jeff reached for my waist and pulled me over to him. "We kind of came up with a deal. You'll work on getting more passengers for *Zodiac* and he'll let us live onboard until the sailing season starts."

"I don't know that I'm much of an expert anymore when it comes to building a business."

Jeff brushed my bangs away from my forehead and then traced his finger underneath my chin. "That's bullshit—you're just a little gun-shy, is all. I told Tim that once you started marketing his boat, the biggest problem he'd have by next year would be getting a day or two off."

I pondered for a minute. "Well, it probably wouldn't hurt to go talk to him, I guess." I pushed him away and reached for the oven mitts. "I'll go down tomorrow—but only if you go with me."

"*Excellent.* This is going to be good for you—you'll see."

"Mmm, yeah, we'll see. Meanwhile, call the kids and let's eat."

"Sounds good. Just let me get changed first. I stink like fifty-year-old bilge dust." He laughed.

The following evening, Jeff and I boarded the *Zodiac*, the rickety gangplanks twisted and rocked as I stepped aboard. We found the captain crawling underneath the disassembled floor in the main salon. He was busy pulling links of heavy, rusting chain out of the bilge boxes. We watched him work for several minutes before he stuck his head out of the bilge and acknowledged our presence. "Why was it, do ya suppose, that when they put all this stuff in here—back in the '40s—they couldn't have found some uniform-sized chunks of ballast?" He threw the metal onto the sole and it clanged loudly, a small cloud of saffron-colored dust rising into the air.

I turned to Jeffery and asked, "Why'd they replace the ballast anyway? If she was built in the '20s, wouldn't she already have all the ballast she needed?"

Jeff replied, "The original lead was requisitioned for ammunition during World War II. They replaced it with whatever else they could find back then."

"Like all of this crap!" Tim's voice echoed out of the bilge box as he tossed some more rusty chunks up on the sole.

"Huh. So why put the lead back in now?" I asked—leaning down so he could hear me.

Tim paused and replied. "Lead's much denser, and that changes the stability. The lead actually improves her trim—she was initially designed for the heavier ballast. Oh—and because the Coast Guard is now requiring me to do it for our C.O.I."

I wondered what a C.O.I. was, but chose not to pester him with more questions. He appeared to be in a pretty amicable mood and I didn't want to jeopardize it.

"Hey, you—climb out of there and have a beer with us," Jeffery interjected.

"Now *that* is a good idea." Tim pulled himself out of the bilge and brushed off his hands. He unzipped his filthy coveralls and went forward to clean up. Jeffery pulled out three ales from the reefer.

I accepted the bottle from my husband and took a long swallow. While we waited for Tim, we sat down at the galley table and took in the destruction all around us. The old ship really looked a mess. The sole had gaping holes every five or six feet, tools and garbage were haphazardly strewn about the entire galley. "Man, how the hell are they going to get her ready for the sailing season in just two and a half months?" I wondered aloud.

"Tim's pretty sure they can pull it out in time," Jeffrey replied. He'd picked up a small pump motor that sat nearby and studied it, turning it around in his hand and poking his finger into little compartments.

Tim walked back in the galley, grabbed his beer from Jeff, and took a big swig. "Impeller's broken on that darn thing." He pointed his beer bottle at the pump in Jeff's hands. "I can't find a replacement anywhere in town—cheap Chinese crap. I keep telling volunteers that I only want parts we can buy in the United States. Nobody listens."

We spent a few hours on the *Zodiac* chatting with her captain. I learned a lot about donated lead from decommissioned Navy subs, meta-centric height and the current rate for scrap metal at the transfer station. At last Jeff broached the subject of the potential trade. He brought Tim up to speed on the last few months and about the plans we'd hatched for a lifestyle change. Tim sat back on the settee and listened, he didn't interrupt or ask any questions.

As Jeffery continued with his story, I weighed our options. It did make sense to move onboard *Zodiac* once they took her north for the charter season. Jeffery needed us out of the house while he completed the last stretch of our remodel. The real estate agents certainly wouldn't want us present while they showed the house. Plus, I couldn't bear the thought of seeing strangers walk through our home, poking into our cupboards and closets—it upset me to think about it. The *Zodiac* sounded like a good plan, and an emotionally safe one. I just hoped that Captain Tim would agree.

Jeffery wrapped up his tale with the offer to throw his 'marketing-wizard' spouse in trade. Captain Tim set his beer on the table and shot a brief look my way. "It might work—perhaps Chris and I should talk more about it in the next week or two."

Our family spent our weekends traveling to countless marinas up and down the coast and waterways of Puget Sound. The twins quickly lost interest in traipsing around dirty shipyards in search of old boats and invented excuses that kept them close to home. Soon enough we dwindled to a threesome: Jeff, Juliet and myself—the youngest having long since abandoned her enthusiasm. One rainy Sunday evening, we drove back from touring a converted tugboat in LaConnor— Juliet slumped in the backseat, sound asleep. I turned to Jeffery and asked, "Are you sure we'll be able to make this all work?"

"What do you mean?" Jeff focused straight ahead as the rain pelted against the windshield.

"I just mean… if we find a boat, how are we going to purchase it without first selling the house? And how can we sell the house until the remodel is done? How can you finish remodeling if we're out looking for boats every weekend? I just feel like we're chasing our tails."

"We'll make it work—I dunno how yet—We might have to put down a deposit and hope that we can get a contingency, and, you know—the purchase would go through as soon as we sell our house. Lucky for us, the only thing worse than the housing market right now is the yacht sales market." He made the turn down our street. "Trust me honey, the right boat is out there—one that we can afford—we just haven't found it yet."

In February, the disruptive re-ballasting project finally ended and the *Zodiac* fell back into back into some sense of order. I made up my mind to speak with Captain Tim further about the arrangement that Jeff had proposed. I worked up the nerve to approach him during the day—he stayed on the ship alone during middle of the week and I wanted to have this conversation without volunteers eavesdropping on us.

I stopped by the old Metro-dock shop, Tim's white Jeep was parked in the gravel lot and I assumed he'd be inside, operating one of the big machines. I stepped through the double doors and noted how the old mullioned windows of the warehouse were covered in years of sawdust and cobwebs. They acted as a filter lens, softening the sunlight as it braved its way into the catacombs of storage bins and shelving. Antiquated boat parts lay stacked next to bits of signage and scrap metal. A massive ship's saw commanded center stage in the midst of jointers, thickness planers and saw-horses. It reminded me of my father's wood shop in our old barn. I spotted Tim back at the rack of wooden blocks—he stood at the drill press, working on a piece of thick metal.

Tim appeared to be deep in thought as he concentrated on his project. I watched him and mused about the irony of being surrounded by craftsmen and carpenters: my father, Jeffery and now Tim. I approached slowly, making sure that he could see me well before I got too close.

"Hey, Tim."

He nodded at me and turned off his machine. "Hey there."

"So… ya got a minute?"

Chapter 19

Kwaietek

Clankety, clank… the metal platform shook as we plodded down the cheese-grater nonskid surface of the ramp. It was frosty out that morning and our breath hung in front of us like puffy little clouds. "Juliet! Hold onto the railing. I don't want you slipping on the ramp."

"Mom! It's too cold to touch!" she complained.

"Just do it."

Jeffery walked a ways ahead of us, trading shop-talk with Russ, the broker. I followed in the rear, keeping a close eye on Juliet. The docks of the Tom-Mac shipyard were sketchy and looked like they could use a few more supports. Slimy moss, dusted with frost, grew up from the planking.

We were on the north fork of the Fraser River, its frigid water flowing swiftly by us. I looked over to the opposite bank. Giant logjams were packed in tightly, skirted together with thick ropes to keep the fallen trees from escaping. A few mavericks had got away from the herd and drifted by on their way out to sea, sure to wreak havoc for boats along the way. The distant skyline of Vancouver poked up from behind the trees of the opposite shore. Old, tired fishing trawlers and tugs nosed into the dock like horses lined up in their stalls. Their many different colors popped brightly out of the icy palette of frozen white sky: turquoise blues, salmon pinks and pale yellows covered the hulls of the '50s-era vessels, rust stains bleeding down to their waterlines. Several ancient behemoths had assumed the oxidized-red monotone that came with decades of exposure to the elements. They all shared the same used-up appearance. However, as with all the work boats we'd seen over the past month, they possessed an air of stubborn pride that made me fond of each one of them.

"Which one is the *Kwah-ee-tek*?" Juliet asked. She pronounced each of the Salish syllables with emphasis.

"Well, do you remember the picture we saw of her online?" I asked her. "Do you see a boat that looks like that photo anywhere?"

She craned her neck and scanned the ships on the dock. "Is it that one over there?"

I followed the direction of her finger and spied the sheer wooden prow of a 1920s looking hull. "That kinda looks like her—yeah." I grabbed Juliet's hand. "Let's go see."

We carefully picked our way down the slippery dock and saw that Jeffery had paused near the boat. As we drew closer, it became clear that this was indeed the old British Columbia Forestry boat we knew was for sale.

She loomed tall above us as we approached. I stopped and admired her bow that stood several feet above my head and dropped straight down to the water in a graceful line. Her stem was a solid chunk of oak. On her starboard side was a billboard made of Brazilian ipe. The planks followed the curve of her hull and protected the underlying frame from the large iron anchor resting against her side. The tarnished bronze letters—K W A I E T E K—were widely spaced along her forward bulwarks. Her hull and superstructure were painted traditional enamel white and her trim was dark burgundy—quite pretty. Upon her large smoke stack sat a dark green oval with a lone pine tree in the center and "British Columbia Forestry Service" inscribed around the border.

As we walked around her port side, we looked up at the wheelhouse. It sprung from the deck roughly eight feet aft of the bow. She had large plate windows around the entire front of her house, with varnished fir panels and sills. In front of the house was a short mast and on it hung a brass ship's bell. A faded FOR SALE sign was taped in the window.

Jeffery climbed aboard and offered his hand; Juliet ignored him and jumped on deck, but I smiled as I took his hand, carefully stepping on the boat. She withstood the addition of our extra weight without even bobbing in the water. "She's a sturdy old gal," Jeffery commented.

"You're not kidding," Russ said. "The provincial government spent a lot of money on the fleet over the sixty-or-so years they employed 'em. Old *BC Forester* here, that was her old name, was their headquarters launch for the first couple decades she was on the water. She got a lot of tender loving care."

I left Jeff to discuss the history of the boat with Russ and followed Juliet to the stern. A rounded scuttle hatch protruded from the deckhouse and I was curious to see where it led. Juliet had already disappeared down the companionway before I rounded the corner. "Hey! Wait up!"

"Look at this, Mom!" she called from below.

I backed down the steep ladder and turned to get a look at the room below. As my eyes adjusted to the dimmer light, I saw a truly cozy galley. Varnished fir panels covered the walls, and the ceilings were painted white with darkly stained, thick beams running overhead every foot or so. The white enameled diesel oven had a cast-iron stovetop with a lid on the surface that you

161

could lift up to check on the fire inside. Above the stovetop was a separate warming compartment—very nice. The whole thing was in great condition.

Separating the "kitchen" part of the galley from the dining area was a partial bulkhead that transitioned into shelves for plates and glasses halfway up. It allowed light to filter into both sections. Thick, round portlights lined both sides of the ship. The large table could seat eight people easily. "Wow," I whispered.

"Mom! Come see the big engine in here!"

Following her voice, I approached a long passageway that dissected the engine room. Juliet stood beside a *huge* engine. I counted six cylinders and tried to follow the maze of coils and parts. A stamped metal plaque on each cylinder read GARDNER. "Oh, man. Your dad is gonna love this." The portlights continued throughout the engine room, making the entire passageway breezy and light. I walked around the engine and noticed a countertop, generator and large bank of batteries. Near these was a small head with a sink, shelves and toilet.

"That one's for Dad," Juliet stated matter-of-factly.

"Are you sure this isn't the only one on the boat?"

"Oh no, I already found the big one. Come see it."

"Hang on I want to see everything else first." I walked past the engine room and poked my head into a stateroom. The bunk was a large twin bed with cabinetry built next to it. "I bet this would be your cabin, Juliet," I said. But she'd already moved into the next room and didn't hear me.

I liked the smell of this old boat. It was just the perfect balance that came with years of oil soaked wood and dampness. Too many of the boats we'd been on during the last month stunk of fuel or had an overpowering scent of mildew and age. *Kwaietek* retained enough of the old wood and varnish aroma that no other odors assaulted my senses. The way I looked at it, if we were going to be making our home on a boat for the next several decades, then it better damn well smell good.

Including offensive smells, I had a pretty good checklist of what I did *not* want on any boat I was going to consider buying: missing deck beams, rotten framing, low headroom, engine rooms that were larger than living space…. I'd come across enough negatives on vessels during our search to know that, when the right combination of them came together, the sum was only one thing: Divorce Boat. In order to be polite, I shortened the name to *D*-boat.

After many weeks of touring marinas with brokers, I reached the point where I could walk the dock and spot the D-boats without even stepping on board. On one occasion we drove to Tacoma to meet a broker and tour a former prison boat. We'd tramped down a winding labyrinth of docks and piers, the broker chatting incessantly about the charm and history of the vessel. "You ever heard of Al Capone? Well, when this was a prison boat at Alcatraz, Mr. Capone was a passenger. I bet that'll make some great dinner conversations, huh?"

As we made our way to the last dock, a swan stood preening on a finger pier of one of the empty slips. "Wow, would ya look at that!" The broker didn't miss an opportunity. "I'd say that's a good omen! A swan right there in front of the boat you guys were meant to own!"

I'd wondered if he noticed the opposing omen—the greasy green pile of swan poop the bird deposited on the pier as it dove back into the water. The prison boat the beaming broker was standing beside listed at dock and showed pieces of rotten wood all along the railing right at eye-level. Forward, patched portions of the decking had been covered with plywood to hide what I could only guess were gaping holes.

"Uhm, Jeffery? ...D-boat." I'd already turned to walk to the car. As I traipsed back across the rambling docks, the swan glided alongside and looked at me sideways. "Yeah, thanks for the warning, buddy," I told him. He ducked his head a couple of times and paddled away.

I remembered that incident as I headed forward to join Juliet in the forepeak of *Kwaietek*. So far so good—no bad omens, no bad smells, not an obvious D-boat. And then I walked into the master stateroom and gasped. It had the distinct feel of a cozy log cabin, definitely not something I expected. The walls and bulkhead were varnished hemlock, floorboards made of polished cherry, and cabinetry constructed of old growth fir. I could actually picture some of my paintings and belongings in this room. I almost wanted to pause right there and make a detailed sketch of it to help me plan what would go where. The master head sported a full shower and a vanity cabinet. It needed a good paint job and some of Jeffery's carpentry skills to make it really nice, but I could envision the potential as I stood there in the middle of the room. *Heck, I bet even Megan would like this boat!* I wanted to get both the of the twins onboard to check everything out.

"Mom, you're taking too long. I wanna go upstairs now!"

We climbed the steps and rejoined Jeffery and Russ, who stood in the middle of a long sunny room just behind the wheelhouse. Five large windows on each side of the deckhouse gave it an open and cheerful look. Fir floorboards ran the length of the room.

"This is the main salon, kiddo," said Jeffery.

"Whoa! Cool!"

I followed Juliet into the room and turned around full-circle. "It's really beautiful," I said and stepped over to examine the trim that ran along the base of the windows on both sides.

"Wow! There's a woodstove here!" Juliet opened the grate and peeked into the little cast-iron stove.

"That little stove can heat this entire level," Russ said. "The owner Doug, told me he often had to open these windows when he got it stoked up." With that he showed us how the wooden framed windows each slid into a pocket-drawer inside the walls of the boat. They could be opened at different heights with small wooden wedges that accompanied each sill.

As Jeff and I played with opening and shutting the windows in the salon, Juliet walked into the wheelhouse and cranked on the gearshift. It was a round bronze wheel that moved forward and reverse; the middle was reserved for neutral.

"How simple is that?" quipped Jeff as he came up behind her.

The *Kwaietek*'s helm looked like a miniature version of the *Zodiac*'s large wheel. The spokes were spun into the traditional spindle shapes and the center band was inlaid with a bronze strap. On the fir dash above the wheel sat a boxed compass and bronze lamp. Crispy, yellowing charts were rolled and stored above in wooden slatted pockets. Everything had its place.

I looked at Jeffery and smiled. He, too, seemed pleased with what he had seen already. And Juliet turned to me on her

165

way out the wheelhouse door and informed us, "I want this boat." She clambered onto the wheelhouse roof and dropped her head down over the side. "Hey! Can I ride up here when we're driving?" Her yellow hair hung down, blocking the view out the window.

I called up to her, "Not if you're hanging upside down out there. We won't be able to see where we're steering—you nut!"

"Right." She disappeared.

Jeffery and the broker went below and spent nearly an hour in the engine room pouring over her mechanics. As predicted, Jeff fawned over the old Gardner diesel engine and for the next several hours could talk about little else.

Russ wisely noticed that Jeff and I wanted some private time, so he excused himself and walked back to his car. Jeffery turned to me and asked, "Well? What do you think?"

Juliet didn't wait for me to answer. "This is the one! This is the one!" She jumped up and down as she yelled.

"Hey. Let your mother have a turn please," Jeffery scolded.

"I like it. This is the first one that I can actually see us living in," I replied matter-of-factly.

"That's a good thing," Jeffery said smiling, putting his hand to my shoulder. "Because I told Russ that if it were up to me, I'd hand him a deposit right now!"

We chatted about *Kwaietek*'s possibilities. Jeffery showed me places he wanted to add cabinetry and where he planned to modify certain areas to make more functional space. "There isn't much to be done though," he said. "Doug kept good care of all the structural stuff over the past twenty years."

"Sure sounds like it's already our boat, hon," I said. "So, why's Doug selling it?"

"The broker says it's because Doug's brother passed away last year and it made him realize that life's too short to put off doing things you've always wanted to do. I guess Doug always wanted to own a piece of land up north. So he bought a little farm in Powell River."

"That's wild!" I laughed. "And here we are, making the move onto a boat because life's too short to spend it doing something we don't want to do!"

"Yeah. Ironic, but pretty damn cool," he agreed. "Oh, and get this—her name means 'sea bird' in one of the Salish dialects... remember hearing that name before—only in Scandinavian?"

"Are you kidding me?" I laughed. "Well, sea-bird didn't fit Sugaree, but somehow it works for me on this boat."

"Yeah, I guess there's something about that name that's supposed to be a part of us."

After snapping some photos to take with us, we said goodbye to *Kwaietek* and walked back to the parking lot. I felt sort of sad to be leaving her and turned at the top of the ramp. "Bye *Kwaietek*. Don't worry, we'll be back!"

167

Chapter 20

Casting Off

S tanding in the center of my bedroom, I stared at the piles of belongings scattered everywhere. *Jumping Jeezus, where to begin?* I pressed my fingers against my temples and tried to focus... create a mental inventory of all my things. Some of it would go with me and some would be boxed away—taken to a storage unit until who knew when.

Now that the purchase agreement had been signed— making *Kwaietek* ours once we sold the house— the pressure was on. Our actual moving date was over two months away, but for me, the process of leaving a place required a complex protocol of detachment... an emotional *bon voyage* of sorts, so that when it came time to depart, I was already long gone.

I chose to start with my dresser—that way Jeff could move the heavy antique out of our room once it was empty. I bent over and yanked at the bottom drawer, a little too forcefully—its entire contents tumbled out onto the carpet. Amid the unmatched socks, nightgowns and old journals, a rough ceramic plate caught my eye. It was thick and lumpy and unevenly glazed. "What in the heck...whose is this?"

Dane walked past the doorway at that moment, with Sasha close behind him. He spotted me crouching in front of the drawer and paused. "Hey Mom, I just stopped by to grab my weights and... what are you doin'?"

"Huh? Oh hey. Good to see ya." I turned over the little plate and examined it on both sides. "I'm just sorting through some stuff—hey, check it out. It's yours… from kindergarten." I held up the ceramic mold with a tiny handprint in the center. "I completely forgot that I'd had it for all these years."

Dane gave it a cursory glance and handed it back. "Yeah, I remember making that. You keep way too much stuff *Madre*, you oughta just chuck some of it."

"Not on your life, Dude. This is definitely not the kind of thing one just 'chucks.'"

"Huh… OK, good luck then. I'm headin' out—but tell Jeff I grabbed those speakers he said I could have." With that Dane, took his leave; Sasha followed, happily wagging her tail.

I placed Dane's handprint platter into a pile of "keepers" and continued to sift through the items on my floor. Eventually I headed into my closet and began to pick through the clothes that I'd no longer need on a boat. Many of my outfits were bought specifically for my former role as a corporate executive; those were the easy ones to part with. High heels, silk blouses and any pieces that required dry-cleaning were removed from their hangers and boxed away. My comfortable dress clothes caused a conundrum, however, as I could envision wearing most of them in my new role as a liveaboard. Just because we were moving onto a boat didn't mean I couldn't do it with a little style.

Never having considered myself much of a clothes horse before, I was surprised to behold the mountains of clothing strewn everywhere. I scrutinized the boxes and bags of shoes that I owned and felt a little like Imelda Marcos.

In due course, the ambiguous mounds of what to keep, what to toss and what to store began to meld into one giant,

169

undulating mass that spanned across the entire bedroom. I temporarily abandoned my project in lieu of microwaved popcorn and a game of catch with the dogs.

Packing wouldn't be so difficult for me if I didn't sentimentalize every little thing in my life. My inclination to attribute feelings to inanimate objects has made it damn near impossible to get rid of certain items like broken Christmas ornaments, fearing they'd be traumatized by the experience. I'm convinced this is a type of mental instability, but I've managed to live with it.

Once the clothes and personal knickknacks had been dealt with, I moved onto my second and more daunting task: sorting through our enormous collection of reading material. Shelves of books occupied three walls of our library—and held places of distinction in our bathroom, bedrooms, hallways and offices. Jeffery also had bookshelves crammed full of manuals and magazine volumes in his basement woodshop. My first order of business was to identify the ones that I couldn't live without, then progress to the books that I'd been saving to read. I placed them all in the same pile and labeled them 'Books—to go on boat.' …And so on.

Jeffery walked into the library as I sat on the floor, surrounded by various piles of books, He paused and looked around. "Well, here's one thing we don't have to worry about: putting extra ballast in *Kwaietek*—what with all the books you've set aside to bring."

"Oh, don't you even *start* with me," I replied. "I've seen the six crates of *Wooden Boat* magazines that you've been stockpiling to sneak onboard."

Over the next couple of weeks, I sorted and packed away books. We'd agreed that most of our general collection would be left behind to "dress" the rooms for open house visitors. So I inventoried only the ones that belonged to me. It began to feel like parting with old friends—especially since it was unclear when we'd meet again. I had never had to box up my things with no assurance as to when they'd ever be opened again. Eventually, I altered my labeling system to include tags that read 'Goes to boat—if there's space,' and 'For storage—in front of unit.' It became my compromise with the purge.

One morning, Jeffery found me crying with a first-edition copy of my old book, *The Pocket Doula,* in my lap. Concerned that my depression from the previous months might creep back in as I culled my things, he pulled me out of my chair, handed me Sasha's leash and sent me out of the house for a walk.

Several days passed and I found my way back to sorting and packing. The house took on a transitory look as more and more of my belongings were stacked in corners of every room. The kids continuously complained. "Mom, I can't move around here, your piles of stuff are in front of the TV."

"Mom! Porter just knocked over your boxes in the dining room!"

"Hey Mom—did you already pack away the thesaurus? I needed that!"

Jeff brought home a sturdy plastic container and I boxed up all of the glass and crystal awards that I'd garnered over the past few years. I wrapped each trophy in tissue and tucked them all securely into the storage bin. Oddly, it hadn't been very long ago that these were some of my most treasured possessions—testimonies of success and accomplishment. I sealed the lid and taped up the bin. I wrote 'Storage—long term' across the top of the container.

Once my belongings had been stowed away, I moved on to the next stage of the detachment process: avoidance of my favorite haunts.

The spare bedroom that we'd transformed into my office and the kids' craft space, with its colorful, sun-drenched walls had too many powerful memories for me—I needed to make a clean slate. So, instead of children's paintings and posters splattered around the room, there now were barren expanses of bleached wall. Where the Persian rug had been strategically placed to hide a grape juice stain, there was nothing but cardboard boxes. The site for the dogs' beds that were positioned to catch optimum sunlight was now occupied by an upside down chair with boxes stuffed inside it. The room was spartan, devoid, emotionless.

That was my system: remove the emotion.

Yet emotion still welled within. My mind was plagued with the conundrum of consolidating a four-story house and decades of memories onto a 63-foot boat—and how to reconcile the dissolution of my family.

Already, Megan and Justine were busy with preparations to move to their dad's for the remainder of the school year, and after that—who knew. Breaking up the family circle struck at my core; I was the woman who'd built a profession around supporting and building families.

The next item on my checklist was to say farewell to our close friends.

On the night of our going-away party, we were touched by how many of our friends showed up—representative of connections that had been forged throughout the years—both old and new. Several *Zodiac* crew-members came by as well. Everyone who had shared our life in this old house in some way and witnessed the changes over the years had come to say goodbye.

Thanks in part to my emotional baggage-packing of the previous six weeks, I was relatively calm throughout the evening. As the house filled to capacity, I stepped outside to grab some fresh air. The porch swing was vacant, so I sat down and gave a gentle push with my foot. As it rocked back and forth, I looked through the picture window at the gathering inside. Scores of people congregated in the dining room while Jeff recounted a tale of apparent hilarity—judging by the laughter of those who surrounded him. I observed three toddlers sharing some of Juliet's Breyer horses. Their mothers stood behind them chatting and sipping wine as the babies played. I recognized the parents and smiled to myself, I had helped to bring each of those children into the world.

The front door opened, allowing the clamor of voices and music to escape onto the porch. Dane stepped outside and walked over to the keg, followed by Craig—one of our Gracewinds dads. They were deep in conversation about the Seattle Seahawks and didn't notice me sitting in the shadows. Dane filled both cups without disrupting their animated evaluation of the players' performances the past season. As they turned to head back indoors, he spied me on the swing. "Oh hey, *Madre*. Good party!"

"Yeah, I think so too."

He hesitated in the doorway for a few seconds and then nodded as Craig went back inside. Dane sat down on the swing next to me and took a few sips from his plastic cup. We rocked together slowly for several minutes. "You doin' OK?" he asked.

I sighed. "Yeah, it's sort of bittersweet though. You know… it's pretty cool to see all our different friends—all here at the same time. It's kind of that whole 'when worlds collide' thing, huh?"

Dane tossed back his beer and patted my shoulder. "Well *Madre*, you've always been kinda the one that brings everybody together, haven't ya?"

I smiled at him as he stood to go back in the house. "Glad you came by for the party," I said. He yawned and removed his Mariner's baseball cap long enough to scratch his head with the bill.

"Yeah, there's some cool people in there I s'pose. Anyways, I should probably get back and set Craig straight about Hasselbeck's season—man, that old fart can't pass for shit." With that he returned to the keg and refilled his cup, then walked back inside the busy house. From my shadowy perch, I watched him resume his armchair-quarterbacking with Craig and one of our neighbors. Sasha wriggled between their legs as they conversed.

I'd never fully realized to what extent our home had impacted the lives of so many people. That night I saw my house from the perspective of our vast and diverse group of friends, most who would not be meeting again now that their common ground was moving away.

By early April it was time for the final step in saying goodbye. We gathered the family together in the house one last time.

I decided to use a holiday celebration as the excuse, and chose Easter—though not technically on Easter weekend (more like a week early)—because it worked for everyone's schedule. Trent and his family arrived the night before. The girls fought for turns to play with their four-year-old nephew, William. Juliet and her nephew Kairen, played *Guitar Hero* until they fell asleep on the couch. Trent and Dane stepped out onto the porch to catch up without any parents, wives or girlfriends hanging around.

"It's brotherly bonding," Justine said.

"Smoking a blunt is more like it," Megan scoffed.

We played card games and board games and drinking games and then, when the kids went to sleep, we just drank and talked.

Sunday morning arrived just scant hours later, and I'd been nominated to play the Easter Bunny. I rose early, tiptoed downstairs and poured myself a glass of water. After setting the kettle on the burner, I proceeded to hide three dozen brightly colored eggs throughout the house. Sasha kept pace with me, puzzled by this perceived game. She poked her nose into every hiding spot and looked at me as if to say *you want me to fetch all of these?* I padded back into the kitchen and waited for the early risers.

By my second cup of coffee, the baskets I'd placed in front of beds had been discovered and sleepy squeals rent the morning solitude. Kids of all ages raced down the stairs so as not to be left behind in the mad dash for eggs. And for one last time, I enjoyed the sounds that had echoed from countless Easters-past in our old house.

"Remember to leave the E-A-S-Y ones for the little kids, Juliet."

"Duh, Mom." She sounded annoyed, and suddenly much older.

"Hey, no fair! I saw that one from over by the couch!"

"Well, you didn't call it, and I got to it first!"

The rest of the adults had finally risen and showered, and I made breakfast. We enjoyed it outside on the back deck; the air still had a spring chill to it, but the sun was shining and I wanted to enjoy the backyard as much as possible.

The kids laughed and joked with each other and took turns re-hiding the eggs for William in the damp grass. There was no fighting or whining. I savored every moment and tried to burn the images into my memory—willing them all to remain unchanged forever. Even the two dogs were relatively well-behaved. Everyone sensed that this was a special day and nobody wanted to ruin it.

At last the time came when Trent and his family had to leave. Kairen had school the next morning, and their six-hour drive back to Corvallis would keep them on the road for most of the day. Jeffery walked out front and helped Trent load some of the furniture and boxes of things we'd given them into the back of his pickup. Dane went to help and I watched the three of them standing in the street talking and laughing. The twins sat on the porch swing with Jessica, and traded stories about life in our house. Juliet and Kairen chased each other around the yard one last time.

Finally, when we could avoid it no longer, the hugs and kisses and 'we'll come and visit you soon' promises were doled out. Trent called Porter over to the truck and, with Jeff's help, coaxed him into the dog crate. He was going to be a farm dog now. As they drove off, we all kept up the sad waves and blown kisses until we could no longer hear Porter's farewell barking.

The last time our family would be together in our own home was now ending. With Trent and his family gone, the first heart-wrenching moment had broken the spell, and it made little sense to prolong the myth of my nuclear family. I turned to the twins and said, "Well guys, the car's all packed and Jeff's ready to drive Juliet and me up to Bellingham. I guess we'd better just say goodbye right now and get this over with."

The girls, who were staying behind with Dane until their dad came to pick them up, knew exactly what that meant. In their characteristic, identical-twin style, they simultaneously burst into tears. Juliet ran over to her sisters and threw her arms around them both. Sasha got in on the act and pushed her face into the huddle.

I looked over at Dane, who stood apart from his sisters. There was sadness written on his face as he looked over and smiled at me. "I love you, *Madre*."

Jeff stood by the car, unsure whether he should hurry me along or allow the sob-fest to continue. I walked over to my daughters and placed my hand on top of their heads. I buried my face in their hair and started to cry as well. We stood like that for several minutes, and then I motioned for Dane to come join us.

He walked over to his siblings and gave them each a bear hug. In his best big-brother voice, he said, "Come on sissies,

Mom's just going to Bellingham. It's like, an hour away... They'll be back down when they get the new boat."

Even in my distraught state of mind, I loved hearing Dane call the girls "sissies." It had been his nickname for them both since childhood. And I loved that he helped bring a sense of reality to the goodbyes—it wasn't for *forever*. I kissed the kids and told them that I'd drive down to pick them up for a visit in a couple of weeks. "We'll spend the entire weekend on the *Zodiac* and maybe go for a hike in the hills outside Bellingham." I reminded them that I'd be back for their birthdays in a month, and that we'd be seeing each other "all the time."

"Soon enough, you both are going to be in college, and be living on your own anyway!" I composed myself and rubbed their heads. "We knew this was going to have to happen sooner or later—it's just a few months sooner. And just think, instead of a stuffy old house, you'll come home for breaks and get to be on the water!"

The twins wiped their eyes and managed to slow the tears. Juliet wiped her runny nose on her sweatshirt and the kids all cried out in disgust, "Gross! *Eeew!* Juliet!"

Their teasing caused Juliet to laugh and blow a giant snot bubble out her nose, which caused everyone *else* to laugh and probably saved the day. At last I said a heartfelt, non-weepy goodbye to my kids and pushed Juliet and Sasha into the car.

Jeffery leaned over the seat and gave me a kiss on my forehead. He started the car and pulled away from the curb, and I turned to wave to my children, and then took one long last look at my home. "I can't ever go back there again," I whispered to no one in particular. The tears rolled down my face the entire drive from Seattle to Bellingham.

Chapter 21

A Favor

Zodiac awaited us at her dock. Her masts towered above the adjacent ferry terminal's roof. As we traveled though the parking lot, Juliet rolled down her window and hung her head outside to get a better view of the ship. Sasha crowded in as well, instigating a tussle in the backseat. Before the dog-daughter encounter had a chance to escalate into a fight, Jeff pulled up to the gate. "OK. Everybody out!"

We piled out of the car and stretched. The salt breeze relaxed me instantly and the familiar sensation of grounded contentment came rushing back. Standing outside the car for a few minutes, I took in the view. *Zodiac* bobbed only slightly in the swells of the bay. Her decks were deserted and clearly in mid-restoration work, but the familiar mahogany trim still gleamed in the sunshine.

Jeff popped open the trunk and unloaded our belongings into several dock carts. I packed enough gear and clothing to last both of us for the next three months. Juliet's bags of stuffed animals and homeschool books took up an entire cart to themselves. "Don't forget the dog food!" I called back to Jeffery.

I went down the ramp first, with Sasha dragging me toward the dock. The two seagulls that stood several yards ahead of us picking apart a starfish eyed her suspiciously. They waited until the charging pitbull made it necessary to flap upwards to safety, leaving behind a perfectly good meal. Sasha rushed to where they'd been just seconds previously and snorted as she sniffed their leavings.

After a few trips back and forth for all the loaded dock carts, we piled our things onto the deck of the ship, and I stepped below to turn on heaters and some lights. *Zodiac* was cold and deserted. I poked around the engine room in total darkness and found the switches on the diesel-fired boiler. I flipped the ignition toggle, and the circulation pumps clicked on to drive the warmth into various sections of the ship. I peered down the passageway to the forepeak and could barely make out the bunks and staterooms. It was an eerie contrast to the bustle and energy that usually filled the old schooner during her cruising season. Sasha grew tired of waiting for me and trotted back to the salon, crisscrossing around to stick her nose into each of the lower bunks on her path. She jumped onto the settee in the center of the room and looked back at me with her tongue hanging out the side of her mouth, her eyes alight. "Yep, this is your new home for a while, Pig-dog." I told her.

The past several months of projects were still evident all around me. Tools and refuse from the sole reconstruction and varnish jobs littered the salon, the galley and the charthouse. A thick coat of dust had settled upon all of the surfaces, and even the usual glowing mahogany panels were nondescript and dull. I glanced toward the kitchen portion of the galley and sighed, dirty dishes covered the counters near the sink from the last work party. "Well, let's get to it," I told the dog.

Jeffery and Juliet pounded down the companionway loaded with boxes and bags. I directed Juliet forward to where her bunk was located and removed a few of the heavier items from Jeff's bundle.

"Wow, the place is still pretty much a wreck," he commented.

"Yeah, looks like I'll have plenty to keep me busy for the next couple weeks—I'm sure I'll barely miss you."

Sasha rushed past us to the foc'sle, intent to find Juliet and, no doubt, cause havoc with the unpacking. We soon heard the aggravated screams from our youngest. "Sa-*shaaaaa*! You stupid dog! I hate you!" The dog came barreling back through the galley on her way to a hiding place in one of the salon bunks.

"Ah, it feels just like home already!" Jeffery said.

We brewed some coffee and unpacked the chocolate chip cookies Juliet made. Then the three of us sat around and talked about the many plans we had for our next few months on the *Zodiac*. Jeffery listed off the items that needed finishing on the remodel, and his strategy—if all went well, for what we would do once we purchased *Kwaietek*. I wanted to keep the verbal momentum going—the mapping out of our new lives—but Jeffery needed to get back to Seattle and orchestrate some of his tasks for the next day. "Trust me Chris, I'd like nothing more than to stay tonight, but my goal is to plow through these last details and start getting on with our lives. I want that house completely done and sold as soon as possible."

The time had come to say one more painful goodbye. Jeffery was my strength and I could feel my confidence begin to erode as he gathered up his coat and keys. Barring the weekends, we would be living apart for several months now—at least until the house sold. The reality of our situation became crystal clear as Jeff walked back up the ramp and waved good bye at the gate. Juliet's tears did nothing to help my inadequate attempt at stoicism. "Don't be so sad, Bug. Your dad's gonna be back up every weekend to see us. And we've got Sasha here to keep us company."

"I hate that stupid dog!" She stomped below.

Lying alone in my bunk that first night, I listened to the unfamiliar noises of our new surroundings. Freight trains rumbled along the waterfront every few hours, whistles heralding their arrivals. I could gauge the strength of the wind by the frequency and volume of the flag halyards banging against their metal poles outside the ferry building. What I did *not* hear was the sound of my husband's breathing next to me, the cedar branches scraping against our bedroom rooftop, and the noises from my children as they settled in for the night in their rooms. I lay awake in the dark, with *Zodiac*'s subtle rocking, and grieved for my old life.

Sasha stirred in the bunk below me and sighed in her sleep. I rolled over and looked at my dog. She seemed unaffected by the big change and smiled in her doggy-dreams. I crept out of bed and walked across to Juliet's bunk, just outside my stateroom door. She was curled up in her blankets. Family photos and her drawings were already taped onto the walls encircling her bunk, making it appear cozy and uniquely hers. *OK, if Sasha and Juliet can handle this, then dammit, so can I.*

For the next several days Juliet and I cleaned house, or rather boat. I scoured the galley and main salon while she swept and dusted. Soon *Zodiac* started to resemble her old self again. By the time Jeffery returned for the first weekend, we had our homey, familial routine established onboard.

"Has Tim been by to see you guys yet?" Jeffery asked as we cleared our dinner dishes from the salon table.

"Nope, he phoned to check on us two days ago, but I haven't seen him."

"Well, he'll be pleased with how you have her looking."

Our days and nights on the ship became a normal routine. Juliet sat in the charthouse with me, immersed in her homeschool lessons as I worked on the marketing campaign for the ship's next season. Captain Tim began dropping by the ship once or twice a week for coffee in the galley before he set to work on his projects in the nearby shop. And for two precious days a week we had Jeffery to ourselves. He showed up for dinner on Friday evenings and left at dawn on Monday. Occasionally, the girls would join him for a weekend visit. The tears that Juliet shed during our Monday breakfasts faded as the weeks wore on.

As we settled in, I felt the urge to do something more tangible than sit at the computer. One morning, I asked Tim if I could paint below decks. "Take on whatever you're willing to do," he replied. "She needs some freshening up in almost every department."

That next day, I started Juliet on her school assignments and went up to the shop. I returned laden with white enamel, thinner, sandpaper, buckets, tarps and brushes. By midafternoon the galley and companionway were sanded and prepped for paint. I threw myself into the physical work, and it somehow helped me to not think about the past few months, the house, the kids, our old friends. Once I let my mind recall those memories, it usually resulted in the same empty and hopeless emotions that paralyzed me last winter. I didn't want to go there again.

For the most part, I enjoyed living full time with *Zodiac*. And it was as if I was living *with* her and not simply *on* her. She became like a friend to me, and I figured that she liked having people around her. She was warm and dry, her passageways sported new coats of paint, and there was a constant smell of baking cookies or bread emanating from her galley. Plus an energetic child and rambunctious dog skittered across her decks every day. I imagined she could only be happier with a full crew and passengers on board—her sails filled. In my characteristic manner, I'd already anthropomorphized her to the point that we could carry on conversations.

One evening during a substantial south-westerly blow, Juliet, Sasha and I lay in our bunks listening to the wind whip around the rigging. *Zodiac's* shrouds were particularly noisy. She creaked and groaned as she rolled in the choppy water. Juliet finally called into my stateroom, "Mom! I can't sleep. It's way too noisy."

"Yeah, she's getting banged around a bit, huh?" I climbed out of my bunk, reluctant to go up on deck and face the chill of the winds. Throwing on my jacket, I walked past Juliet's berth. "I'll go have a talk with her and see if we can't calm her down a little."

"OK. Tell her I'm trying to go to sleep." Juliet flung herself around to face the wall of her bunk.

When I pushed open the charthouse doors, a severe blast of wind struck me head-on. I braced myself and stepped onto the deck, staggering as *Zodiac* rocked from side to side. Once I regained my balance, I went back to the quarter-bits and checked the mooring lines: all good. I then walked forward and confirmed that her bow lines were fast. "Well, girl, what's all this fuss? You're making quite a lot of racket up here." Another big gust blew past me and I heard the moaning thud that had been pestering us below. I walked around the charthouse and watched as the fore-boom swung back and forth.

"Hah! So that's what is going on... Come here, you." I picked up the secondary preventer and tethered the boom athwart-ship to a cleat near the gangway. With her boom cinched in tightly, she quieted right down.

"That's a good girl!" I patted her mast as I walked back toward the deckhouse. "Now, how about let's all get some rest tonight, huh?"

The sailing season gradually drew nearer and preparations to get *Zodiac* ready for her charters were well underway. I finished my painting projects below, and the varnishing work above-decks had wrapped up days before. It was time to re-rig and bend on her sails.

Early on a sunny Saturday morning, crewmembers and other volunteers arrived to begin the re-rigging. Jeffery drove up from Seattle as usual the night before and was on hand to direct the process; he'd recently become the lead-rigger for the ship. First, we hauled the running rigging down from the shop and began to lay them out in order. It was Jeff and Tim's job to go aloft and attach the blocks and halyards to both of the masts. I stood by on the deck to operate the gantline, hauling the heavy tackle upwards to the men high above. Everyone had to wear hardhats while they were on deck, as the rigging being performed aloft was over a hundred feet up the masts. Even a shackle pin dropped from that height could put a serious dent in someone's skull.

Once the running rigging had been reinstalled, we brought the canvas sails down to the ship. *Zodiac*'s mainsail alone—over 4,000 square feet of it—weighed several hundred pounds. Using block and tackle, the volunteers hoisted each sail up on deck, and we worked together for the entire afternoon to bend-on the four big sails. Once all was done, *Zodiac* had regained her exemplary schooner look and she was ready to set sails once more. Before dark, the volunteers put the finishing touches on our day's work by tying on the green sail covers.

The next morning was quietly domestic; with Jeffery, we were once again the sole inhabitants of the boat. I stood in the galley and sipped my first cup of coffee, watching the bacon sizzle and pop in the skillet. Jeffery lounged at the galley table and perused the latest issue of *Workboat* magazine, and Juliet nestled at the far end of the settee, her face buried in her *Harry Potter and the Deathly Hallows* book.

"Hey, I think I hear somebody on deck," I said, pausing my coffee cup mid-way to my lips. "Juliet, go see who just came on board."

"Can't, I'm still in my pajamas," she mumbled, without looking up from her page.

Sasha didn't wait for a request or permission and dashed straight into the charthouse, barking at the unseen intruder. "Sasha! That's enough!" I called after her.

I heard the charthouse doors open. "Hey-hey, Sasha, it's just me," Tim laughed. He stepped down the companionway stairs making every effort to avoid Sasha as she jumped up and entangled herself around his legs.

"Sasha! Hey, Pig-dog—get down!" I ordered. She ignored me and proceeded to make a nuisance of herself until Jeffery stood up and grabbed her by the collar.

"Sit, stay!" he scolded the dog and then grinned at Tim, "Did you come all the way down here for coffee?"

"No, but I'll take a cup if offered one." Tim took a seat and scratched Sasha's ears.

I poured a cup and set it in front of him. "You'd better watch out—you're going to get used to my espresso-roast and you won't be able to drink that awful swill you guys call coffee." I was gradually letting go of my apprehension toward the captain.

"I don't think that I could ever make as good an elitist as you," Tim replied.

"That's me—an 'elitist.' Champagne tastes and a beer-bottle pocket."

"No doubt," Tim smiled, then he put his coffee down. "But I didn't come down to discuss your views on coffee. I'm needing a favor."

"What kind of favor?" Jeffery asked.

I slid four strips of bacon onto Jeff's plate and called Juliet over to get her breakfast.

"Actually, this one would be from your wife."

"*Me?*" I was momentarily stunned at the prospect of Tim wanting something from me rather than Jeffery. "What exactly are you in need of?"

"Well, it looks like we've lost our cook for April and May. She's apparently enrolled in a class that won't end until the first of June."

"Oh wow—I could *definitely* cook!" I replied. "I've been making meals for the work parties for most of the last two winters. Jeez, it shouldn't be that much different."

"OK—but before you say a definite yes—remember that the first few months are all school trips. They're more difficult than the adult cruises in many ways. For one thing, do you realize how much teenagers can eat?"

"Uh, Tim. *Hullo?* Five kids…"

"Oh. Right." He chuckled. "Well, it pays about a hundred and thirty a day. I know that's a lot less than you're used to, but we're just little guys, you know."

I stifled a laugh and glanced over at Jeffery who winked back. "Don't worry, Tim," I said. "I think we can manage on that *just* fine."

"Well good. That's one load off my mind. Thanks a lot." He rose from the table and hung his cup back on its special hook. "Alright—on to the next thing then."

Sasha ushered Tim into the charthouse. I heard him step off the ship and could barely make out his footsteps clanging up the ramp. As soon as they'd faded away completely, I let out a shriek and executed an impromptu jig around the galley. "*Whoo hoo! Hell's bells, Jeffery, this whole thing might just work out after all!*"

Chapter 22

Pressed into Service

"Whoa! Megan—*duck!*"

Megan crouched as one of the electric griddles shot past her shoulder and came to rest on the galley floor.

"That was close!" I said, laughing. Then I noticed the giant pot of elbow macaroni sliding to the edge of the stovetop. I grabbed for the oven mitts and captured the pot seconds before it pitched off the edge.

The *Zodiac* heeled over once again and with a surging roll, more dishware dislodged from cupboards and careened across the galley. Megan scrambled to contain some tomatoes that stampeded toward the counter's edge. One of the riper ones escaped her grasp and exploded onto the floor, pulp and juice seeping into the holes of the rubber mats at our feet.

"Balls! Why didn't they give us any warning from the helm?" She asked, not bothering to mask the irritation in her voice.

"I dunno—my guess is that they didn't expect it. You never know, maybe it caught them by surprise, too."

I could hear from the pounding footsteps and the banging of wooden blocks onto the deck above me that the crew and passengers were busy adjusting their sails. ET ran down the companionway and paused to grab a handful of pretzels. Stuffing them in his mouth all at once, he said, "Hey, sowwyboudat, wewuda'cawed…"

"What the *hell*, ET?" Megan laughed. "We can't understand a thing you're saying with your mouth full of those things!"

ET stopped long enough to swallow his mouthful of pretzels and then reached for a cup of water. "I said, sorry about that. We would have called down but we sorta got caught off guard." He hung his cup back on the hook and turned to go back on deck. He stopped long enough to grab more pretzels and stuffed several handfuls into the pocket of his pea coat. "Heads up, Tim says there may be more gusts ahead. You might want to batten things down again."

"Not a problem. I just managed to save lunch from hitting the floor." I said.

"Thank god! I'm starving!" He ran back up the stairs.

"I'll ring in an hour!" I yelled after him and heard the faint but distinct, "Roger that!" acknowledgement as he walked back on deck.

"Oh no—my cake!" Megan grabbed the oven mitts from my hands and pulled open the door. "Oh, Mom, it's all lopsided—look!"

I leaned over and looked inside the oven. The chocolate sheet cake had a distinctly undulating appearance to its surface. *Zodiac's* back and forth heeling must have occurred at the exact time that Megan's cake set up.

"Hey, don't worry about it; they're a bunch of high school kids. They don't care." I said, "If you spread enough frosting over the top, it'll all even out."

Megan wasn't buying it. She threw the oven mitts onto the counter and stomped over to the galley table, depositing herself into the chair with a dramatic slump. "I give up!" She exclaimed and buried her head into her arms.

I knew that Megan was trying hard. And yet I also had a hunch that it wasn't just to impress the captain or me. My mother's intuition told me that Megan's sudden interest in culinary prowess was for the sole benefit of our newest crewmember, a wiry little deckhand named Kris. He'd clearly become the cause for her newfound interest in styling her hair and borrowing my clean shirts. Megan had a crush—on a *sailor*.

I set the timer on the oven to allow her cake time to finish baking. While my pasta continued to cook, I poured a cup of tea and sat down next to my daughter. Her plight amused me and at the same time, touched my heart. This was the girl who swore that she would never set foot on a stinky old boat, yet here she sat in the galley of *Zodiac* wearing a ship's apron, trying to win the affections of a salty boy. She'd changed a great deal in the last few months.

It hadn't been easy coaxing her onto the boat. The final enticement had been the promise of a portion of my cook's wages. She had no interest in sailing, but putting some money into her bank account was a big incentive. She needed the cash. Her living arrangement at her father's house hadn't exactly panned out—his method of discipline and rigid house rules didn't jive with Megan. She'd called me almost daily to complain about the difficulties she was experiencing living with her new stepmother and adapting to her dad's parenting style. Finally one afternoon, a few days before *Zodiac's* season was to begin, she called in tears to inform me she'd left his house for good and needed a place to crash.

"You can't just bum around on the Av' and be a street kid. How the heck are you getting to school?" I asked her.

"I quit school. I'll just finish it next fall." She replied.

Oh god. Yet another teenager in crisis, I thought. My mind raced to come up with a solution which would get her back on some sort of path before she veered too far off. The last thing I wanted was to see her becoming an 'Av' Rat' and bumming around on Broadway. I knew that my headstrong daughter would not be receptive to ultimatums, so a hardline approach wouldn't cut it. I thought about it for a few seconds and said, "OK. Here's the thing… I'll try to help you out of this, but first off, you're going to call your father and see if there's anything you guys can do to patch things up." I could hear the beginning of a protest, so I spoke louder to override her resistance. "I'm not saying you have to apologize or anything—just make the effort to talk to him. No doubt he's worried about you. That, by the way, is non-negotiable."

"And what else?" She said. I could make out the brittle tone in her voice.

"Secondly: I don't want you staying on the Av', not even for one night—got it? …also not a negotiable point."

"And?"

"And, well…nothin'. I'll figure something out and then call you back in an hour. No, hold on—I don't know how to get hold of you. You'll have to call me back in an hour, OK?"

"Yeah, alright. I'll call you later." She hung up.

You're welcome, I said to myself. *She only had one semester left of school for Chrissake!* I felt the familiar accusations of guilt creeping back into my mind. Once again, the lack of stability in our family right now probably had everything to do with Megan's recent crisis. I sighed and moved the blame-game aside. I needed to be productive and find a solution, not wallow in self-reprimands. I called Jeffery and explained the situation. We agreed that the best option was to get her on the boat where I could keep an eye on her.

Several phone conversations and much cajoling later, we arranged to transport my 17-year-old daughter up to Bellingham and put her to work as the galley assistant. Soon enough, the Greyhound bus rolled into the station and Megan showed up at the gate, bags in hand and guitar case slung over her shoulder. She'd arrived the day before our first high school trip, a three-day charter in the San Juan Islands.

It took me a while to orient Megan with the basics, such as directions on a boat. The foreign words and descriptions bounced off her ears without really sinking in: *forward, aft, companionway, bulkhead...* they meant nothing to her and she stubbornly clung to her land-terminology as if to spite us for bringing her aboard. It made working with her in the galley a bit of a challenge. The first evening she was aboard, I asked, "Megan, grab me a flat of eggs in the laz, please."

"Where is the *laz* again?"

"It's aft—through the main salon and then up the companionway. It's the hold located on deck, remember?"

"So, I go... that way?"

"Nope. That way's forward," I said and pointed toward the salon. "You go *that* way."

"Jeez, can't you people just use English?!"

"Actually, Smart-ass, it is English; way-old English words that were invented for life on ships," I replied. She didn't care to listen and stomped her way through the salon. I could hear her mumbling to herself as she climbed the companionway ladder. I set my paring knife on the counter and muttered, "Dear god, this is going to be a long spring."

The first trip with Megan in the galley went exactly as I had feared. She complained about the early hours and cramped conditions. She rolled her eyes at the stacks of dishes to wash after every meal and complained about my choice of music. Her reaction to the captain's stern demeanor was predictable as well. "He sure isn't very nice is he?" She grumbled one morning after breakfast had been served.

"Why d'ya say that?" I asked.

"He was sort of a douchebag when he didn't like the coffee I made." She stood next to the sink, washing out the pots and skillets I'd used to prepare the breakfast. "Like I would even know how to make coffee—I hate that crap!" She threw the sponge into the soapy basin and wiped the hair out of her face with the back of her arm. "He just made this grumpy noise and threw the cup in the sink. I told him I'd make another pot, but he said something about *not subjecting people to my coffee twice* or something like that."

I chuckled and nodded. "Yep. That's just Tim in the morning, girlfriend. But he has few enough things to look forward to—and a fresh cup of coffee in the morning is one of the big ones. C'mere, I'll show you how to brew it the right way."

I showed Megan how to operate *Zodiac's* eighties-era coffee brewer and demonstrated the proper amount of beans to make a good, strong pot. "There, now you have it. It's the first test of every new galley cook onboard: make a decent pot of coffee and the captain will let you stay."

"I don't care—he's still a crabby old dude."

"He grows on ya, trust me."

Gradually, Megan began to assimilate into *Zodiac's* routine. Out of boredom, she made friends with a number of the older crewmembers—and actually started being nice to Juliet. She complained less frequently about her 5:30 AM wakeup call and even asked if she could cook some of the lunches. Before long, she'd become a regular part of the crew.

Our third charter was Ballard High School, from our old neighborhood in Seattle. Many of the kids that came aboard were former classmates of the twins and soon Megan was ducking out between meals to hang with her friends. After dinners, she brought her guitar out and played some of her original songs for the kids. I was relieved to see her finally settling in and actually enjoying herself on the ship. And then, the new deckhand hit her radar.

"Mom, who is that boy?" she asked after Kris had returned for his fourth helping of the chicken and rice casserole.

"He's a new guy. I like him. He's as much of a 'bottom-feeder' as Jeffery is, so I rarely have to put away any leftovers when he crews onboard. I don't know where he puts it though... kid's skinny as a rail. I bet he's got a tapeworm."

"How old is he?" she casually inquired.

"I don't know—young. Maybe like 19-ish. What is it to you? Gotta little crush on him, do ya?"

"Mom! Shut *up.*" She walked away in apparent disgust.

Not long after, I spotted Megan sitting on the charthouse roof, serenading Kris with her guitar and her favorite song she'd written about zombies. Kris sat nearby, thoroughly enjoying Megan's apocalyptic song. I watched him for a minute or two as he lounged, splicing the end of a line while she played. His cut-offs and Converse shoes and the plugs in his earlobes made him the quintessential candidate for my daughter's attentions. He definitely had the Seattle hipster look going on. I smiled and wandered off toward the laz.

During the Ballard High School trip and subsequent youth charters, Megan became the center of attention with the students. In their eyes, it must have seemed that this cool-looking girl from the ship's galley with a nose ring and a guitar led the ultimate life of high adventure. As I worked on meals, I overheard comments directed toward Megan from kids, "You're so lucky to live on this boat!" How'd you get this gig, anyways?" "Man, I wish my parents would let me do something like this!" Eventually Megan began to appreciate the situation she'd landed in and started to actually enjoy the experience.

Zodiac leaned into a new tack and items slid back to their former resting places. I finished my cup of tea and left my morose daughter to resolve her baking dilemma. I needed to finish lunch and prepare and a dinner plan. Within the hour, we rang the bell and twenty-six ravenous teenagers descended upon the galley.

Their frenetic energy managed to pull Megan out of her bad mood, and soon enough she was joking with the kids and teasing the volunteer crew. By dinnertime, the cake issue had been fixed with extra frosting and a little creativity—we made up little signs and taped them onto toothpicks that read: 'port tack' and 'starboard tack', then stuck them on the appropriate lumps. Megan beamed as Kris came back for his second helping of her dessert.

As the spring high school portion of the season drew to a close and my stint as ship's cook neared its end, Megan approached me with a question. "Hey, Mom," she asked, "Do you s'pose I could volunteer as a crewmember for some of the trips this summer?"

I paused in my task of loading the dishwasher and turned to look at her. She appeared to be serious. "Uh, well, I imagine you could ask ET and see what he thinks about it," I said. Grabbing a few more bowls, I stacked them inside the racks and continued. "I'm moving up to a deckhand position after next week's trip is over and the new cook shows up. You know that I don't have any say about what happens up on deck, right? I'm just a crewmember like everybody else once I leave the galley."

"Well, I'll ask him and see what happens," she replied, and grabbed the bag of recycle to stow on deck. "I hope he lets me 'cuz I'd really like to learn how to be a deckhand."
I smirked as she turned around and walked up the stairs. *Go figure.*

Chapter 23

The Laz

There's this old saying that people love to toss around: "Be careful what you wish for." I can't even begin to count the times I've heard that phrase and it always gives me pause, because I think the phrase doesn't quite say enough. What it should really conclude with is: "But be really wary of what you *didn't* wish for at all."

Now those are some words of wisdom that I could really have profited from.

My first full season on *Zodiac* was almost at an end. The spring and summer had generally been filled with pleasant days and good winds. My tenure as the ship's cook for the high school and youth trips had been short, after which I'd been reassigned to a fulltime deckhand position for the final four months. Even though I felt like a pretty confident crewmember from my volunteer stints the previous years, my sailing skills had sharpened tenfold that one season.

I was pleased by Megan's about-face attitude toward boats and her interest to continue as a volunteer. She soon moved out of the galley and crewed on a regular basis, often working on the foredeck under my guidance. She'd *also* fallen head over heels for Kris, whom we all took to calling 'Jonesy' to avoid confusion with my name. For her part, Juliet grew to accept the extended stays aboard the ship when *Zodiac* was out sailing, and adapted to others coming aboard what she felt was her home. She even inherited her 'very own' sailing station on the running-backstays, and took every opportunity to tell passengers that she was the youngest crewmember on the ship. Jeffery came up from his "remodel-hell" every chance he could get and occasionally borrowed Sasha back from Dane to bring along with him.

My position as the jib-sail crew leader perfectly suited me. I thanked my lucky stars that ET allowed me to keep that position for every trip. The jib required just enough finessing and fine-tuning to take advantage of my control-oriented personality. Working on the foredeck meant that I was up in front of the ship with two other crewmembers almost all day. We coined the nickname "Foredeck Union" or "FU" for short, and even created a tee-shirt that said "Foredeck Union. Don't make us come back there." Our crew was first into the breakers and the first to get wet, our sail released first in order to force the big ship through the eye of the wind, and we were the bad asses who walked out onto the bowsprit while underway to furl sail. To be on the foredeck meant freedom, pure and simple.

End-of-summer doldrums meant that the sailing was relatively laid-back. The light breezes made for relaxed and undemanding cruises. We had just completed a four-day winery cruise and were in the middle of a regional lighthouse cruise. These were fun and diverse, with interesting passengers. Coming up next on the agenda would be our eagerly anticipated two-week Desolation Sound excursion. This cruise couldn't come soon enough for me, as Jeffery was taking time off work to join us. All in all, life on *Zodiac* was pretty sweet.

Chief mate ET and I had become fast friends and solid coworkers over the season. It didn't matter that he was only 20 years old and I was nearing 47, we just worked well together. ET had obtained a captain's license before he got his driver's license; he was mature and pragmatic—definitely an "old soul" as my grandma would have put it. Together we could work from both ends of the ship to keep sail maneuvers tight and ensure that crew and passengers were positioned where they needed to be (most of the time), when they needed to be there (most of the time). Captain Tim clearly appreciated the domino effect from the teamwork between his chief mate and his foredeck leader; this smoothly running operation created an uncommon amiability in the Z's captain—and made for a very happy crew. Sunny days, calm seas and a benevolent captain. *What more could one wish for?*

And then, one humdrum afternoon, ET pulled me aside. "Hey, Chris, I've got something I want to talk with you about, come with me."

Intrigued, I followed him aft. We sat behind the gearbox on the expansive mahogany fantail and he popped open a can of Dr. Pepper before asking, "So, you know that I head back for fall term at Cal Maritime once we're back from Desolation Sound, right?"

"Yeah, so I heard," I nodded, thinking about the loss of my chief mate. "Go on."

"Well, I've been talkin' with Tim about needing to find a new first mate."

"Ah, you want me to talk with Jeffery, right?" Visions of job searches ran through my brain. I'd have to find a gig right away if we were going to put Jeffery on the ship full time as a volunteer. His freelancing carpentry work kept us afloat.

"No. We want *you* to be the first mate." ET smiled.

"You—*what*!?"

ET finished his Dr. Pepper in two gulps and crushed the can between his hands. He smiled at my reaction. "Yeah, seriously. Tim agrees. He wants you to be the mate. Think about it—you know the crew, you know all the stations, you already fill out the forms for me half the time."

"Yeah, but ET, I'm not an experienced sailor. All the experience I have—the little experience I have—well, most of it, has been on this ship following orders for Chrissake! Not giving orders." The thought of trying to shout commands to some of the *Zodiac*'s old-timers made me shudder.

"Well, Tim thinks it's a good idea. So you oughta think about it."

He rose to go and I caught his sleeve. "Really, ET—I am not at all sure about this."

"So what. I am. Tim is." He patted my head. "Give yourself a bit more credit, Ms. First Mate."

"What the hell—what did I do to deserve this?" I thought glumly. It had been such a nice season. I'd barely managed to hit Tim's radar with any stupid mistakes or newbie responses. I'd even gotten rid of the habit of calling the chart a "map." And I had enjoyed having only a *little* responsibility. I looked around the deck with new eyes, trying to picture being in charge of it all. Well, not in charge—that was the captain's duty—but still... *answerable* for it all. It was overwhelming to imagine.

I stewed on ET's news for the rest of the night. In the morning, after the crew safety meeting, ET approached me about my answer. "Well?"

"Yeah, it's not happening, dude."

"Huh. OK. Well, I'm not going to take that answer until Tim and I sit down with you." He stepped around the coffee table and then paused. "Oh yeah, and it's your turn in the chain locker." He went down the passageway to refill his coffee cup.

Not wanting to give ET's proposal any more thought, I was grateful for something tangible to do. I squeezed down into the narrow hole in the foredeck where the anchor chain was piled. I put on the headphones and waited for the sound of the windlass motor to start, signaling that the heavy chain would be dropping down the spill-pipe for me to flake into neat rows. But as I crouched below in the dark, I couldn't keep my mind off what my two senior officers were considering. *First off: I do not see any of these old guys taking orders from me, a newbie and a woman. Secondly: I can't see Jeffery taking orders from me—at least not very well. Shit, he's the one who knows everything about sailing! Thirdly: I'm not sure I could handle being the buffer between Captain Tim and the rest of the crew. I've seen him take a lot out on the mate.* I spent the rest of my chain locker isolation inventing excuses as to why I could not, would not, be the first mate of the *Zodiac*.

With the anchor hawsed, I climbed back onto the deck. I was covered in silt and needed to wash off before we raised sail. I waved to ET to let him know that I would shut off the windlass on my way to the head. As I stood at the sink, scrubbing at the dirt, I heard him call, "All hands on deck!"

Oh jeez. "See what this means?" I said to myself. Similar situations raced through my brain, such as accounting for the whereabouts of every single deckhand; having to tell Tim whether or not his crew was ready at any given time—like me down here washing my hands when sails had been called. It would be like having a dozen kids. *Shit!* By the time my hands were dry I had already talked myself out of the job. Again.

The rest of the day's sail went without a hitch. We spent the entire day tacking back and forth into the wind to arrive at Reid Harbor on Stuart Island. My passengers and I had dropped our jib sail right before we came upon the island. Then we balanced on the footropes of the bowsprit netting, rolled the jib sail into itself and tied the gaskets with square knots to hold it in place. Once we were done, we admired the banks of evergreens and rocky shores that greeted *Zodiac* as the rest of the crew lowered her remaining sails. The narrow, winding bay was serene and undisturbed save for the small ripple that *Zodiac*'s bow made as she slipped into the entrance.

I watched ET with renewed interest as he ordered one of our older crewmembers up to the bow to ready the anchor. This process involved several complex steps to be ready, and on command, to loosen the brake and drop anchor. It required a good deal of experience and attention to orders. The particular crewmember ET had given this task to had been doing it for over fifteen years. He was approaching seventy-five years old, but it had been his task for as long as he'd been crewing on the *Zodiac*, and he stood ready as Tim put the ship in neutral. Tim let her coast for a few seconds longer and we started to slow down. ET stood by, alert, watching for the mark that signified it was time to drop the anchor. At that moment, a jarring *thunk* came from the bow. Tim swerved from his position at the wheel and looked forward. ET shoved me out of the way and leaned toward the bow. All was still for a moment.

ET strained to see what had happened. He turned back to Tim and said, "It's OK, we're fine. He just forgot to secure the brake—but he caught it before anything happened. I'd just chalk it up to a 'senior moment.'"

"No more of those. Train somebody else, dammit." Tim's face was like stone.

I thought to myself, *what would I have done had I been the mate? How could I know whether my deckhand was able to handle that or not? How could I have fixed it? This would be way too much.* I tapped ET on the shoulder to point out my concerns.

"Not now, Chris." He tersely waved me away.

Well go screw yourself then, ET. I walked away and left him to finish the anchoring detail.

The lazarette on a ship is a hold below decks used for ship's stores, fuel tanks and various other supplies. The hatch to the laz is situated directly in front of the wheel and aft of the scuttle where our radios are located, right near where the captain is usually stationed. The *Zodiac's* lazarette is big enough for a bunk as well, and I had claimed the bunk in the laz for the last several weeks because it was isolated and quiet. This night, once our passengers were busy uncorking bottles of wine and pulling out deck chairs to watch the beginning of a stunning island sunset, I went below to the laz and pouted all by myself. I could sense both Tim and ET watching me as I shut the hatch.

Good. At least ET will know I'm down here and I don't have to go inform him of my whereabouts, I fumed. In truth I knew that ET was right in waving me off when he did. He was still working and I had interrupted him. But I wanted a reason to be mad at him, and an even greater excuse as to why I could not take on the job of first mate.

The hatch on the laz opened up. Amid the glare of fading sunlight I made out the silhouette of the ET's head.

"Hey. I'm coming down," he called.

I made no response, which didn't faze him. He climbed down the ladder.

Before I realized what was happening, the captain followed right behind him. ET perched on a corner of the bunk and Tim pulled a couple of orange crates together and made a seat. The tiny laz looked a little cramped, to say the least.

"Well. Did ET talk to you about our idea?" Tim inquired.

"Yes he did," I answered. "And the events of this evening's anchor fiasco have only served to convince me that I am *not* qualified for it."

ET shook his head and fished one of my rubber boots out from the covers under his butt. "*Nuh* uh. That problem had no bearing on whether you could be a good mate or not," he said. "That was just me putting a raisin on the anchor who had a brain-fart."

"A brain-fart that could take the bow off the ship," I said. "ET, I just don't think that those old guys, any of 'em, are gonna like having me order them around or pull them off of their duties."

"Nobody does," he countered. "Do you think they felt really happy about having a cocky teenager bawl them out? Because I started doing this three years ago y'know, and not too many old timers thought I knew what I was doing—at first."

Tim shifted on his crate. "It doesn't matter whether they like it or don't like it. Everyone on this boat is here to learn. If you're acting on my orders and doing the best you can, you're doing the job right."

I started to interject, but Tim shook his head and continued. "Chris, I can teach anybody to sail in two weeks' time. What I need is somebody with experience in management and leadership."

I pursed my lips and thought about his comment for a few seconds. "Could you just see me trying to order Jeffery about when he comes on board?" I asked them. "I just don't see that flying very well."

"It had better," Tim replied flatly. "If I put you in command as first officer, I would expect Jeff to accept that. I think he would."

ET rocked back and laughed. "Oh *shit!* I hadn't thought about that! I wish I could be here the first time *that* happens!"

"Shut up, ET," Tim and I replied.

We talked for some time in the laz. The dinner bell rang and still we continued talking. Eventually, one of the other older crewmembers climbed down the ladder. He was looking for an item from the bosun's locker. "Oh my! A party!" He said, and turned one of the five-gallon buckets over to make a seat. "What are we celebrating?"

"The fact that we've found our new first mate." answered ET, and he glanced over at me and winked.

I shook my head, but this time it was out of resignation rather than denial. I wasn't sure what this new turn of events would bring, nor how capably I would manage their expectations of me, but I was starting to get a little excited about the possibility.

Chapter 24

Making Way

"Those headsails are killing our tack! Go tell your husband to sheet in his jib—*again*." Tim said. "We're never going to make it through Thatcher Pass at this rate."

Oh dear lord, not again. I drew a deep breath and went forward to relay the captain's orders to my foredeck leader. I seriously doubted he'd be any happier hearing from me this time than he was the last three. "Jeffery, Captain says your jib's still sheeted out too far. It's killing the tack and making us carry too much rudder."

"Christ—I'm doing it *exactly* the way he asked for it last time! If I sheet in any more we'll be backed!"

"All I'm doing is passing along orders; please don't kill the messenger." I spun around and returned to my new position at the quarterdeck, complaining under my breath all the while. "Talk about getting caught between a rock and a hard place…" I shook my head and silently counted the hours until we'd drop anchor and I could go hide in my stateroom. "This totally sucks. Why did I ever think I could actually pull this off?"

It didn't help that on this, my first trip out as a mate, I had a fractious captain and a partner who didn't appear to be adjusting very well to taking orders from his wife—especially when those orders often contradicted themselves. I wasn't certain whether Tim was testing me or just being testy—either way, it made for a long day. It felt like I'd already logged countless miles on-deck, relaying commands and responses to and from the foredeck.

I walked up to Tim and inquired if the headsail was now to his liking and received a reply that was more of a muffled grunt. I chose to interpret it as a sound of approval. My next duty was to walk around the deck and make sure everything was *ship-shape*. I began capsizing a few coils, only to hear the captain's voice from the quarterdeck. "Chris—hands in your pockets! Your job is to delegate. You can't keep an eye on everything if you're busy coiling lines!"

I sighed. I missed my old job as a deckhand where I could just manage my sail, stow my lines and retire below to read or chat with friends. There was no such thing as standing down for me any longer, and no reprieve from the constant vigilance. Now I had *four* sails to manage—over 7,000 square feet of them—with two or three stations per sail. I had to watch over *all* the passengers now, not just the ones who were assigned to my station. Worst of all, I had to keep a look-out for eight other deckhands, a few of whom were beginning to stand out as accidents waiting to happen.

I finished my lap of the deck and collared the appropriate crew to tidy up their lines. In doing so, I was met with several annoyed expressions and one unruly complaint from a little blonde deckhand on the back-stays. "*Mom*! I hung it on the pin just like Tim told me to! I don't wanna coil it again!"

"This is the mate telling you to recoil it, *not* your mom. You can't argue with the mate—if you don't like it, go talk to the captain." Juliet pouted and went back to her station to tidy up lines.

Once we cleared Thatcher Pass, Tim told me to sheet-out to a beam reach and order the main and foresail crews to rig preventers—cables that inhibited the booms from swinging back on an accidental jibe. I called my crew and their passengers on deck to start rigging their preventers. I walked forward to supervise the process and noticed that the main preventer cable looked strange; the mainsail team had run it inboard of the jib sheet. "Hey Ron, I think you've led it wrong. It's gonna conflict with the jib once you sheet out...I'm pretty sure." I scratched my cheek as I studied the layout, and said, "Let's redo it; I'm not happy."

Ron glanced down at the preventer and shook his head. "Nah, this is the way it's supposed to look. I've done it this way a hundred times." He continued to lead his cable aft to connect it to the boom. I shook my head and stared at the mess of lines; now the jib sheet, main and fore preventers were laying one atop the other. My memories from my former position as the foredeck leader told me that things were askew. *It doesn't seem right somehow...Well, he's been doing this a helluva lot longer than I have. I guess he knows better.*

Tim called to ease out all sails for our new course and as the main boom stretched outboard, I heard the *twang* of my jib sheet springing tight. *Dammit! I knew it!*

"Chris! Get that preventer fixed—before that ferry crosses in front of us and we have to move out of his way—I do *not* want to jibe!" Tim yelled at me.

I nodded my head and glared at Ron, who was too busy trying to free the preventer to bother with my silent reproach. Once their line had slacked, we struggled as a group to untangle the main cable. Tim shouted at me to quit doing the deckhand's work and to supervise, but I pretended not to hear him—I could see that Ron and his passengers were unable to cope with it on their own. I leaned overboard to help disconnect the hasp, when suddenly a gust of wind grabbed the mainsail and back-winded it, sweeping the sail and all its hardware toward the opposite side of the ship. I instinctively ducked and at the same time heard Tim yell, "Everybody—out of the way!" The massive boom caught on the throttle of our inflatable tender that hung over the starboard rail. It wrenched the throttle mechanism off the console with a resounding *smack!* The tender jerked upwards, then fell back into the boat-falls.

The thermal eased as quickly as it started, and the boom slowed its swing just enough that we were able to counteract a complete jibe. I looked back at Tim's face and had no doubt as to what might be on his mind. He glowered as he spun the wheel around to keep our sails in their rightful positions. *Oh balls. I'm gonna hear about this one.* Deckhands ran to the rail and helped the mainsail crew secure the preventer correctly. I stood by and pretended to supervise, but inwardly I felt foolish and superfluous. At that moment, my husband appeared beside me. "Whoa! How'd all this happen?" He inquired.

"Don't even ask. I think I'm in big trouble."

"They shouldn't have led their preventers like that… didn't you stop them?"

"Aren't you supposed to be up on the foredeck?" My irritation started to get the better of me—I was jealous that my husband had the ability to just come and go during my crisis. I resented that he could identify the problem so quickly and furnish a solution so assuredly.

"Alright, I'll stay out of your way. I get the hint," Jeff said and went back to the charthouse to read his magazine.

Tim called Worley and Jeff back to the helm. "Get on the tender and see if you can repair that throttle before we anchor this afternoon. We're going to need it to shuttle passengers to shore." The guys went down to the engine room to find the appropriate tools. I leaned against the lifelines, hands finally in my pockets, and awaited the reprimand that I knew was forthcoming.

Tim ignored me for the most part, and concentrated on keeping his sails full. Ron sat in the captain's chair and avoided all eye contact. Eventually, Tim handed the wheel over to a crewmember and walked over to where I stood. "What went wrong?"

"The boom jibed because we didn't have the preventer hooked..." I started to explain.

"No. I know all that—I could see it from the wheel. What did *you* do wrong?"

I gulped. *Oh, that.* "Well, I didn't trust my instincts and let a deckhand overrule my decision... I didn't step back and delegate to the crew when I needed to and as a result, I didn't catch what was happening with the boom."

"Yep, pretty much. You would have seen that we were about to clear the lee of Willow Island—and you probably would've held off on releasing the preventer until you knew whether or not we'd get a gust."

"I'm sorry Tim. I… I guess I'm just struggling with how to be the boss. I know I shouldn't worry about how much everybody else knows and, well, start believing in what I know." I looked down at the deck and fumbled with my words; at that point I didn't feel like I knew much at all.

"You got that right—you *have* to be the authority on the ship. I need to know that you're watching all this stuff and that you can give orders that will be obeyed—otherwise stuff like this happens." He nodded in the direction of the tender, where Jeff and Worley were crawling around trying to reattach the throttle.

"Yeah, I know, but—these guys—like Ron… He's ex-Navy and he's been crew on here for years. I realize that I have to tell 'em what to do, but it's hard to make 'em listen sometimes," I said.

Tim looked unsympathetic. "If you don't believe in yourself, then why should any of them believe in you?" He gestured toward Ron, who was now snoozing in the chair. "Ron's probably forgotten more about sailing than you and I've ever known—but the problem is, he doesn't realize he's forgotten it."

"I understand."

"Alright then, let's tack and then we'll drop in about thirty minutes or so. Get ready to slack preventers." He turned back to the helm and then paused to add, "Hands in your pockets."

"Yes sir. I got it."

Later that evening, with the hook down and our passengers occupied in conversation and cherry cobbler on deck, I stole away to my little cabin. The mate's stateroom had become my favorite place on the ship; a solitary confine where I could curl up in my bunk and lick my wounds from the day. And by this time, I'd develop some substantial wounds to care for—after the throttle debacle, we'd encountered another mishap as my crew launched the tender. I'd assigned several of the younger crewmembers to the boat-falls and instructed them to listen for my commands. Unfortunately, one of the old timers took matters into his own hands, calling for the bow to lower first. This resulted in a rather ungainly and rapid entrance into the water for our poor inflatable. I'd pondered briefly about which of us was having the worse day: our little tender or myself. Before Tim had the chance to start yelling, I went back to the helm to explain. "I know, I know..."

"Get control of your crew," Tim said.

"I will—I swear. Mitch just jumped in without asking. I'll come down on him next time."

"Yes, *well,* Mitch... having him as crew is like losing ten good men." Tim grabbed his sweater and newspaper from the scuttle. "You either have command of your deckhands or you have... anarchy. It's your choice." With that he walked below.

"Aye boss." I said aloud to myself.

A soft *tap, tap* at my cabin door shook me out of my contemplation. "Yeah?" I said.

Jeff's voice emanated from the other side of the door. "Hey, you up for a little company?"

"I s'pose so." I leaned over and unhooked the latch. "Just don't mention anything about today's events, please." I thought to myself, *If Jeffery had been the first mate, there wouldn't have been any arguments or insubordinate looks... nobody would have presumed to call orders out of turn.* My ego felt trampled and my insecurities ganged up on me.

"Can I get you anything—you hungry?" Jeff asked.

"Nah, I'm good."

"Well, you don't look good," he piled several armloads of clothes onto the sole so that he could sit next to my bunk. "Are you in here feeling sorry for yourself?"

"Perhaps. It's been a sucky kind of day. I think Tim may have overestimated my ability to take charge."

"He told me you might be feeling that way," Jeff replied. "He also said that you're doing OK... all things considered." Jeff repositioned himself on my tiny bench seat; my cabin was not built for a tall individual such as himself. "Wanna know what I think?"

"I guess."

"I think that you're just going to have to commit to this thing—make your decisions, right or wrong, and stick to them. You're going to get blamed regardless, so rather than getting chewed out for somebody else's mistakes, you might as well get chewed out for your own. Does that make any sense?"

"Yeah—yes, I reckon it does." I moved to the edge of my bunk. "What you're basically saying is that I just need to 'cowboy up' and grow a pair."

"Exactly!"

I sighed, "Alrighty then, starting tomorrow I'm gonna *own* this whole mate's job," and then added with a smile, "There's just *one* thing babe."

"What's that?"

"Sheet that jib in tighter when we come about—you're killin' the tacks."

Jeff chuckled and got up to kiss my forehead. "You got it *Madame* Mate. You got it."

Chapter 25

Stick Our Nose Out

S till sleepy, I flipped on the marine radio. When the mechanized female voice began the weather forecast for our region—the northern inland waters—I listened more intently. The monotone, emotionless voice offered nothing to ease my apprehension. A gale-force warning predicted winds of 25-30, gusting to 50 knots in our location of the Salish Sea. *Zodiac* was anything but a small craft, and still safely tucked away in Echo bay, she bobbed and swayed with ease in the increasing swells. But we wouldn't be able to stay in the protection of Sucia Island—it was the final day of a four-day charter and our passengers had flights to catch and connections to make. There was no choice but to weigh anchor and push for home.

With a length overall of 160 feet and a depth of 16 feet, *Zodiac* could easily plow through the predicted six to eight foot waves under power. However, Captain Tim always preferred to sail if at all possible, and a gale force warning was not an insurmountable obstacle to his way of thinking—not on the *Zodiac*.

It was my fourth trip as mate; Jeff was back working on land and Justine and Megan were volunteer deckhands—they'd yet to experience having their mother as their "boss." The previous cruise, a three-day jaunt around the islands, had been a walk in the park with clear skies and calm seas. Even with my initial insecurities and shaky self-esteem, I now handled the ship's crew pretty well—Jeffery's advice had been taken to heart. However, this forecasted stormy weather was completely different, and I worried about what lay ahead. If Tim chose to raise sail, we'd have to reef to reduce canvas and keep *Z* from getting overpowered. I had yet to supervise this process, and many of my volunteer deckhands had little to no practice at reefing. My mounting insecurities made me feel a little queasy and I dreaded what was to come.

I waited at the helm as Worley raised the anchor. As soon as the *Zodiac*'s hook untethered itself from the muddy bottom, the ship began to bounce and pitch as the rolling waves had their way with her. I leaned against the wheel deep in thought, and the chatter of the ship's radio reminded me to check in with Vessel Traffic.

"Seattle Traffic, Schooner *Zodiac*," I hailed.

"*Zodiac*, Traffic," came the response.

"Yeah, Traffic, we're preparing to get underway from Echo Bay, Sucia Island, and cross Rosario Strait, returning to dock in Bellingham at 1500."

"*Zodiac*, Traffic. Will you be under power or sail?"

I paused, holding the mic near my face, and took a deep breath. "Traffic, that's unknown at this time. I'll get back to you. Over."

"*Zodiac*, Traffic. Copy. Please call underway. Traffic out."

I hung up the mic and looked around, watching the spray blow off of the whitecaps across the bay. I waited for word from the captain.

As if on cue, Captain Tim appeared from the charthouse and walked toward the quarterdeck. His foul-weather gear was fastened and he folded his collar up against the wind as he approached.

"OK, fire her up and let's go for a ride," he quipped and took his seat behind the wheel.

I pushed the green button on the gear box; spun the wheel a full turn; put her in forward and pointed the big ship toward the entrance of the bay. "Give her some juice," Tim directed.

"Shall we just motor back to Bellingham Bay then?" I asked.

He squinted for a short while—searching the open water and weighing his options.

"Nah, let's raise some sail. We'll stick our nose out there to see what happens."

Goddamn. He's so predictable.

My expression didn't faze the captain as he gave me his official command. "Get 'em all up on deck and make *sure* that they know how to reef that main." He took the wheel from me.

I heaved an audible sigh and went for the intercom. "All hands on deck. Prepare to raise sails—we're reefing."

I could hear the groans and chuckles from the main salon as the passengers abandoned their mugs of coffee and magazines for rain gear. Obviously, the comfort of below-deck was preferable to the howling wind and spitting rain above-deck.

The crew and passengers worked together to ready their sails while the big ship pitched through the pounding waves. The occasional yelp could be heard as a crashing wall of water doused an unsuspecting sailor. I walked the deck, offering encouragement and urging my deckhands to pick up their pace.

"Way to go gang, don't forget to stow the gaskets where you can find 'em… Let's pick up the pace. Jib-crew, I need sails up in five."

I hoped that my voice conveyed confidence and strength and not the anxiety building rapidly inside of me. I worried that the task ahead of us would prove too great for my crewmembers, especially for Megan and Justine, who were still considered raw recruits. And I doubted my own ability to oversee the entire operation under such adverse conditions. But—I had no choice. The time had come to raise the sail.

"All hands to the main!" I called.

Zodiac suddenly lurched to port, allowing a giant wall of water to drench me from head to toe. *Fantastic.* This was a fine way to start the day.

While the passengers were familiar by now with raising the sails, conditions like these were new to them. Nevertheless, they all pulled together to raise the mainsail. The rising canvas slapped as the wind beat it about—and combined with the pounding waves, the result was deafening. I had to raise my voice louder than I thought possible for the crew to hear my commands. We reached the grommet point midway up and I called for my crew to reef the sail. The deckhands looked toward me; their faces showed their uncertainty and their actions were disjointed. Many mistakes were made as they struggled to find their positions and perform the job in the correct order.

The captain grew impatient as he watched the mishaps from the quarterdeck. "Get it done right—you're killing the sails, guys!" he bellowed. "Do it faster!"

The passengers stood by, hands on halyards, watching my struggling crew. Wind whipped all around us and spray came over the sides of the ship at regular intervals. We fought to tie the nettles around the main boom and secure the sail—which insisted on billowing away from us. Megan and Justine fought with the nettles; the process completely alien to them.

"I want reef-knots—square-knots! *NO* granny-knots!" I yelled at everyone.

Frustration emanated from Captain Tim. "Your daughters are useless!" He yelled at me as I hurried past.

Megan and Justine were in tears as I leaned over to correct their knots. The intensity of the increasing wind alarmed me, and the flapping sail would not behave.

At last and with great effort we got the mainsail reefed. We finished raising the peak gaff to its full height and put a stopper knot ahead of the block. I called to the passengers, "Drop the halyard on the count of one-two-*three!*"

Finished at last! Every soul on deck looked wiped out as they moved forward to the next sail. I was shaky and spent—and this was just the first sail. We managed to raise the foresail next and made it fast. I then called on my headsail crew to 'go ahead on the stay.' As the triangular sail rose above us I felt the ship immediately heel over with great force. We'd just cleared the lee of the island and were now out in open water, the wind raging across our beam with *Zodiac* at its mercy. Our indicator read sustained wind speeds of 40 to 50 knots, gusting to more than 60.

Any items that weren't fastened down were immediately pitched across the deck. Passengers raced to find a handhold, and the crew scrambled to secure the tenders that violently swung from their boat-falls. The noise and commotion became utterly riotous. I stood for a moment, as if frozen to the deck. My heart was pounding in my chest.

"Drop all sails NOW!" I barely heard Tim command from the quarterdeck.

Yes! Do that! Like a coil suddenly released, I sprang back into action. "Drop your sails!"

We ran forward to the staysail first, and fought to keep our footing and not slide into the rails. The boat had heeled so far over that the thrashing water was washing over the bulwarks. "Let it loose!" I yelled to Joe, my foredeck leader.

He cast off the halyard and we stepped away from the fife rail, expecting the sail to tumble down to the deck. Nothing happened. We looked up, dumbfounded—we could clearly see that the line was off the belaying pin as it should be. *Why hadn't it dropped?*

"It's too full! The sail's too full of wind and it can't come down!" yelled Joe.

I screamed back, "Get it down! Somehow! Anyhow!" I could see behind me, toward the helm, Tim pointing and yelling, gesturing for us to '*douse* the damn sails.' The wind roared around me and the rig creaked and moaned. I could hear nothing except its fury. More crew rushed forward to help, and we urgently tugged on the heavy canvas sail; inch by inch we got it down onto the deck. "Get some straps on that thing!" I yelled. I could hardly hear my own words and only hoped someone on the crew could.

The remaining hands managed to lower the foresail and the remaining mainsail at last, but *Zodiac* still heeled dramatically as she rushed through the turbulent waves. The wind blew the canvas of our mainsail into a colossal balloon—gusting over the starboard side of the ship. With so much wind power still filling the sail, we couldn't get any gaskets around to contain it.

"Get them on the boom!" Tim yelled.

I looked frantically around me; I had four deckhands nearby able to help, including Megan. My heart sank. "You heard the captain," I shouted. Everybody on that boom—bring—in—that—sail!"

All four deckhands yelled back "Aye!" and scrambled up and onto the slippery boom. They braced themselves as *Zodiac* dove into the oncoming swells, rising and falling with each violent onset of waves. She was laid well over and making intense speed as I, too, clambered onto the boom and made my way out toward the tip.

"Grab what you can of the sail and stuff it into itself!" I shouted into the rushing wind.

Nobody could hear me, but most of the crew knew what to do. Still, it was a struggle—the wind had filled the sail to the point where there was no slack to gather. We fought against the gale's sheer force to pull it in. From my vantage point at the tip of the boom, I watched my crew reach precariously outboard to pull in the canvas. I looked down at the roiling water and a desperate fear gripped me: if anybody fell overboard right now they'd be lost. *Gone.* There would be no possible way to turn the big ship around in time and no possibility of launching our inflatable in these winds. "Oh shit, shit, shit," I mumbled as I leaned forward, looking down the line of my crew. My glance fell upon Megan. Pure panic was written on her face, but her actions were determined. I looked at the faces of all of my volunteers—each of them wore the same expression. I shouted as loudly as I could, "Everybody! Hold on tight!"

We continued to work together, intent and silent, nothing but the raging wind about us. At last, we were able to bundle the unruly mainsail and gasket it around the boom. My crew dropped down to the main deck in utter exhaustion as *Zodiac* righted herself and powered on though the storm.

Without her sails up, the *Zodiac* returned to a much calmer state and everyone resumed a more 'even-keeled' routine, passengers visibly relaxed. I walked up and down the deck to double-check all the lines and overheard several animated conversations regarding the previous excitement.

"I couldn't believe how far we were tipping over!" Exclaimed an elderly woman with a floral scarf tucked into her bib overalls.

Her friend replied, "The crew was so brave, getting on the boom like that. It's a wonder that none of them slipped or fell overboard!"

I walked toward the charthouse to drop off my wet gloves and listened to a small group commenting on the photographs that they'd captured from the last forty-five minutes. "*Oooh,* that's a keeper!" and "Check out the spray over those rails!"

In short order, my deckhands were able to release their anxieties, the heighted adrenaline from the last hour's episode totally spent. Laughter and jokes came from the warmth of the charthouse as they recounted their individual experiences with the sails.

Zodiac crashed onward through the surf, appearing not to give one whit that conditions had almost overwhelmed her crew. The old girl seemed to be unruffled by the wind and waves. After all, she hailed from the heyday of the great American fishing schooners—the mammoth ships designed to beat into windward gales, fish holds brimming. But the Grand Banks and rocky shores of Gloucester were notorious for deadly storms, and the careers of countless ships and mariners had ended there. Yet *Zodiac,* the last of her contemporaries, sailed on, plying the waters of the Pacific coast.

A shiver ran down my back and jerked me away from my reverie. I was freezing and exhausted. I looked down at my soaking wet clothes and the ordeal we had just gone through flashed back in vivid detail. The stinging comment from Tim suddenly rang in my ears: 'Your daughters are *useless!*'

The anger of a mother bear welled up inside of me and I went back up on deck. I marched to the quarterdeck where Captain Tim was holding our course, smiling widely as he traded sea stories with an older gentlemen passenger. His smile vanished as he saw me approach, and guessing my mood he offered an encouraging, "Good job. Nobody died."

Usually his understated sarcastic comments, often meant as a form of praise, would elicit a chuckle from me. Instead I just glared at him.

"What's wrong?" He looked perplexed.

I recognized the warning signs of my runaway Scottish temper as I stood in front of him, shaking with anger. Heedless of the crewmember and passengers who were standing around us, I blurted out, "You will never again say that my daughters are useless. *Never!*"

Tim stood in front of me in a stunned silence. I continued with my tirade, my voice sounded shrill. "Did you notice Megan standing out on that boom, risking her life—to bring in that damn sail? Is that your idea of *useless*?!"

Passengers backed away and awkwardly looked out at the horizon, pretending that they were unaware of the situation occurring between *Zodiac*'s two officers. Tim adopted a conciliatory tone as he replied, "I meant that they couldn't tie the proper knots. They would have been better off to stand aside in that instance."

"I don't care if they could or they couldn't. You cannot say such abusive stuff about my kids—and you shouldn't say it about any of your deckhands!" My voice had lowered and I spit the words out through clenched teeth. Without giving the captain time to respond, I spun on my heel and stormed back to the charthouse, ignoring the glances from my crew as I brushed past them.

The rest of the day was spent in a series of icy exchanges between Captain Tim and me. His orders came out in curt commands and I acknowledged with terse responses. The crew and passengers walked about on deck as if on eggshells whenever they got close to the quarterdeck. Once below-decks and away from the intensity above, they were able to drink their coffee and eat lunch in relative calm. By the time *Zodiac* entered Bellingham

Bay, our guests returned above-deck to snap photos and trade contact information. Even the twins were chatting and laughing—everyone had forgotten the day's earlier physical and emotional turbulence. Everyone except me.

By mid-afternoon, the time for our arrival drew near and my crew worked together to haul the inflatable back on deck, prepare the fenders, and take care of the other tasks necessary for our approach. *Zodiac* glided through the calmer water of the bay, barely cutting a ripple through the water's surface which by now presented just small chops. From a distance, we could see family members, friends and passing tourists awaiting us from the pier. They waved and shouted excited greetings and watched closely as we navigated into our narrow slip at dock.

Captain Tim backed the ship toward the dock and nodded to me, signaling the start of the docking procedure. I pointed to my bow and sternline deckhands to stand by, ready to throw their lines on command. Two of my more agile hands stepped onto the caprail, waiting for the opportunity to leap onto the dock as the *Z* approached. I watched them follow their orders smartly. *Pretty good work for a bunch of volunteers.*

I looked over my shoulder to watch Tim complete his docking maneuvers, difficult in light of how narrow *Zodiac*'s slip was. Even though I was still angry, I couldn't help but admire how adeptly he handled the giant ship. I never grew tired of watching as he finessed *Zodiac* forward and backwards, nudging her stern close enough so as to deposit the line handlers onto the dock seconds before contact and then powering forward to align her for the final approach. Once the crewmembers were ashore, the familiar *whack* of lines hitting concrete was heard and they were made fast around the bull rail.

"Bowline secure!" I called back to Tim.

He acknowledged the information with a quick nod and spun the wheel a complete turn. The underlying current caught the ship and pushed her toward the opposite side of our slip, an overhanging pier made of thick cement attached to tremendous, barnacle-encrusted pilings. The onlookers who stood above us gasped as the ship's boom moved closer to the platform. I chewed on my lower lip; I was familiar with Tim's tendency to goose *Zodiac* forward while shifting his rudder. The ship responded and slipped forward just before the boom kissed the overhanging pier.

Balls! I could never imagine doing that.

A loud and unexpected splash made me whirl around. The sternline had fallen short of the dock and hit the water. "OK. Bring it in fast and throw it again—but do it now!" I yelled, as I made my way aft to reinforce the rattled deckhand.

She managed to recoil her line before the propeller sucked it under the transom, then she sent the dock-line soaring with a twisted, overhand throw. The toss made contact and the line-handler on the dock quickly secured it to the bull rail. "Stern line's secure," I said to Tim and made my way back to midship to call distances from the dock.

"Take up slack and get a turn around the bit," the captain ordered. The deckhand repeated the order and checked her line.

For the next several minutes crowds on the dock and on deck watched as the captain and his crew brought the hundred-and-sixty-foot ship alongside her dock. Finally, Tim crossed his forearms over his head, signaling to the crewman at the bow to make the lines fast. Tim walked over to the gearbox and pushed the red stop button. The throaty growl of the engine ceased.

In unison, passengers broke into applause—as did many of the onlookers from the pier above. I smiled, Captain Tim's capabilities in close-quarters maneuvering never failed to impress.

I stepped over to the ship's radio to clear-out with Seattle Traffic. As I leaned into the microphone, Tim brushed by me and tapped my elbow as he prepared to go below-deck. "Stay behind, we need to talk."

I winced and gave a brief nod. "OK."

Once Traffic cleared us, I assembled the passengers together and thanked them for coming aboard. Hugs and handshakes ensued as shipmates said their goodbyes. I stood aside and witnessed the camaraderie that had developed amongst passengers and crew. A few passengers came over to me before departing.

"You have a *really* great crew and you all handled things so well today," exclaimed a woman as she shook my hand.

Her husband chimed in, "You did a good job today, little lady. That was a rough one."

"We were so impressed by your two daughters, and how mature they are. You must be so proud of them," another passenger confided as she passed by me.

"Thank you," I responded. "They're learning more every time we go out."

The deckhands lined the caprails and called out their goodbyes as passengers walked past the ship toward the gate. "So long!" and "Come back again!" could be heard at intervals from every crewmember. I smiled as I watched the ritual transpire. *This is what it's all about.* I turned to go below, feeling good about things big and small— and then it hit me: *Oh, jumpin' Jeezus. We have to have the 'talk.'*

I squared my shoulders and walked down the stairs into the galley, steeling myself for whatever lay ahead. *This might be the shortest first mate career on record.* Although I hadn't been raised with a military background, I knew about the hierarchy of command on board a vessel and I'd learned the golden rule: 'The captain is always right.' I had no delusion what my outburst on the quarterdeck signified. *This may not be pretty.*

Tim sat alone at the galley table. He had a half-full bottle of beer in front of him and an unopened one next to it. I pulled up a chair across from him and sat down, grateful for the wide expanse of mahogany that separated us. He didn't say anything, but he pushed the unopened bottle toward me. I managed a smile of thanks and twisted off the cap. We each took a few quiet sips before he cleared his throat to speak.

"I want to talk with you about this morning," he began.

"I know… I'm very sorry that I jumped all over you in front of the passengers," I blurted out.

Tim held up his hand, "No. Listen." He paused. "First: We should *not* have raised our sails first thing today—you're all still too green. That's on me." He paused to take another sip. "Next: You're right, I shouldn't have said that about your girls and I am feeling badly about it. There is no excuse."

Not having a response ready, I just took another long drink. Finally I was able to say, "Thanks, Tim… and, well, I'm sorry that the 'mom' part of me got the best of the 'mate' part of me. I should have cooled down before I spoke with you about it."

I wavered for a minute and then pressed on. "The truth of the matter though Tim, is that if you're going to keep abusing the crew like today—whether it's my daughters or anyone who's busting their butt and doing their best for *Zodiac*... you're likely just gonna end up with a really pretty boat that sits at dock all the time because nobody will crew on it."

Tim took a long, slow pull on his bottle and paused. A couple of the deckhands bounded down the steps into the galley, holding beers and laughing. They drew up short when they saw us. Tim nodded his head toward the stairs and said, "Give us a few minutes, please guys."

"Sure thing, Skipper" they replied and hastened back up the companionway. The only sound in the galley was the *tick, tick, tick* of the ship's clock.

After some time, Tim spoke again. "I know you have a temper, Chris—believe me. It's a little intimidating."

Wait a minute—he's intimidated by... me? I set my beer down for a brief moment.

The captain continued. "On the other hand, what scares me even more is my own temper and what happens when I lose control of it—like today." He paused briefly and frowned as if recalling something he didn't relish remembering. "I understand what you're saying and I am really working on changing some things. That's part of the reason why I asked you to be mate."

He looked straight at me and continued, "But, you have to understand this—and this is important: it's a thankless job, being the first mate. Everybody wants to be the captain, but folks don't last too long as the mate. It is always *your* fault when things go badly and there is very little thanks when things go right."

This remark made me smile, as I had become all too familiar with that fact. We sat at the table, nursing our beers for a while longer. Tim gave me a half-smile and said, "I'd like for you to continue on in this role—as long as you're willing to work with me… and we can both work on our tempers."

I nodded. "Yeah, that sounds about right." We clinked our bottles together in a mock toast. No more needed to be said.

Chapter 26

Eagle Harbor

The day started with a foggy mist that clung low in the sky, the weak July sun failed to dry the moisture droplets off of *Zodiac*'s deck. My deckhands were reluctant to vacate the cozy charthouse for their morning duties. I couldn't really blame them—even I felt a wee bit groggy and unmotivated. However, the banter from the galley indicated that the passengers had recovered from their prior evening of wine-tasting and were ready for another day at sea. I admired their stamina.

During our morning crew-meeting, Tim told us that the thick, low-lying fog would prevent us from sailing right away. We would raise anchor and motor through Peavine Pass. I doubled up the bow watches and increased the range on our radar.

Zodiac's engine idled while the anchor was hoisted and rinsed. I waited at the wheel for the captain to reappear. Eventually, Tim ambled back to the quarterdeck. He pulled his wool sweater over his head and settled back into his large teak chair. "You take her out," he said to me, and unfolded his magazine across his lap.

I motored *Zodiac* toward home, passing though Upright Channel. The Lopez Island ferry pulled away from the dock at Humphrey Head and blew her fog horn, then disappeared into the grey. We had four hours remaining before our arrival in Bellingham and were making about seven knots over the water.

The passengers marked time by reading, knot-tying and snapping photos until they could uncork the remaining wine bottles with their last meal. I handed the wheel back to Tim so I could check in with Ian—before I even reached the first step of the stern passageway, I smelled the unmistakable aroma of roasting garlic. My mouth began to water.

"Whatcha cooking? Smells great!" I asked.

"Oh, you know, just bilge-scrapings," Ian responded.

"Well, when might we expect said delicacies?"

"Only the best for you, Your Highness," he said and scratched his chin with his forearm while squinting at the galley clock. "Give me about forty-five more minutes and I'll ring the bell."

I returned to the helm and relayed Ian's message to Tim and then scrambled back to the fantail and took a seat next to Calen.

He acknowledged me with an absentminded shrug. "My neck's sore. Gimme a massage."

"I gave you a neck massage yesterday, you spoiled brat."

"Yeah, but it didn't take."

"My *god*, I spoil you," I said, but sat down behind him to rub his shoulders.

Tim craned around to look at us and nodded in agreement. "Yes. You do spoil him, and you should really stop it."

"Ignore him—he's a grumpy old man," said Calen. The sun gradually cut through the fog, and one by one we shed our coats and heavy sweaters. *Zodiac* passed through Peavine Pass and headed toward Cypress Island. I chatted with Calen while I massaged his shoulders, but paused when I noticed Tim hastily rise from his chair.

"Hey, did you hear anything just now?" I asked Calen.

He raised his head up and looked around. "Nah, I don't think so… wasn't really paying attention, though."

I straightened up and looked over at the gear box. Tim now stood at the entrance to the aft scuttle with the mic in his hand, one foot on a lower step with the other resting on the scuttle ledge. He leaned his elbow upon the scuttle rooftop and surveyed the water. I could see his serious expression from my seat on the transom.

"Heads up, Calen. Go see what's happening with your dad."

Calen grudgingly got up to check in with his father. Several minutes later, he waved me over. I walked to the scuttle, but before I could inquire, the receiver crackled and I heard a woman's voice. There was panic in her tone.

"We're in Eagle Harbor. There are about six other boats anchored nearby—we're on a green and white boat. It's about, I'm not sure… 30 feet or so long."

I frowned at the radio and shot Calen a questioning glance.

"Mayday call," he whispered.

Ahhh. I stood by in silence and listened in to the conversation. There was a lot of chatter back and forth between the woman in distress and the Coast Guard. At one point I jumped, startled at the mention of our ship's name.

"*Schooner Zodiac,* this is U.S. Coast Guard. I understand you are underway, approaching Cypress Island? Over."

Tim pressed the *speak* button on the mic. "Affirmative Coast Guard. We're abeam of Towhead Island, westbound currently. Over."

"Copy that *Zodiac*. Do you have the ability to render assistance at this time? Over."

Tim cleared his throat and replied, "That's affirmative. We're prepared to send our tender over with several of my crew. Over."

"*Zodiac,* do you have any crew with medical training that you can send with this party? Over."

Tim looked directly at me and I nodded in reply. "Bryan used to be an army medic—he should go with me as well," I said.

Tim returned to the mic and relayed to the operator that his mate and another crewmember had medical backgrounds. "We're sending them over now, with our AED," he added.

"*Zodiac,* understood. What is your estimated time to arrive in Eagle Harbor? Over."

Tim glanced at Calen and pointed to the tender. Calen tore off down the deck. "Coast Guard, we're lowering our boat right now. I estimate we can have them over there within eight to ten minutes. Over."

"Copy *Zodiac*. Be advised we have a Coast Guard response vessel en route. They're about fifteen minutes behind you. Over."

I didn't wait for Tim to finish his conversation with the Coast Guard operator. I ran forward and shouted for Bryan to follow me. "Grab your PFD and the AED—we've got a *mayday* and we're the closest vessel to respond."

Bryan said, "I'm on it," and dashed down the charthouse stairs to grab his gear.

I stood by the gangway as the deckhands lowered away. The fast-attack boat slapped against the surf as it made contact. Calen leapt into the tender and started the motor. He called up for the boat-falls to be released and waved for me to jump down. I yelled over my shoulder, "Bryan! Time to go." I watched him tear up from the charthouse with the AED in tow.

Tim strode forward as the deckhands tossed the bow and stern painters to us. He looked down at the tender and yelled, "Winds are picking up—be careful out there! Have you got your running lights on?"

Calen reached for the switch. "Yeah, I got 'em!"

"Radio back in when you arrive—and watch *out*!" Tim called after us.

I gave a hasty wave to Juliet who stood anxiously next to the boatfalls. She'd been in her bunk during the unfolding drama and had just discovered what was going on. Calen put the throttle in full forward and we ripped away from *Zodiac*'s hull.

The waves shouldered against each other to crash into our bow as we pounded forward. Bryan sat on the sole of the rigid inflatable, his head ducked low to lessen the effects of the wind. We all leaned into the small radio on the tender's console as more information was exchanged. The Coasties were now speaking directly with the woman on the distress vessel; it was difficult to make out all of her words through the panic and cries.

I heard them say that the vessel *Zodiac* was sending assistance and they relayed our ETA. We then heard the broadcast to all vessels.

"*Mayday, mayday, mayday.* All Stations. This is United States Coast Guard Puget Sound. We have received a distress call in the area of Eagle Harbor on Cypress Island. Vessel in distress indicates occupant has suffered a massive heart attack. Coast Guard Rescue boat is en route. All stations stand by and monitor channel one-six. Over."

At the mention of the word 'massive,' I shouted instructions over the roar of the boat's outboard while we sped on our way. "OK guys, a *massive* heart attack means this guy may already be gone by the time we get there."

Bryan was nodding his head. Calen shot me a look of grave concern before he returned his attention to driving.

"Bryan, you'll need to board first and get CPR started right away. We don't know if whoever's on board has even been doing it—let's hope so. I'll take care of the wife and anybody else. Calen, you secure the boat and fill the Coasties in when they get here. Everybody got it?"

Bryan replied with, "Roger that." And Calen tersely said, "Yup."

Eagle Harbor lay before us, enveloped in the low-lying fog that refused to burn off. Calen throttled down as we approached the entrance. As our outboard's wake caught up with our tender, we bounced about like a toy in bathwater. The secluded harbor was eerily hushed, the tree-lined shore encircled a half-dozen boats silently resting on their anchors. "Over there—that has to be the one." Bryan pointed toward a green-and-white-hulled Bayliner. Calen turned our tender in the direction of the vessel and we came alongside her.

Bryan climbed aboard and vanished immediately into the deckhouse. Calen brought the tender astern and I stepped onto the swim platform. He tossed me the AED with a look that conveyed *good luck*. I smiled and said "Thanks. Give us a heads up when you spot the Coasties, OK?"

The cabin was dimly lit and I noticed that the shades were drawn. As I stepped across several piles of clothing, I saw a man on the floor lying spread-eagled. He was naked save for a towel draped across his mid-section. Bryan was kneeling by his torso applying chest compressions—he'd taken over from an elderly gentleman who squatted beside the body, breathing heavily. I watched for a few seconds longer and assessed the events around me. Bryan's rhythmic compressions caused the man's belly to slosh to and fro. His hands and feet had assumed a waxy yellow tint and his face was a pallid grey. *He's gone... I wonder if Bryan realizes this.*

Bryan glanced up at me as I walked around the body. I could see in his eyes that he knew the man's fate as well. I knelt beside the victim's shoulders and unpacked the AED. We worked quickly and wordlessly. No matter what our opinions of the outcome, we were trained to continue life-saving procedures until the professionals arrived. I handed Bryan the electrode pads and he ripped the sticky seals off, applying them to the man's chest. The machine announced *'apply shock'* and we sat back as the AED transmitted the electrical current. The man flopped upward and fell back. There was no other change. Bryan resumed his compressions.

I scanned the cabin. A heavyset young woman stood by the counter anxiously watching the process. She hugged her shoulder with one arm while her other hand covered her mouth. She nodded at me briefly. The man next to Bryan leaned forward, hands on his jeans. He looked expectantly at Bryan after every compression.

I moved to the side and saw a fragile-looking woman in her mid-fifties emerge from below. She wore nothing but jeans and a bra and her tangled hair looked like it had been hastily bunched together away from her face. She looked dazed, her face expressionless. She stopped midway up the steps and blankly stared at Bryan as he worked.

I moved nearer to the woman and introduced myself. I asked her name. She didn't answer at first but then replied, "Uh, what? Oh, uhm, Janice. I'm Janice—I'm his wife." She continued to stare, her countenance disconnected and remote.

Then she turned to me suddenly and said, "He just got out of bed and fell right over. He didn't say a word." Her gaze wandered around the room and rested near the galley counter. "Oh, I should get those dishes off the counter before the Coast Guard come inside… the space is… there's just no room to move about in here is there?"

I took her gently by the arm and said, "Don't worry about that, Janice. They won't notice. Say, can I find a sweater for you? It's getting a little chilly in here isn't it?"

"Oh. Yes… yes, OK. Maybe it's over there?"

I asked the young woman to fetch something to throw over Janice and cleared a spot for her on a bench near her husband's feet. She passively sat, hands clasped in her lap. When I handed her a sweatshirt she looked up at me and smiled. "He's not that terribly old, you know. He's been in good health now for several years."

241

I placed my hand on her shoulder, "Bryan's going to keep doing CPR until the Coast Guard gets here. I'll stay right here with you."

"Thank you all so much," she said.

The atmosphere in the room was solemn and unnatural. The hollow whooshing sounds the man's empty lungs emitted as Bryan continued CPR were the only noises inside the cabin. We hung on the performance in front of us, mute witnesses of an unfinished drama. Outside came the slap, slap, slap of waves knocking against the fiberglass hull.

Calen's footsteps on the swim-deck stirred us from our trance-like state. "Coast Guard's here," he said and ducked back outside.

I stepped outside to quickly update the three Coast Guard officers of our actions and observations, and then allow them enough room below to work. With their arrival, the couple who'd come to help from their neighboring vessel said goodbye and paddled back to their own boat. We waited. Eventually the team of blue-uniformed men came out of the cabin with the heart attack victim; a bedspread wrapped around him as a sling. Bryan remained inside to pack up our equipment. The Coasties worked together with the help of Calen to lower the body into their rescue boat. We cast off their lines and watched as the red inflatable peeled out of the harbor. As the sound of their twin engines faded into the distance we were left alone once more in the oppressive stillness of the bay.

The visibility was decreasing with the growing fog. Calen stepped down into the tender and stood beside the console, sucking on his teeth as he squinted into the distance. It struck me that he looked very much like his father at that moment.

Bryan joined me on the stern. His hair and brow were drenched in sweat, and stress was etched across his face. Behind him followed Janice with a blanket wrapped around her shoulders. "Are we meeting them at the hospital in Anacortes?" she asked us. "It's OK—I'm ready to go now. Will I be able to see him when he's in the emergency room?"

Calen sat down on the bench seat of the tender and fiddled with the ignition key. Bryan knelt down and checked the AED machine. I took a quick breath and said, "Sure thing, we'll get you over to Anacortes as fast as we can, Janice. I'm sure they'll call you once they're ashore." I hoped that my tone conveyed more optimism than I felt.

I motioned for her to join Calen in the tender; he helped her don a lifejacket and made room for her on the bench seat next to him. Bryan and I piled in after her and secured the AED below the seat. The seas were beginning to build with confused waves hitting us from all sides. The fog began to creep back in across the horizon. I leaned over to whisper to Calen, "Running lights."

We sped off in the direction of the Coast Guard's wake, and I radioed to *Zodiac* about our plan to follow them into Anacortes. Our route took us from Cypress Island across Bellingham Channel and into Guemes Channel. The misty shroud that filled in all around us gave Calen less than a quarter-mile visibility as he negotiated the choppy waves and hidden reefs. Our running lights were no match for the soupy fog that now covered the entire archipelago.

Calen raced the boat forward and we crashed into the mounting seas one after another, slamming down hard in the valley of each cresting swell. Bryan held onto the straps of the inflatable's chambers; he was getting thrown repeatedly onto the rigid sole and fought to keep himself inboard. I watched with concern as the grim expression on his face darkened and his brooding silences intensified. He'd only recently returned from his second deployment in Iraq as an intelligence officer. I wondered if this trauma might be bringing back some pretty rough memories for him.

From my position on the sole I could see Janice shiver involuntarily as she huddled next to Calen. The blanket wrapped around her was covered in droplets of condensation and spray. I began to recognize some familiar signs of shock. I nudged her on the knee and said, "Hey, Janice! Can you hear me?"

"Huh?" She looked down with a puzzled look, the roar of our engine surpassed our voices.

"Hey! We're just about there. Have you got your cell phone?" I yelled into her ear.
She nodded yes.

"Good—hold onto it and we'll hear from them soon. Are you doin' OK right now?" Once more she nodded her head. It was indistinguishable from the wracking shakes of the rest of her body.

Calen pulled the tender alongside the floating dock near the shipyards of Anacortes. We narrowly missed colliding with a couple of south-bound fishing boats in the thick mass of fog, and I was relieved to be on shore at last.

Bryan assisted Janice out of the tender and handed up her purse. Calen secured the tender to the bull rail and followed us up to the gravel parking lot. I posted myself next to her as she sat on a cement block to await the taxi cab.

"I don't smoke anymore … but I carry a few around with me. I don't know why." She dug the pack of cigarettes out of her bag. "This seems like a good time to have one." Her hands shook so violently that she couldn't operate the lighter. I helped her light her cigarette and briefly toyed with the concept of smoking one myself. Her phone rang from inside her purse.

My heart skipped a beat as I heard the ring. I stood by in silence, placing my hand gently on her shoulder and glanced over at Calen and Bryan who'd moved away from us—to put some distance on the intimate tableau that developed before them. I bowed my head and looked away as Janice listened, but I could hear the Anacortes Fire Department Medic reporting that her husband had been pronounced dead upon arrival at the marina. They informed her that his body would be transported to the mortuary rather than the hospital. She nodded into the cell phone as she listened, pausing to take long drags on her cigarette. I mouthed 'get the cab' to Bryan and he hustled up to the road to flag down the taxi we'd hailed.

I overheard the officer on the other end of the line ask whether Janice had any friends or family with her at the moment. I saw her hesitate and involuntarily look around. I rubbed her shoulder and said, "You're not alone, Janice. I'll be here as long as you need me."

She paused and said, "Yes, I have a few nice folks from a sailboat who've offered to help me. I'll call our... *my*, friends from Bellingham to meet me at the funeral home."

With Bryan on the street corner and Calen at the tender, I sat alone with Janice and waited. After five or six minutes, the taxi pulled into the parking lot. I saw Bryan explain the situation to the driver. Janice stubbed out her cigarette and fumbled in her purse for fare. I told her, "Don't bother Janice, they won't charge you for this ride." Then I watched her square her shoulders and make her way over to the taxi, thinking to myself, *that's got to be a long walk.*

Calen approached me. His hands were shoved deep into the pockets of his jeans, his head hung low. "What do ya think we oughta do now?" he asked.

I heaved a sigh. "Well, I guess you should take Bryan back to the Z," I answered. "I think I ought to stay here with Janice; she's gonna need somebody until her friends can get here." I smiled at him. "Better radio Tim and let him know what's going on."

A look of relief washed over Calen's face. "Hey, you!" I called after him. "Keep an eye on Bryan, will ya? I think this whole event may have been sort of hard on him."

Calen gave me a wave of acknowledgement as he headed back to the dock. Bryan passed by me on his way to the tender and gave me a hug. "Hang in there, tough chick."

I waved goodbye to my shipmates, suddenly feeling very homesick for *Zodiac*. I followed Janice toward the cab and opened the back door, slipping in behind the driver.

The afternoon at the funeral home was a long ordeal. Our cab ride took only a matter of five or ten minutes, but it felt like an eternity. Janice wavered between the brutal acknowledgement of her husband's sudden death and the numbness that comes with all-encompassing shock. She fought back tears as she searched her cell phone for numbers of friends. She wondered how to break the news to her husband's elderly mother. The thought of this sent her into wracking sobs and howls of painful grief. I didn't say anything—just sat behind her and kept my hand on her shoulder. She occasionally reached for my hand as if it was an anchor to hold onto.

As the taxi pulled up to the mortuary, the funeral director was waiting for us outside. He had the composed look of one accustomed to greeting people in such a state. He gently ushered Janice into the parlor and offered her a place on the oversized loveseat; he handed her a box of tissues and leaned forward to ask if there was anything that he could do. They spoke together for a while and I excused myself to go outside and call my husband.

"Absolutely, I'll stay here with Janice," the man said.

I stepped outside the swinging glass door and took a deep breath. The skies over Anacortes were much clearer than those over the islands. It was still daylight—I had completely lost all sense of time. I glanced around the block and saw cars driving down the road, heard someone mowing their lawn, smelled smoke from a patio grill. Life moved on as it always did. I wondered how many other people around the world were coping with grief at this moment, pulled outside of their ordinary lives by the suddenness of death. It seemed so weird, so *unnatural*.

I dialed Jeffery's number and he picked up on the second ring. "Hey, you! How's it going?" He asked.

"Oh, well… Not so good. I'm not on the boat right now actually… It's a really long story, but can you come pick me up in Anacortes?"

"What? Why? What's happened? Are you OK?"

"Yeah, well… I'm fine. I just need you to come get me when you can. I'm at the Anacortes funeral home. I need to stay here for at least another couple of hours, but then I sure could use a ride home."

"What the hell! Is everyone on the ship alright? Is Tim OK? What *happened*?" He asked again.

"I'm fine. Juliet… Tim, everyone on board is fine. We just had to respond to a *mayday* on our way home, that's all. The victim is the one who's not OK. I'm with the wife, *er*, widow, right now."

"Oh god, I'm so sorry. Well, I'm on my way back up from the airport with my mom. We'll be in Anacortes in… oh, in about two-and-a-half hours then. I'll call you when we get into town."

"Thanks—by the way, I really love you." I hung up, took a deep breath and went back inside.

The funeral director looked up at me and smiled. "Janice was able to reach her friends and they're on their way here. I'm going to make a call. If you need me I'll be right in there." He pointed toward the small office in the hallway.

I took my place next to Janice and gave her a gentle hug. She hunched over, whimpering softly into a tissue. "Can I do anything for you, Janice?" I asked.

She shook her head and rocked back and forth. "He won't let me drive the boat. What am I going to do about our boat?" She said. "I ought to go back out there. There's nobody to take care of it. I want to be back on the boat. It was the last place we were together… Oh, god! Oh, *god*!"

I smoothed her hair and rocked in time with her. There seemed to be nothing to say, so I just let her pass through the waves of her grief. "We were, you know, he might still be alive if we hadn't…" She looked up at me. "We were in bed when it happened. Maybe if we hadn't..." She bent over in tears, crying inconsolably.

I let her pain run its course. "Janice, I'm no expert, but it seems to me that if I was allowed to spend my last moments on earth in a little bay out on the water—and if I was making love with my partner... well, I don't believe that there's a much better way to leave this life. He was where he wanted to be—with you." I felt her sobbing lessen; her body stopped shaking so terribly. "It might have been the nicest thing you could have done."

We sat together for the next hour, her grief rose and fell in the same manner as contractions peak and subside during labor. I came to understand the patterns and found that I could comfort her in the same way that I had with my pregnant mothers. I realized that just as one could not remove the pain of a strong contraction, there was no way to dispel the sorrow when it occurred. I stayed beside her as she rode out the grief, doing what I always did—remaining present.

Eventually the doors swung open and Janice's friends rushed into the room. They swallowed her up in tearful embraces and comforting words. They held her as she broke down anew, patting her and supporting her as she cried. I stood up quietly and excused myself from the room. It was a relief to be removed from the burden of her sadness and yet I felt a slight reluctance to leave. We'd shared something extremely important and I wanted to stay and ensure she'd be taken care of properly.

As I retrieved my bag and coat, Janice looked up from her friends' arms and said, "You guys, this is my guardian angel, Chris. She's been with me through the whole thing. I don't think I could have made it without her." She smiled at me through tears and asked if she could give me a hug before I left.

"Of course you can." I went over to the couch and we shared a long embrace.

"Thank you, thank you, *thank* you. God bless you," she said repeatedly. Her friends smiled at me and offered their appreciation as well.

"You take care, Janice. I'm so glad that your friends are here for you," I smiled, and then headed for the front door. The funeral director stood there waiting for the ambulance to arrive with the body. I shook his hand and thanked him for being so nice. "It's nothing," he said. "This has been a long week, though—lots of deaths in town this weekend." I decided right then that it took a really extraordinary person to do his kind of job willingly, day in and out.

Jeffery and his mother pulled up at that moment and I ran over to the car. Jeff opened the door and before he was able to straighten up, I threw myself into his arms.

"Hey there you, are you gonna be OK?" He asked.

"I am now that you're here."

After we pulled away from the funeral home, I pushed my seat back and let Jeff's mother chatter on about the cross-country flight and her east coast grandchildren for the entire ride to Bellingham. The day's emotional stress began to seep into my consciousness and I held it at bay, allowing her voice to drizzle over my thoughts. It felt good to not have to say anything or make any decisions, to just stare out the car window as the scenery blurred past me.

When we reached *Zodiac*'s dock, the passengers had already disembarked. Tim sat on one of the deck boxes surrounded by all of our crew. They were enjoying their customary post-cruise beers. I followed Jeff down the ramp and we climbed up the boarding ladder. Juliet ran over when she saw her grandma and gave a hug to both of us. Tim waved me over—he smiled and held up a beer. I gratefully accepted the bottle and found a shady spot nearby. He didn't ask me about what happened or even how I was doing—thankfully, the rest of the crew followed his lead. We leaned back against the lifelines and relaxed, trading stories with our friends.

Chapter 27

The Service

The following week Tim brought over the obituary for Janice's husband that ran in the *Bellingham Herald*. Her husband's name was Gus, and he had been a professional musician, a writer, a ham-radio operator and a small business owner. The article mentioned his love of boating. At the bottom of the obituary was a short sentence that read *Gus' wife, Janice, would like to express her deep gratitude to the Schooner Zodiac's First Mate and crewmembers for their help and great kindness.*

"You ought to attend his service if you feel up to it," Tim said.

"I think I might like to. Jeff's working here in Bellingham this week—maybe he could take me."

"OK, we'll make it happen."

The timing of the funeral service coincided with the first day of another cruise. We were scheduled to drop our passengers off at Lummi Island's winery, and Tim pressed *Zodiac* harder than usual, allowing Calen time to ferry me to the mainland. The rain that started earlier in the day refused to let up, and I was still wearing my foul weather pants and jacket. I leapt from the tender as Calen slid in near the sandy beach.

"Catch ya later," he yelled as I picked my way through the driftwood on shore.

I walked up the beach and saw Jeffery waiting for me in the car. He took the afternoon off work so that he could drive me over to the gravesite ceremony.

It was a busy day for funerals. We drove around the maze of lanes and plots, and saw several tents dotting the grounds; mourners huddled underneath to stay out of the rain. When we found Gus' site, the service had already begun, so we walked toward the edge of the lawn and waited. After the many family members and friends said farewell and told their stories, the pastor asked Janice to speak. I saw her rise from the front row and walk to the microphone. She looked totally different than the disheveled and disoriented woman I spent time with last week. She wore a black dress with a burgundy shawl and low heels; her hair was combed back and lay in loose curls around her shoulders.

In a clear voice, she thanked their loved ones and associates for coming to pay respects. She mentioned how uncomfortable her husband would have felt at all of the high praise. She motioned toward the vases of roses that were placed around the graveside and commented about how Gus used to tease her for spending so much time with her flowers. "I never really guessed that they would be covering his casket, though."

After the service, people lined up to offer her their condolences and support. I turned to Jeffery and said, "We should probably leave now, don'tcha think?"

He shrugged and said, "Don't you want to at least go over and say 'hi'?"

"I'm really not dressed for this." My outfit of red Gore-Tex overalls with the black patches on the knees and seat was a striking contrast to the somber attire of the other mourners.

Jeff leaned over and said, "You're crew from the *Zodiac*—it's kind of appropriate that you look like this."

I sighed and said, "Alright." Cautiously, I picked a path around the other guests, giving them a wide berth. As I rounded the tent where Janice stood amongst a long line of people, she spotted me. "Oh, my gosh—it's my guardian angel!" She pointed in my direction. I felt my cheeks flush as the crowd of people turned to stare at me—standing there in my foulies and boots.

Janice pushed past the group of friends and rushed toward me. "Oh Chris! I'm so glad you came! Everyone, look here! This is the first mate of the *Zodiac*. She helped me *so* much on that day…" She paused. "I have always believed that everyone has a guardian angel and I know that I've found mine!"

I couldn't believe anyone would ever refer to me as an angel. My eyes began to tear up and I knew that I'd soon lose my composure, so I hugged her and wished her the best, adding that the captain and crew of *Zodiac* wanted her to come sail with us someday when she felt able.

She squeezed me tightly and said that she'd like that. "Tell your skipper thanks so very much for allowing you to be here today."

I waved goodbye to Janice and her many friends and headed back to my husband. Clearing my throat, I said, "Well. I'm glad we showed up—but now let's get out of here."

Jeffery threw an arm around my shoulder and said, "You're my favorite, you know."

On our route back to the pick-up spot on the beach, we stopped at the liquor store so I could grab a bottle of Pusser's rum. "I want to have a toast for Janice's husband on the boat tonight," I said as I slid into my seat and shut the car door. Jeffery drove back to the beach where Calen waited for me in the tender.

Jeff paused before handing me the bottle. "You know, I wouldn't mind sharing a shot with you right now." I unscrewed the cap and we both tossed back a quick swallow. He leaned over and gave me a peck on my cheek. "Have a good trip and I'll see you in three days."

"Thanks so much for taking me," I said and stepped out of the car.

Later that night on *Zodiac*, when the passengers were comfortable below-deck, I asked the crew to gather at the helm. Tim came out of his stateroom and joined us. We passed around the bottle of Pusser's, each pouring a shot into our glasses. In the dwindling light, I raised my glass and simply said, "To Gus."

"To Gus," they echoed and we silently tipped back our shots.

Chapter 28

Obtaining Clearance

The day had come at last: our boat *Kwaietek,* was finally ours. Almost two years had passed since we'd found her, and now on this crisp September morning, Jeffery prepared to head north to take possession. Before departing for British Columbia, he stopped by the *Zodiac* to say goodbye. I stood next to the chart table and filled out forms for the charter group due to board shortly. Jeff ticked off the items in his duffle bag, and for the third time recited the list of documents he was carrying into Canada to complete the purchase. "My god, I haven't seen you this nervous since our wedding!"

"Yeah, I'm a little excited I suppose." he replied. "Maybe I should have stuck to just three cups of coffee—but I don't want to get up there and have a Customs' official stop me for missing a document."

"I'm kind of jealous that you guys get to go pick her up. I wanted to bring her down with you, too. Are both Rory and Barney going to be onboard?"

"They're meeting me up in the parking lot in about ten minutes. Both of 'em have their captain's tickets so that should help with Customs at the border.' Jeff said. He zipped up the duffle bag and threw it over his shoulder. "I gotta run to the market and grab a couple days provisions for us. I should probably get going."

"You don't have time for breakfast? I wanted to make some eggs or something."

"I'm not feeling too hungry, actually."

I could tell that Jeff wanted to get on the road and begin his adventure. I envied him—bringing *Kwaietek* home across the border. I thought briefly about taking this charter off and hopping in the car with him—but no, this was a significant event for Jeffery and he deserved it. This trip was Jeffery's reward for staying behind and working. He'd even unpacked his father's military flag to run up *Kwaietek*'s halyard as they crossed the border. With our two friends there to share in it, he would finally get to realize his much-anticipated dream.

I glanced up toward the gate and spied a horde of teens leaning over the railing: *Zodiac's* passengers had arrived. I rose to locate the rest of my crew as Jeffery reached for my hand and squeezed. "Hey, the next time we see each other, we'll have our new home!"

"Man, I can*not* wait for that," I told him, standing on my tiptoes to kiss his forehead. The thought of a place to call our very own again made me feel giddy. He grabbed the rest of his bags and jumped down onto the dock, stopping to wave one last time as he made his way through the crowd of kids at the top.

After the seventeen excited students and four harried-looking chaperones were welcomed aboard the *Zodiac,* I gave the orientation lecture and passed out bunk assignments, stretching the process as long as I reasonably could in order to allow the captain time to arrive. Finally, I sent the entire group of eager kids below deck to unpack just as Tim strolled down the dock with his gear; he smiled as he came up the gangway. "I saw your hubby in the parking lot. Is he all set to pick up that boat of yours today?"

"Oh, you better believe it… and trust me, he's made his list and checked it twice."

Tim gave a cursory glance around, assessed the deck, and inquired, "So, we ready to go?"

"Security sweep's complete, the rig-check's done, water tanks full—fuel tanks dipped and everything's been logged. Twenty-one passengers onboard."

"Sounds good. Let's go for a ride."

While Tim went below to stow his gear, I went to the helm and passed out the orders, "OK, let's single up now." I watched two of my deckhands leap over the rails, landing solidly on the dock—one headed toward the bow and the other walked aft to remove the extra stern line. It didn't take long to complete our tasks for departure. I radioed Traffic with our information, and soon, with the captain's presence on deck, steered the ship away from the dock. I coaxed her to starboard as we eased out of the slip, and just then I heard my name shouted from the pier above us. Looking back I could see Jeffery standing at the rail.

"We'll be waiting here on *Kwaietek* for you guys on Sunday!" he called after us.

"Save me a beer!" I shouted.

Juliet ran up from below. "I love you, Daddy! I'll see you in three days!" *Zodiac* skimmed slowly out into the bay as Jeffery waved us off.

The Edmonds Heights kids were familiar with *Zodiac*. Most of them had been on board for two previous seasons, and some of the older kids sought out their favorite crew from last year's trip. They felt right at home and took to their duties quickly, and it was an easy job to raise the sails as we cruised across the bay. Soon, the overcast skies relented and the sun broke through the patchy clouds. We sailed *Zodiac* across Rosario Strait and through Peavine Pass with a fair wind for the remainder of the day. As the afternoon drew to a close with steady seas, Tim decided to 'sail onto the hook' and summoned me to the quarterdeck to inform me of his plan. I enjoyed sailing onto the anchorage with a solid bunch of deckhands. I saw it as the ultimate compliment Tim could bestow upon his crew—he'd never attempt anchoring without the engine if he doubted we had the skill to pull it off.

Zodiac rounded Frost Island and glided toward Spencer Spit. As we sailed into the lee of the island, Tim nodded to me and I shouted the command, "Douse your jib!"

A young girl ran past me pulling on the line and the foremost sail tumbled down in a matter of seconds. Next to drop would be the staysail; I pointed at Juliet and she relayed the command to her passengers. A freckle-faced boy by her side let loose the halyard and the staysail flew down in hasty folds, splayed across the foredeck.

The remaining crew stood by their stations, waiting for their orders. Tim gave the nod and I called, "Lower the main and the fore!" The heavy gaff booms sank in time with each other, flapping canvas collapsing beneath them. It was a sight that I found lovely to behold. A familiar, jarring "*ka-thunk*" could be felt and heard as the crewman at the bow removed the devil's claw from the heavy anchor chain. He stood by the windlass, eyes fixed upon the captain for the signal. Before the last of the mainsail fluttered down to the deck, Tim pointed toward the bow, and like clockwork, a crewmember released the windlass brake. A chain of two-hundred-and-seventy-feet could be heard thundering through the hawse-hole on its way to the muddy seabed.

The rest of that afternoon and evening flew by as the kids were tendered to shore and back again, fed dinner and allowed to play on deck until lights out. More than half of the group elected to sleep above deck, underneath a clear, star-filled canopy of night sky. Groggy teens tromped down the companionways in the early morning as a misty rain rousted them from sleep. We spent the second day sailing from island to island. "Tire 'em out," Tim had requested—we were doing our best.

Sunday morning dawned: our final day of the charter. The exhausted kids were still sound asleep below-deck. The charthouse was quiet and warm and I nursed my coffee while I penned the watches into the logbook. Tim sat nearby, reading Friday's newspaper. Below us in the galley, Ian could be heard pulling pans of freshly-baked cinnamon rolls out of the oven. The smell made its way up the companionway and my stomach growled. Just before seven-thirty, my crew straggled up the steps for our morning safety meeting, sporting their usual third-day-out hair styles. Their respective expressions hinted at the quality of their night's sleep.

After breakfast, I summoned the passengers on deck for their own morning meeting. Captain Tim sat on one of the deck boxes, leaning against the lifelines, his cup of coffee balanced on his leg. It fascinated me to observe the rapport between passengers and the captain. The school kids were always able to forge a cheeky kind of relationship with Tim and I found it amusing—especially compared to the awed respect that the adults showed him.

The phone in my pocket vibrated and made me jump. It was Jeffery. I stepped away from the group and answered it. "What's up?"

"Hey, you," Jeff answered. "We just left the Fraser River and all went smoothly. Next stop: good ole' *U.S. of A.*"

"Wow—I'm so excited! Where are you now?"

Jeff replied that they were making eight knots just north of Point Roberts and would be clearing into U.S. Customs in the next hour or two. He spent the next five minutes extolling the virtues of *Kwaietek*'s engine. As I listened to him go on about cylinders and heat exchangers, I chuckled. I could easily imagine the three salty men crawling around the engine room last night with a seventy-year old manual and a six-pack of beer. It must have been like heaven on board a boat.

"So, what does it feel like to sleep on your own ship?" I asked him.

"Amazing!" he replied. "You'll see for yourself tonight. I can't wait until you come on board."

"Yeah—and I can't wait to sleep in the same damn bed as my husband again. I've kind of forgotten what that feels like."

"Yes, well, heavy is the head that wears the crown, and all that…" he replied, and I smiled at the tone in his voice.

Out of the corner of my eye, I could see the group of passengers dispersing from their morning chat with Tim, which could only mean it was time to go. "It's looking like Tim's getting ready to start things up. I'll see you for pizza and beer on the fantail this afternoon, honey. Jeez, I'm so excited to see her again!"

Sure enough, having disbanded the meeting, Tim was antsy to get underway. As I approached him on the quarterdeck, he was scanning the harbor with binoculars. "We may get a little wind here shortly, so let's motor out and see if we can find anything out there."

I nodded and called for the crew. The sun poked through the clouds and we fired up the engine and weighed anchor. The breeze played cat and mouse with us as we motored north through President Channel. Tim caught the tell-tale signs of a wind-line on the water further north, and said, "Let's just raise the sails and see what we can get out of it."

Thirty minutes later, under full sail, we cut the engine and turned *Zodiac*'s bow into the freshening breeze. The canvas made a big *whoosh* as it filled with air. We could feel the lift as the sails were drawn forward. The kids coiled and capsized their lines, then checked in with their crew leaders. Several of the kids who'd been on board multiple times approached me for permission to sit on the boom. I hesitated for a moment and looked back at Tim for some guidance. The kids loved to climb up onto the boom when we were sailing close-hauled. They'd scoot down the length and lean back into the belly of the main when the winds were light. I had to admit that it was a pretty awesome vantage point.

Tim examined the sky and shook his head. "Sorry guys, I think the wind is gonna get a little fluky when we reach that point of land up there. I won't want anybody up in the sail when that happens."

The kids returned to their classmates. As lunchtime approached, Tim's prediction proved to be correct. A williwaw rolled off the crest of Point Doughty and caught *Zodiac* on the starboard side. The ship heeled to port and her sails popped full with a steady wind. We coursed ahead, gaining speed as we went. "Yeehaw!" I cried. "*Now* we're sailing!"

We trimmed our sails to maximize the lift and felt *Zodiac* gain momentum. This was definitely her kind of wind. Hoots and squeals of delight emanated from the kids as she heeled over on her course. By the time everyone had finished their lunch, we were up to eight-and-a-half knots and picking up speed.

Zodiac sailed on, making toward Village Point on Lummi Island. The solid wind had tempered slightly, but in exchange, the sun was out in full force. The kids entertained themselves with card games, knot-tying and sun-bathing. It seemed to have shaped into a fine afternoon's sail for the last day of their trip.

Chapter 29

Lower the Boom

I rose from my napping spot on the fantail in order to stretch my legs, and strolled forward to check our position on the plotter located in the aft scuttle. The GPS showed our speed to be 6.2 knots over ground with the current running against us. Our heading appeared to be just east-southeast of Clark Island.

Jeffery phoned to give me an update on their journey home in *Kwaietek*: they'd crossed the international border, just past Blaine. U.S. Customs had waved them off from check-in at Point Roberts and once again in Blaine—*Kwaietek*'s length was too much of a bother for their small marinas. They were being routed directly to Bellingham where the officials would meet them at the dock on arrival.

"Well, that cinches it I guess," I said. "You're definitely going to beat us to the dock now."

Juliet tugged at my sleeve, so I handed her the phone. While she recounted her weekend and the new friends that she'd met on board, I surveyed the deck. The kids were lounging around in groups, scattered everywhere. The mood on deck was definitely relaxed. Juliet handed back my phone. "I'll see you later this afternoon—can't wait," I said and hung up the phone.

I moved aside to allow a chaperone to go down the passageway, and Juliet asked, "Mom, do you think we'll get to sleep on *Kwaietek* tonight?"

"I don't know sweetie, it all really depends on—"

CRRRRACK

A splintering crash froze the rest of the words in my throat. We both looked up. Twelve feet in front of my eyes, I watched the giant main mast disintegrate. As if in slow-motion, the air around us filled with dust and particles—fragments of what used to be solid wood. Juliet and I stood in disbelief as the unthinkable became real. The towering, 128-foot spar had literally exploded—disappeared, leaving in its place a jagged stump only fourteen feet high. The only lucid thought that surfaced from the turmoil in my mind: *How can this be happening?*

Kids screamed. Panicked crew rushed to the starboard side of the ship. Juliet stood next to me, clutching my arm as she stared straight ahead, crying repeatedly, "Mommy…, Mommy…, Mommy…."

I looked down, and bending over her, I grasped her firmly. "It's OK honey, we're going to be OK." Trying to calm us both, I had to shout over the din around us. I saw a passenger standing nearby, one of the older girls that Juliet was fond of. I grabbed her by the arm. "Can you take Juliet? Juliet, go with Cheryl and stand by the wheel. It's safer there—Mom has to go help Tim now."

I straightened up and looked around the deck for Tim and the crew. I saw him dash over to where the boom had fallen across the port side of the deck. *Oh shit! He's looking for people trapped underneath it!* I sprinted forward to help him, catching my shin on the shrouds that now stretched across the width of the deck. I toppled over, breaking my fall with my wrists; I barely even noticed.

When Tim saw me, he yelled at once, "Chris, I need you back at the wheel!"

I nodded my head and spun back toward the helm. The *Zodiac*'s man-overboard and fire-drill protocols flashed though my brain. *Manifest! We need a manifest!* I called out to one of the deckhands to bring me the clipboard with the passenger and crew roster. I hurried to the helm and did what I could to account for all of the people onboard.

Tim rushed by me as he went for an extra emergency knife. He pointed toward the three remaining sails and shouted, "Chris—lose those sails now! We're getting blown onto the shore and I can't turn on the engine. *Hurry!*"

I yelled for all available hands to follow me forward. "We gotta bring everything down—as fast as we can!" My words were muffled by the wind and flapping sails as I made my way up the deck. I looked over my shoulder and saw the shore of Lummi Island looming much closer than I expected. The crew responded promptly and both the headsails tumbled down in unison. I left them to lower the foresail and ran back to the quarterdeck, this time taking care to jump over the cables strewn across deck.

With passengers and crew accounted for, I quickly tended to two with minor injuries: one girl had bruised her elbow while scrambling out of harm's way and an elderly volunteer had been pinned underneath the rigid-inflatable tender. I called to the school's teacher to distribute life jackets to those who had not already donned them. Juliet looked frightened and begged for me to stay with her, but the older kids hugged her and gave her distractions, allowing me to return to all the immediate demands, including the crew at the foresail.

I got back to mid-ship and saw three of my deckhands struggling with the sail. "What's going on? Why hasn't it come down?"

"The rookie let the goddamned peak halyard drop and the goose-neck came free from the mast!" Worley panted.

"*Christ!* We can't get it to come down!" yelled Ian.

I shielded my eyes and looked up at the gaff boom. It had detached from the mast and swung dangerously free. Without the gaff jaws secure around the vertical mast, there was no easy way to bring it down. My gaze continued up the mast, beyond the dangling gaff and luffing sail. I caught my breath and winced at what I saw. There above us—seventy-five feet in the air—hung the heavy steel mast cap from the main topmast. It remained attached to the fore-stay cable and dangled haphazardly from the top of the foremast. The twenty-foot cable swung it from side to side like a gigantic pendulum. I mutely pointed up at the foremast to warn my crew. They looked up in unison and collectively groaned. Worley said, "Watch yer heads, boys an' girls."

We pulled the gaff boom back down by tugging on the edges of the sail. The resistance made it difficult, but at last we were able to grab the boom and lower it toward the decks.

Breathing a sigh of relief as we laid the gaff boom on the deck, I gasped out, "No offense you guys—I love ya and all—but I was thinking the entire time, if that damn thing comes down, please don't let it be on *my* head!" I was grateful for my crew's chuckles.

With all joking aside, I barked, "Passengers and crew—everyone: remain aft of the salon deckhouse." It was just a matter of time, in my opinion, before that masthead cap came crashing to the deck below. Returning to the quarterdeck, I looked around for Tim. It was strange to see no one at the wheel. *But then, with no steerage, what was the point?*

I found Tim and three of my crewmembers hanging over the lifelines of the port rail. They hacked away at the myriad of cables that were strung over the rail. I climbed across the debris and looked into the water. Floating alongside the *Zodiac*, like entrails, were her shrouds and halyards. The tangled mess acted like an umbilical cord, tethering what remained of her main mast to the ship. *Zodiac*'s proud mainsail, which we routinely touted as "the largest working mainsail in North America," now hung in the water like a monstrous sea-anchor. I watched Tim cut through the lines and realized what was happening. We were being pulled into the shore and with literally miles of cable and line beneath her hull, we could not even attempt to turn on *Zodiac*'s engine. If we did, the five-foot-diameter propeller would suck in the wreckage and freeze the mechanism. We were dead in the water.

Tim looked up; as he noticed me he said, "Oh good, I need you to monitor Traffic and stay on one-six for the Coast Guard. I made the call ten minutes ago and they've dispatched a cutter, but I think one of their rescue boats will be here sooner."

I hesitated. "Don't you need me here?" I felt disappointed that I couldn't take part in the action.

"Do as I say," he replied and returned to his job.

I walked back to the scuttle and positioned myself in front of the radios. I didn't like the prospect of standing around. For one thing, the adrenaline was taking its toll, and the longer I remained in one place, the more I began to shake. Soon, I spent almost all of my concentration trying to stop my arms and legs from trembling. The passengers huddled around the quarterdeck. I turned to address them as cheerfully as possible. "Hey, gang, the Coasties are on their way. Everything is going to be A-OK," I said. The kids surrounded me and fired questions all at once.

"Are we going to get towed back to Bellingham?"

"Will they send a rescue helicopter?"

"Can I go below and get my camera?"

"Hey! Listen up!" I yelled. "Quiet down, everybody." The entire group hushed. I looked around me, at the faces of the kids and their chaperones. "First off, kudos to all of you guys, you've remained calm and you've followed orders; you've stayed out of the way, and… well, I'm super impressed with the whole bunch of you." I meant it.

One of the chaperones called out, "Three cheers for Captain Tim and the crew of *Zodiac*!"

"Hip-hip hurrah! Hip-hip hurrah! Hip-hip hurrah!" they all cried out.

I allowed the kids to go below in groups of three, but not to leave anyone alone. "You all got it, right?" I confirmed. I placed the rookie in charge of the below-deck forays and stayed at the radios to monitor channels five-alpha and sixteen. The chatter on the radios was abuzz with the news of a tall ship being dismasted. Tugs, fishing vessels and recreational power boats were calling in to Traffic to report that Schooner *Zodiac* had lost its mast off of Lummi Island. Soon enough over a dozen small boats were standing off our beam, taking video and offering possible assistance.

Tim came over to me, wiping the sweat off of his forehead. He whispered, "Sheesh, this is all we need!"

"What do you want me to do?" I asked.

"Tell 'em not to leave a damn wake," he said, shaking his head as he turned to go below.

"What's going on?" I asked, puzzled that he was heading down the companionway.

He smiled sardonically and quipped, "I gotta go pee in a cup."

Huh? I thought. *Oh, right… the Coast Guard!* I suddenly remembered that the protocol for any maritime accident over a certain amount of damages would require the captain, and very likely the crew, to submit to a drug and alcohol test. I attempted to take a deep breath but found it difficult to fill my lungs properly. I had to force the air in several times before I could feel my heart rate begin to slow down. For the first time since the dismasting, I stopped everything else I was doing and inspected the damage.

Gigantic splinters of wood, some of them two or three feet long, were strewn across the deck. The remnant of the mast resembled a tree split by lightning—woodchips and dust covered everything. The starboard shrouds and rigging had been swept across the deck, dissecting the ship in their wake; the inch-thick cables were stretched out at knee-height. I involuntarily flinched as I imagined the fate of anyone so unfortunate as to have been caught underneath their path.

Right then it struck me hard, *how had we been so lucky to escape any casualties?* I recalled the groups of kids who'd been lolling on the salon roof where the rig and shrouds now lay. The boom now rested on a deck box and caprail where at least two teenagers were sitting minutes before. My gaze followed the length of the boom as it stretched down the rail and hung out over the water; it had missed crushing the helm station by a mere eight feet. "What are the odds?" I wondered.

The images of what might have been were too unnerving and I began to feel lightheaded. At that precise moment a familiar voice cut through the buzz on channel sixteen. "*Zodiac, Zodiac, Zodiac.* This is *Kwaietek* on one-six."

For a few seconds I couldn't place where the voice was coming from. I recognized it as Jeffery's immediately, but my mind refused to connect it to our ship's radio. Finally, I reached for the mic and responded, "*Kwaietek,* this is *Zodiac.* Switch to six-eight. Over." I switched the channel on the radio and waited for my husband's voice.

"Hey, you, what's going on over there?" Jeffery asked.

The sound of Jeff's voice chipped away at my composure. "Oh, nothin' much really—we just got dismasted, that's all." I tried my best to make light of the situation.

"*Jesus Christ*—it's true then!" he said. I could hear the tone of his voice change to alarm.

"Yep. True enough."

"Holy shit."

I overheard Barney and Rory in the background, anxiously grilling him for details. After a few more of his questions were answered, Jeffery said, "Look, we're about forty minutes from your position. I'm going to try and get Customs to allow us to divert and assist. Let me see if I can get 'em on the phone and I'll call you right back."

271

"OK. But use the cell phone. Tim wants me to monitor one-six and Traffic."

"Copy that," Jeff said, and then added, "Hey, is everybody doin' OK?"

"Affirmative. All is good. I'll talk to you shortly. *Zodiac* back to one-six." I hung up the mic. I didn't dare allow myself to be his wife at that moment. I needed to keep my emotions at bay for as long as I could. It was difficult enough to witness the fear in Juliet's face and yet leave her in the care of others while I carried out my job.

"...*Zodiac.*" I heard the tail-end of the hail on the radio and I quickly grabbed the mic once more.

"Yes! *Er...*" I responded, grappling for the correct lingo. "Uh... Coast Guard. This is the *Zodiac.*"

"Schooner *Zodiac,* this is U.S. Coast Guard. We have two response vessels approaching your starboard beam. Is your ship able to receive them if we raft-to?" said a male voice.

"Affirmative, Coast Guard. We'll stand by to secure you on our starboard rail. *Zodiac* out," I replied.

I replaced the microphone and went in search of Tim. I found him supervising the crew as they gathered up the flotsam. One of the tenders had been salvaged and two crewmembers were using it to retrieve pieces of the rig and mast. They had abandoned efforts to cut the rig free, as the cables were too thick for any tools onboard. Instead, they attempted to consolidate the wreckage and secure it as best they could alongside the ship's hull. I walked over to Tim and told him the Coasties were about a mile off and would raft to our starboard side.

Tim paused and deliberated. Finally he said, "I've got to get this mess sucked up tight to the rail here, Chris. Their big cutter will be here within the hour for a tow. If I can't get the mast and spreaders secured, we'll be in trouble if we get hit with heavy seas on the way back." He looked over the starboard side to where the two bright red response vessels approached, and said, "This is gonna have to be on you for now. You think you can handle it?"

I nodded.

Tim continued, "Work with them and give 'em whatever they need but *only* what they ask for."

"Understood."

I walked across the deck and pondered Tim's orders. It dawned on me that all of us were under the microscope now. The instant that our mast hit the water, everything we would do from that point forward and, in fact, many things we had done previously would be scrutinized. I realized that as events unfolded, it would become imperative to be honest and yet refrain from volunteering my opinion or any theories. It also occurred to me that *Zodiac* was a certified charter vessel and the largest wooden schooner on the west coast. She was considered the flagship of the northwest windjammer fleet; of course the news would spread.

The twin outboard engines on the Coasties' inflatable *go-fast* boats revved into high reverse, causing the water to roil all around the transoms. They slid alongside our hull, and one of the young men tossed his bowline up, which I made fast to our stanchion post. He fastened his stern line and walked atop the inflatable chambers of the boat, cinching their vessel closer to our hull. I stood by the gangway ready to meet their senior officer.

Three uniformed young men climbed aboard *Zodiac* followed by a brown-haired woman in her mid-twenties. All of them were outfitted exactly the same: navy blue pants and shirts with bright-orange life vests emblazoned with *USCG*. I turned toward the young men, anticipating an introduction.

"Are you first mate?" asked the female officer using a very authoritative voice.

"Yes, ma'am, I am," I replied, and immediately felt chagrined for overlooking her as the ranking officer.

She either didn't notice my blunder or she chose to brush it off. "My name is Lieutenant Spencer. How are you all faring?" I told her all were fine, and she proceeded to confirm my full name, my rank and the name and spelling of the ship's captain. She noted my responses in a black notebook full of checklists and little boxes. I guided the four of them back to the quarterdeck and handed over the trip manifest. Two of the officers remained with the passengers to conduct a more comprehensive triage of injuries. The lieutenant asked me to direct her toward the captain. Pointing toward Tim at the aft portside rail, I explained our decision to keep him on the task of battening down the fallen rig.

"I'll just need a few minutes of his time," she stated. "I can work my way over to him and keep out of his way."

As the officer left to find Tim, I went below and filled up my water bottle. Then I sat down on the salon roof and drained the entire bottle. I couldn't remember when I'd ever felt so parched. My cell phone rang again, rousting me from my brief respite. Jeff was calling back. I answered it with quivering hands.

"Hey there, listen—Customs just gave us clearance to alter course for *Zodiac*. We can be over to you guys in about thirty minutes," he said, and then added, "Do you think you'll want to offload any of your passengers?"

I looked skyward as he spoke. My fears about the masthead cap swinging above our heads had not abated. I looked down again and made a swift appraisal of the deck. Broken, twisted pieces of equipment and rigging were strewn haphazardly around me. Tangled piles of rope, knotted and kinked, lay about the usually fastidious deck. I became overwhelmed as I struggled to make order out of the chaos. Everywhere I looked I saw potential hazards. With a sigh, I answered. "Yeah. I think we'll need to get everyone off of the ship."

When Jeffery hung up, I went in search of Lieutenant Spencer. She had finished her conversation with the captain and spoke into her handheld radio with Coast Guard Sector Seattle. After she'd completed her transmission, I requested permission to transfer our passengers to safety. The lieutenant disagreed, preferring to transport just the injured in their rescue boats and leave the others on board. She said that she believed the ship was sufficiently stabilized to handle the ride back with all passengers.

Lieutenant Spencer reached for her handheld in preparation to inform their headquarters and I tapped her on the shoulder, pointing to the top of the foremast. She paused momentarily and then said into her radio, "Stand by just a minute." She stared at the masthead cap for several more seconds and then turned to face me.

"How far away is that vessel that you mentioned?"

"They're no further away than fifteen or twenty minutes now," I replied.

"And they have a licensed captain on board?"

"Yeah, as a matter of fact, they've got two captains onboard."

"Can you hail them and get them to come in?"

"I can," I said, knowing that my husband was already on his way regardless of whether the Coast Guard granted him permission.

She informed Sector Seattle of the change in plans and I returned to the quarterdeck to radio *Kwaietek*. Next, I needed to inform our passengers of the news.

We made preparations to disembark our passengers. All luggage would remain on board to be retrieved later. Kids and adults were allowed below to fetch their identification or wallets. The Coasties finalized their inspection and crossed items off the lists in their little black books. I opted to stay near the kids for the remaining time, holding Juliet's hand as I addressed the group. We joked and laughed and talked about the amazing stories they'd be able to share with family and friends for years to come. Soon I heard the welcome sound of a slow-turning engine and looked up.

My heart started to race and I felt my throat tighten. I scanned the horizon in search of *Kwaietek*.

She appeared, cutting through the waves like a furrow. The translucent smoke rings that puffed from her stack expanded and evaporated in the pale blue sky. I felt butterflies in my stomach and found myself smiling widely. Juliet caught sight of *Kwaietek* at the same time and jumped up and down with excitement. The stately old forestry boat circled behind the schooner and came alongside. I fought down a sob that suddenly welled in my throat and drew a steady breath to keep it from escaping. Barney's smiling, bearded face poked out of *Kwaietek*'s wheelhouse, and I saw Rory appear from the fantail to throw a stern line. Jeffery stepped out of the doorway, and bent down to speak with the Coast Guard officer. He waved when he looked up and saw me. I couldn't contain the tears that ran down my face and quickly wiped them away, grateful for the polarized aviators that I wore.

It struck me then—my two worlds had collided in these surreal circumstances. I watched my long-awaited for home pull alongside what had become my *de facto* home for the past two years. Two beloved ships, meeting at last, albeit not in the way I had envisioned.

Tim took a short break to watch them arrive. He walked over to the rail and stood beside me, shouting over to the guys, "Where ya been? You missed all the fun!"

"Hey Timmy!" Barney yelled, "Did you know that you're a sloop now?"

Their banter helped to stabilize my topsy-turvy emotions and allowed me a few minutes to regroup. I retrieved the clipboard with the manifest and, clearing my throat, I summoned the chaperones to me.

It was determined that the passengers would first climb down *Zodiac*'s gangway and then on to the inflatable Coast Guard boats. The officers posted themselves strategically on their pontoons and assisted the kids with the traverse. One by one the passengers, including Juliet, stepped up to my position at the gangway. One by one, they gave me their name and I checked them off of the manifest. I smiled and teased them as they passed by me and wished everyone a safe ride back; I thanked them for their bravery. It hurt to see them leave. Some of the kids had picked up souvenirs along their path from the quarterdeck. I noticed fragments of rope: what might have been once a gantline or halyard were now keepsakes to be treasured as a token of our fateful day.

At last, Juliet filed past me. She looked so small in the puffy orange life jacket. I could see the conflict in her face, desperately wanting to be with her father on our new boat but hating to leave her mom behind. I felt the rise of unchecked emotions build again—not daring to trust my voice, I opted to kiss her on her forehead as I helped her down toward the young officer. He assisted her onto the inflatable chambers of the rescue boat and showed her where to walk. She turned briefly before ducking into the cockpit. "I love you, Mom!"

I summoned all my willpower and called back, "You too, babe!" I waved and she disappeared into the rescue boat.

The lieutenant checked Barney's credentials before handing the lines up to Rory and Jeffery. I watched my husband, my daughter, my friends and my former passengers motor away from us on what was now my new home.

The Coast Guard officers finished their reports and prepared to cast off as well. The lieutenant called up to me, "The cutter *Terrapin* is only two miles off. You guys will be on your way back to Bellingham before you know it!"

I thanked them as they pulled away from our ship; both their vessels rose onto a plane within seconds as they sped away. We were alone. I stood next to *Zodiac*'s wheel, holding onto her spokes out of habit. The familiar sensation of wrapping my fingers around the worn Turkshead on the kingspoke gave me comfort right then. Without the passengers to attend to, radio chatter to monitor or a workable helm for me to steer, I felt lost. The rest of the crew rushed around me to complete their jobs before the cutter arrived.

At that moment, Tim walked up to me, wiping his hands across the front of his shirt. I noticed for the first time that his usually immaculate white tee shirt was covered with sweat and grime and mud.

"You want to help me drag that jib sail back up and put some gaskets around it before they hook on their towline?"

"Hell yes."

We clambered over the obstacles en route to the foredeck. When we reached the bow, I leaned over the bulwarks. I could see my old jib, floating dejectedly, half submerged in the water. I hated seeing it hanging there. I climbed over the breastwork and Tim followed me out onto the bow-netting.

For the past two years, my station had been back on the quarterdeck with the captain. And yet here we now were—both of us all the way forward on the bowsprit. For a few minutes, it felt like we were just two deckhands completing a task on a routine cruise. We hauled the sodden jib sail on to the bow sprit and furled it in place. Once the gaskets were tied, I reached above my head to grab the fore-stay: the thick cable that ran from the top of the foremast to the tip of the bowsprit. The maneuver usually consisted of pulling oneself up by holding onto the stay. I grabbed for the cable and as I transferred my weight, the massive stay flexed and came down to my shoulders. Tim and I exchanged glances.

"Hmmm, not much support there anymore, huh?" he said with a sidelong glance.

I stared at our remaining mast. Other than by sheer gravity, our foremast was indeed not very well supported. *Damn.* I cautiously grabbed onto the bowsprit and made my way back onboard.

The *Terrapin*, an eighty-five-foot Coast Guard cutter, motored toward us. Tim went below for a jacket to throw over his dirty shirt, then he grabbed a hand-held radio off the wall in preparation for hooking up the *Terrapin*'s tow line. I followed him to the charthouse. Before he left, he asked me to pull the log books from the past two years and scan through them, page by page. "I want you to go through each one and look for *any* entry of a rig check—anything that refers to the rig at all. I want you to highlight those entries." He paused briefly, "Don't correct anything or remove anything—just use a highlighter. These are our official ship's logs and after today, I can guarantee you, there will be a lot of eyes poring over them."

The ride back into Bellingham Bay normally took about three hours. On this day, our ride lasted over seven and a half grueling hours. By the time the *Terrapin*'s 300 foot tow-line had been fastened to the Samson posts at *Zodiac*'s bow, winds began to whip up Rosario Strait. I switched our radio onto the marine weather broadcast and learned that Bellingham Bay reported sustained winds of 25-30 knots. We did our best to reinforce the debris tied down to our hull, but there was nothing we could do to prevent the steel spreaders from slamming into the planks as the waves struck the *Zodiac* broadside.

Tim stationed me at the helm for the first watch and then went below to take a short rest. As the *Terrapin* gained momentum, I felt the *Zodiac* straighten out in her course, the initial yaw subsided and my task became easier. I pointed our bowsprit directly at the *Terrapin's* mast. It felt strange to stand at the controls, yet have absolutely no influence over our propulsion. Neither wind nor mechanics determined our speed or course; just the tenuous cable connecting us to the cutter ahead. I remained at the helm, alone on deck save for Ian, who seemed aimless without a load of people to cook for. He sat in silence on one of the deck boxes forward of the scuttle with a can of soda perched on one knee.

After a couple of hours, we rounded Eliza Island. The remaining light slowly faded into the west. As I turned the wheel to make our gradual sweep into Bellingham Bay, six-foot waves smacked *Zodiac's* starboard beam. I glanced up at our foremast and wondered just how secure it really was. The waves continued to build as we committed our beam to the full force of the elements. I felt the ship rock side to side. *Boom! Boom! Boom!* The *Zodiac's* frame shuddered as the giant cross-trees slammed into the planks of her hull. I drew a long, slow breath and concentrated on my course. There wasn't anything I could do about the waves, so I stuck to the task at hand.

Tim came up the aft scuttle, his foul weather pants on and he pulled his coat over his wool sweater as he emerged. He paused at the top step and looked across the bay. The intermittent banging of the mast's spreaders against the hull had summoned him, but he, like me, could do nothing about it. I sensed his unease with our current situation.

Tim pulled the mic from its hanger and hailed *Terrapin*. He leaned down into the scuttle as he spoke, so that the wind would not interfere with their conversation. I didn't need to hear what they were saying to guess that Tim had requested a change in our speed. Never one to let a situation dictate his course of action, I figured that he'd make some sort of change in the variables. Sure enough, the tension on the towline was reduced and *Zodiac* settled a little bit. The booming noise of the steel spreaders on the hull lessened slightly.

"Is there a risk that we'll be holed if this gets any worse?" I asked him.

Tim walked over to the port side and looked over the rail, his hands jammed down into the pockets of his jacket. He stood there for some time and studied the condition of the wreckage. I switched sides on the helm, so that I could steer it from the port side with one hand on the spoke. I stretched over to stare at the flotsam. *Zodiac*'s wake streamed over the exposed mast trunk and whirled around the mangled bits of sail bound next to the ship. Seafoam bubbled inside of the mass of cables as the water churned though the entire mess. Scanning along the topsides, I spotted a patch of raw wood on her white hull where the edges of the crosstrees banged forcefully into her planks with every crash of the waves.

Tim stepped back and took the wheel from me. "She's taking a real beating, but those are oak planks on top of solid oak frames. They can handle it… I think." He smiled and winked. "You've been up here for long enough now. Go down and warm up. I'll take it from here."

I hesitated to leave and offered to stand watch with him. "Nah, head below and grab something to eat. It's going to be a long night." He searched through his foul weather gear and fished out his cell phone. Placing it on the gear box, he smiled and added, "I need to call Betsy and let her know what's happened before she hears about it from somebody else."

"Ah, wise move," I said. The recent turn of events hit me with renewed force. I was relieved that my husband had been on the scene. He had visual confirmation that we'd survived and were coping with our situation. I imagined how anxious Tim's wife would feel upon learning what had occurred. Then another thought hit me. *Oh no! The Skipper was waiting at dock for our return!* Tim's 86-year-old father was the captain onboard *Zodiac* before Tim took the helm fourteen years ago. He and his son had restored the old schooner to her current condition. This news would hit Karl very hard. I could imagine the old skipper on his bench at our dock—awaiting the sight of *Zodiac*'s masts in the distance. They wouldn't be piercing the skyline on this evening.

I had the sudden urge to call my own family. I rang Jeffery's cell and Juliet's voice cracked through the receiver. "Hey Mommy! Where are you guys? Are you here yet?"

"No honey, we won't be back for a while yet. We're moving really slowly because of the stuff that's dragging in the water."

"Oh."

"Don't worry, we'll get back before midnight and I promise that you can come over to *Zodiac* when we're back—alright?"

"Yeah. Is *Zodiac* doing OK?"

"She's hangin' in there. She'll be happy to be back at her dock, I'm sure of that."

"Are you scared?"

"Hmmm, I'm better now that I know you and Dad got back OK. Did all the school kids like our new boat?" I asked her.

"Yeah—boy, we were rocking back and forth all the way home. *Kwaietek* is a tipsy boat in big waves!" She said. "But they were all having fun. Dad had to chase some of them out of the engine room, but they liked the ride home."

"Good news. Hey, is Dad there? Would you put him on for me?"

"Yep—be careful, Mom. I love you lots!" She said and then screamed for her father so loudly that I held the phone away from my ear.

Jeff's voice came on the line. "Hey, you. How are things going out there? It's getting pretty windy over on this end of the bay."

"Yeah, not enjoying it very much." I replied. "Hey, by any chance was Skipper on the dock when you guys pulled in?"

"Boy, was he ever." Jeff answered. "He'd heard from one of the guys in the terminal that *Zodiac* had been dismasted. He was in a pretty bad state- worried about Tim."

"Shit. Is he OK now do you think?"

"He's doing just fine. He's sitting here in the galley of our boat with a shot of rum as a matter of fact."

I was relieved to hear this news. "I'll tell Tim that Karl is with you guys—that's one less thing for him to worry about."

Jeff laughed, "It's actually a good thing that *Kwaietek* is here to distract him. He's really enjoyed looking around the boat. He's been poking around the engine and that old boiler since we brought him down. I've got Barney and Rory in the galley keeping him company. He'll be alright."

I sighed and then asked him about their trip back to port with all of the kids. Jeffery relayed that the weather in Bellingham Bay had turned pretty rough by the time they motored in. "Jeez, I had kids and chaperones spread all over the damn boat when the waves picked up," he said. "It took a while to corral them all into the deckhouse so I didn't have to worry about losing anybody over the side. I tell ya this little boat may have been built for seven rangers, a cook and a captain—but definitely not for nineteen kids and a handful of adults!" He went on, "She's a bit of a roller unless you can head into the waves or take them on the quarter... Barney was at the wheel as we made a big turn and she rolled over about 15 degrees. When we finished the turn, she started riding pretty nicely with a following sea... and so Barney pipes up with, 'This old girl sure is ass-friendly!' I can only imagine how the teacher felt about that!"

I laughed. "Well, it will definitely be a trip that they will talk about for school reunions to come."

"Something else... "Jeff said, "Those guys from U.S. Customs were great. They met us down on dock and took a head count of the kids, then came aboard, looked around and 'slam-bam-thank-you-ma'am,' that was that. I've never heard of it being so easy. I guess rescuing a boat-load of school kids off a damaged vessel gives you bonus points with the Customs' officials!"

The sound of Jeff's voice acted as a salve on my raw nerves. I still had a rough few hours in front of me and relished the few minutes I had on the phone with him "I'll call ya when we get to the Post Point buoy," I said and we signed off.

The rest of the crew had gathered around the galley table. Several of them slept in their seats. One or two others quietly chatted over their dinner. I grabbed a plate and took a small helping of Ian's leftovers. I sat down next to a snoring deckhand and barely lifted the fork to my mouth when I heard my name being yelled from the aft scuttle. I slid back the plate and ran back through the salon. I peered up the companionway into the darkness and called out, "Hey Tim- whaddaya need?"

From the blackness on deck I heard Tim's disconnected voice, "C'mere and take the wheel—they're hailing me."

I climbed the stairs and immediately wished I'd grabbed my coat that I left slung on the back of my chair. There was no chance to go grab it right then; Tim needed to answer the hail and I needed to take the wheel. I gritted my teeth and braced myself against the wind.

Tim ducked into the scuttle and responded to the Coasties' hail. I shivered in the dark and kept *Zodiac* on course. Suddenly out of the roar of the wind and the banging of the spreaders alongside came a thunderous crash.

I jumped and crouched down beside the wheel. Tim's head appeared from the scuttle, as he searched for the cause of the huge noise. Seconds later deckhands came running from below.

"Stay down!" Tim commanded. "Nobody move!"

He turned back to me, "Did you see anything?"

"No," and then it occurred to me. I replayed the scene from earlier that day. *The masthead cap!* "Tim! Look up—is the cap still swinging loose?"

Tim stepped up on deck and stared into the night. "I can't see from here. I'll go check."

He disappeared into the shadows. Whatever made that noise might happen again. I began to imagine all sorts of heavy objects raining down from above. My panic subsided as I heard Tim's footsteps returning to the quarterdeck.

"You called it. That steel cap just landed on the foredeck—it missed the deckhouse by inches. I think everything else is stable for now."

"Good lord. What else is going to happen tonight?"

"Good question."

Tim asked me to keep the wheel long enough to go to the head and grab a cup of coffee. When he came back on deck, he handed me my coat. "Why the hell aren't you wearing this?" he asked as he tossed it toward me.

By midnight, the *Terrapin* had guided us to our resting spot—about three-hundred feet from our dock. It seemed to me that the lights of Fairhaven's houses and streets had never looked more inviting or familiar. We dropped our anchor and waved the *Terrapin* off as she motored over to her own moorage. After we hung our anchor light and switched off the radios, we collapsed as a group in the galley. Jordan walked over to the cupboard where we stashed our liquor; as he reached for the bottle Tim said, "Hold off on that, please."

"You're kidding, right? Man, if ever we deserved a drink, this would be the night... wouldn't it?"

Tim smiled as he pulled off his wool sweater. "You've never said a truer word, but we aren't finished yet. And until we are, *no*body drinks." He slapped Jordan on the shoulder, and added, "Then I get the bottle first!"

Soon enough, his intuition proved spot-on. We heard a voice from the water calling "Ahoy *Zodiac*!"

Crewmembers filed up on deck and observed a small tender that held three new Coast Guard officials, waiting for permission to board. Several deckhands helped them come aboard and showed them to our charthouse.

For over an hour we convened with the officials individually and recounted our experiences for the record. After thorough interviews and a deck inspection, the Coasties were satisfied. Sometime shortly after 1 AM, they disembarked. They thanked and congratulated us for having carried off the crisis with so few casualties, then motored back to shore.

The crew stood around on deck in a circle, looking and feeling tired. Tim came up from below with the bottle of rum and a handful of shot glasses. He pulled up a chunk of the splintered mast, rolled it over onto its side and sat down with a heavy sigh. "OK gang. *Now* we are officially finished with our day. And I gotta say, outstanding job—everyone. You all did great under pressure and I've been impressed with everybody's performance." He poured out some shots on the deck and then looked over where I was sitting. He handed me over a glass and said, "And you—well done."

I tossed back my rum and smiled.

Chapter 30

Salvage Operations

Alackluster haze enveloped Fairhaven the next morning. The crippled *Zodiac* lay at anchor off shore, unable to reach her moorings due to the cumbersome wreckage that clung to her side.

The handful of deckhands who still remained awoke late. The neglected seven AM wake up call, which normally heralded our safety meeting, spoke volumes about the condition of the *Zodiac* and her crew on this day. We sat together at the galley mess and drank our coffee quietly. Ian cooked up a small breakfast of bacon and eggs, but nobody had much of an appetite. At last, Tim rose from his chair and hung his coffee mug on the hook overhead. With a sigh that conveyed both physical and mental weariness, he announced, "Alright gang, let's go see what's in store for us."

We stood and grabbed our coats. I detoured into my stateroom and grabbed the camera from my shelf; it seemed logical to document the condition of the ship for our upcoming inspections, but I also wanted to record these images for myself. Perhaps someday it would be worth reflecting upon. I certainly didn't want to reflect on anything just then.

As I stepped out of the charthouse, I blinked and forced my eyes to adjust to the blank whiteness that surrounded the ship. I gazed around the shambles—it looked much worse in the stark reality of day. What used to be such an orderly deck now looked like a disaster zone. *Zodiac* reminded me of a wounded animal: motionless, quietly beseeching comfort. Her eerie silence unnerved me. The only sounds were the quiet mumbling of crewmembers as they surveyed the damaged vessel.

I stood by myself in the midst of the rubble and attempted to grow accustomed to the new settings. Try as I might, it was difficult to focus on one simple task; there seemed to be an endless amount of work that needed attention. Tim stood next to the fallen boom, his hands on his hips as he assessed the destruction. I could tell he was pondering the same thought. *Where to begin?*

From somewhere off of our starboard beam, I could make out the disconnected sound of Juliet's voice, followed by Jeffery's familiar laughter. I walked over to the rail and looked out in the direction of shore. A little rowboat appeared from out of the mist. Rory and Jeff rowed in unison as Juliet sat between them, holding a pink cardboard box of doughnuts. She looked up at the railing and waved, catching the box before it slid off of her lap. "Hey Mom!" She called, "We brought some breakfast for you guys!"

Two of the deckhands lowered the ladder and helped bring the tender alongside. Juliet stepped up and handed me the box. She looked around the deck and declared, "This place is a mess! I'm going below." And with that she took the pastry box out of my hands and disappeared into the charthouse.

Jeff stepped onto the gangway and handed me a latte. "I don't know how hot this is anymore." He reached around my waist. "I cannot even tell you how difficult it was to sleep on *Kwaietek* alone, knowing you were just right out here."

I pressed my face into his shoulders and smiled. His sweater was warm and smelled faintly of our old house in Seattle. I didn't fully realize until that moment how much I'd missed him.

A voice called from below, "Hey! Do you two lovebirds want to move out of the gangway so I can come aboard?"

I looked past Jeff's shoulder and saw Rory standing in the tender with one hand on the ladder, the other holding an oversized pair of wire cutters. I pointed to the cutters in his hand and said, "You're a little late, you know. We already brought the shrouds down—as you can see for yourself."

Rory climbed on deck and chuckled, "To hell with that, I'm collecting scrap metal—I could make a killing off of all this!"

We walked over to the group that assembled around Captain Tim. They were staring over the side of the vessel and discussing how to free the remaining mast from the fouled cable and sail. Rory placed the giant wire cutters on the scuttle, next to the boom. Tim glanced over and said, "Thanks for grabbing those; we're going to need 'em soon."

I left the guys to break into work teams and proceeded to photograph the deck. I snapped pictures and then carefully arranged the pieces of broken equipment or rigging into small piles, categorizing them as best I could. By noon, I'd managed to clear a path from the quarterdeck to midship. It lightened my mood, just a little bit, to put some order back to the chaos.

Several hours later, we broke for lunch. Jeff and Rory brought their lunch up on deck and sat down beside me. We began to chat about the last twenty-four hours, it was eerie to hear the story from their point of view. They related the radio chatter as other vessels had discussed *Zodiac's* dismasting. "It was tough hearing what you guys were going through—not being there to see it for ourselves," Rory said.

Jeff agreed, "Yeah, I'm just really glad that we were monitoring five-alpha when it happened."

Our conversation lapsed for a short period and we ate in silence, each pondering the events of yesterday. My eyes wandered around the deck and I noticed Tim back on the quarterdeck, standing alone with one of the damaged blocks in his hand. He seemed bent in thought.

I nodded toward the captain and asked Jeff if we should take him some lunch. "I know he's not in the mood to join the rest of us, but maybe we oughta grab him something to eat?"

Jeff watched Tim for a while. Finally he responded, "Nah, I wouldn't. My guess is that he doesn't have much of an appetite. The shock has probably worn off and he's realizing how much this is gonna cost—and what fixing her will entail." He paused for a moment. "There's a chance y'know that she may not be sailing for the next few years."

I raised my eyebrows in surprise. It hadn't occurred to me yet, the depth of this catastrophe. "Whoa. We—I mean—*he*, couldn't survive a year without revenue… not if he has to pay to replace and repair everything, too!" The enormity of what lay ahead took shape in my mind. His business that he'd poured everything into… *just gone*. Old feelings of loss and grief flooded back. I looked at Tim with renewed empathy.

We finished up our lunch and returned to the clean-up work. Once the guys cut the wire and cables free from the ship, Jeff and Rory climbed into the tender and pulled the waterlogged mast remnant away from the ship. They attached large fenders to each end of the fragment to prevent it from sinking to the bottom of the bay. I stood at the railing with the rest of the deckhands and watched as they slowly hauled the body of our main mast toward the shipyard's drydock. Tim brushed past me to head below deck. I wished that I had something reassuring to say, but knew him well enough to hold my tongue.

As dusk fell about us, we finished up our salvage work and motored *Zodiac* back to her dock. I was sore and achy like I hadn't been in a long time. The job hadn't been that strenuous, but it must have been the stress that wore on me. The rest of the crew had the same downtrodden look about them as well. It had been a long and taxing day for all of us. I sat down and twisted the bottle cap from my beer. I wanted nothing more than a hot shower and bed.

Jeffery squeezed in next to me and threw his arm around my shoulders. "So m'dear, have you had enough of all this? Are you ready to come see your new boat now?"

"Man, I completely forgot about *Kwaietek*!" There she sat, waiting for us at dock, just a few hundred yards away! All of the weariness vanished and I suddenly felt jittery about stepping aboard *Kwaietek* as her new owner.

I grabbed a few of my things and headed toward the gangway. As I made my way down the boarding steps I stopped to pat *Zodiac's* caprail and said, "Don't you worry girl—we'll be back tomorrow. You're not down and out yet. We got masts back in *Sugaree,* and we can get yours back as well."

Jeff turned to look over his shoulder as he walked in front of me—he smiled and I could hear him chuckle under his breath. "I love you, Chris Wallace," he said softly as we walked up the dock.

Chapter 31

Restoration

J eff walked forward and opened the double doors of *Kwaietek's* wheelhouse, and with an exaggerated bow, motioned for me to enter. As I stepped through the hatch, the raw, woody aroma of *Kwaietek* overwhelmed me. "She smells so good—and so different than the *Z*!"

"Isn't it weird how no two wooden boats smell the same?" Jeffery commented. He reached above his head and switched on the charthouse light. The cabin filled with a golden, warm glow. "Y'know, I think that they're just like people. Their environment and occupations—their 'genetics' play a big part in how they end up as they grow older." Then adding pragmatically, "She'll smell a little more like *Zodiac* once we've been onboard for a few weeks."

Jeff walked over to the companionway and grabbed my duffle bag; he pulled it after him as he climbed below. Once he'd reached the bottom of the companionway, he extended his hand. "Come on down, our bed's already made."

I took his hand and stepped down the ladder. The stairs were much steeper and narrower than *Zodiac's*. As I placed my last foot on the sole, I glanced around to see how *Kwaietek* looked from this perspective. Jeff's gear had been piled near the bunk in our stateroom and there were several plastic crates of tools and manuals stacked about the room, but it already felt like home to me. I paused in the doorway to stare about the forepeak cabin. I liked what I saw.

Jeff stood close behind me and placed his arms around my shoulders. He buried his face in my hair and whispered, "Welcome to your home, Chris Wallace."

I leaned back against him and sighed. "This is *so* very cool indeed."

"Hey, Mom?" Juliet's excited voice reverberated down the passageway. "Come see my stateroom! I already know where I'm going to hang Woodsy the Owl!"

We walked aft into the passageway to peek inside Juliet's room. I looked at Jeffery and raised my eyebrows. "Oh, really? And who told you that you could bring that dead, stuffed bird onto the boat?"

"Dad did. He said we could hang Woodsy in my room—didn't you, Dad?" Juliet popped her head out of her doorway and looked at her father.

Trapped for the moment between his wife and daughter, Jeff shrugged his shoulders and smiled. He raised his hands in mock surrender and said, "I give up! I just figured she'd feel more at home if she could put something from the house up on her walls."

"Yeah, but that dusty old owl for gawdsake? I mean—*yccch!* How old is that thing? It's sort of disgusting."

"It is *not!*" Juliet exclaimed. "Dad promised me that I could have it if we moved onto a boat!"

I rolled my eyes and shrugged. "Well, whatever—but when that thing starts to mold because we live on the water… I'm not touching it."

"Wheeeehaw!" Came the squeal of delight from my daughter's stateroom.

"I presume that the mood has been somewhat dampened by our daughter?" Jeff inquired as I returned to our stateroom.

"Somewhat. Although, I am not exactly sure what you were hoping for… she is, after all, only a 2-inch bulkhead away from us." To demonstrate my point, I rapped my knuckle on the panel of our cabin. It was answered almost immediately by an inquisitive, *'Hullo?'* from Juliet's side of the wall.

"See what I mean?" I said.

"Crap," Jeffery said. "I see now that I'll be installing soundboard and some thick bookshelves within the week."

We spent our first night as a family in our new home, and aside from the unfamiliar creaks and systems' noises, I slept soundly. When we awoke the following morning, I called all of the kids—retelling our recent crisis over and over with every phone call. Once they were assured that none of us had been hurt, they expressed concern over *Zodiac's* well-being—especially Megan, who'd spent the most time onboard. I promised that I'd keep them informed of her status.

Jeff and the guys hadn't left me much to work with, but eventually we sat down to plates of scrambled eggs and sausage. "Here's to our first breakfast on *Kwaietek*—and to many more!" I toasted as we clinked our glasses of orange juice together.

During breakfast, Jeff laid out his ideas for some of the projects. "I've got big plans for the entire master head and stateroom. It's going to be really nice—by the time I tear up the sole and rebuild the bunks… I want to rip out that old cabinet and we can stick a nice spalted maple countertop across the side. I've got tiles already picked out for the shower. After that, I'm gonna move into the passageway and frame…"

"OK, OK—*stop*! One thing at a time. Remember, no living through another long remodel. *Please*."

Jeffery took the hint and diverted from the topic of future projects. We talked instead about what items from our old house we would bring onboard *Kwaietek*. I grew more enthusiastic as I remembered my favorite paintings and knick-knacks that could rejoin us. "Let's go over to the storage unit and pick through some of the boxes today!"

"*Uhm*, lets hold off on grabbing our stuff for a while—I'm going to start tearing into the forepeak as early as tomorrow. It's bound to be a little chaotic for a month or so."

Juliet stepped in to help plead my case and at last, we coerced a reluctant Jeffery into picking up a 'small' load from the storage unit. By lunchtime, we'd transferred over four dock-carts of our belongings onto *Kwaietek's* deck. As I piled the last bunch of Juliet's stuffed animals and blankets onto the deckhouse, I noticed my husband standing near the gangway, scratching his head. "How'd I get talked into this?"

"Come on—it's only our important stuff!"

He bent over and picked up my painting of Sasha. "This is something you can't live without?"

"Of course it is—I'm hanging it over our bunk right now." I replied and grabbed it out of his hands to carry below.

All evening long, I sifted through the boxes we'd carried onboard. I stowed my dishes and placed our photos on bulkheads. I found counter space for some of my favorite trinkets—like the jewelry box Jeff made me and the hourglass my father had turned for us. I then hung up our clothes. Jeffery merely shook his head and retired to our bunk with his book.

Unpacking my belongings felt a little bit like Christmas or reuniting with old friends. I was glad to see my personal treasures once more and to make them part of our new life.

I sliced open a box labeled *'Chris' stuff—valuables'* and pulled out one of the crystal awards from 2007. It read "National Winner, Women in Business Champion, Gracewinds Perinatal Services." I held it up to the light in our stateroom and admired the prism effect on the beveled edges. I sighed and wrapped the trophy back in its flannel cloth; it didn't belong on a boat.

For the next few weeks, we alternated between the two ships—I settled aboard *Kwaietek* and helped to repair the *Zodiac*. At times, it felt rather schizophrenic, and I found myself wielding tools to rip apart our stateroom floor as well as to construct a cover for the gaping mast-hole on deck.

Time sped by quickly and before we knew it, winter had arrived.

Chapter 32

Coping Techniques

November introduced itself with a chilly disposition. We were grateful for *Kwaietek's* little wood stove in the salon as snow began to fall. Fat, lazy flakes descended on the bay for a solid week—an uncommon occurrence in the Pacific Northwest. The marina began to resemble Dutch Harbor, Alaska as fishing vessels were concealed under blankets of white.

On the sixth day, snow was replaced by an icy north wind that hurtled down from the Fraser River Valley. *Kwaietek* shook in her moorings as the winds blew through the marina. Several boats had rammed into adjacent vessels as dock-lines broke under the stress.

Jeffery and I worked together in the forepeak, finishing the re-installation of our stateroom floor. Juliet huddled on the floor in the salon and tended the woodstove, a mug of hot chocolate by her feet. Our boat felt cozy and warm in contrast to the raging storm outside.

My cell buzzed from the charthouse and Juliet went to retrieve it. I stepped over to the companionway and listened to her side of the conversation; I concluded that it was Tim on the other end. "Mom, he wants to talk to you or Daddy," Juliet said and handed me down the phone.

"Hiya—its *moi*. What's…? " I began.

Tim didn't wait for me to finish my sentence. "I need you and Jeff down here now—the docks are coming apart."

"*Wha...?*"

"Right now—and call anyone else you can think of to get down here and help too."

"OK—yeah. We'll be right down."

"Thanks. I can't talk anymore." Tim abruptly signed off.

Jeff slid his headphones around his neck and asked, "Who was that?"

"That was Tim—the *Zodiac*'s in trouble... something about the docks are coming apart in Fairhaven." I rifled through our jackets in the passageway and pulled out my foul weather coat. "He needs us down there right away. Can you stop where you're at?"

"Done." Jeff said and tossed his skillsaw onto the sole. He brushed the sawdust off his workpants and went for his coat. "Grab life jackets for all of us—even the Bug's," he said as he climbed up the companionway. "Hey there Miss Bug, we've gotta head over to Fairhaven and help Tim. We need you to come with us, OK?"

"Dad! Why do I have to come? It's too cold out there!"

"Hon, we can't leave you alone in this storm. You'll have to come with us. You can wait inside the cruise terminal while we help Captain Tim, how 'bout that?"

"*Al*right."

We bundled up and made our way down the dock—fighting our way up the ramp against the bracing wind. Our fingers and faces were numb by the time we reached our VW bus. Jeffery tried to start the engine and I clumsily typed in the number of our friends, Jeff and Christine, (the 'other Jeff and Chris'). They agreed to meet us at the cruise terminal. We pulled out of our parking space and raced toward the *Zodiac*.

"Holy *shit!*" Jeff exclaimed, as we watched huge waves crash over the seawall and break into the terminal's parking lot. The wind's ferocity had grown much stronger by the time it reached the south side of the bay. With miles of fetch to build upon, the waves were enormous—frightening, even. I tried to open the car door and found it nearly impossible to push against the wind.

Jeffery stepped out to help Juliet from her seat. A wave breached the wall and doused him with salt water. "Let's get her inside!" He yelled over to me. "I'm going down to the dock and find out what's happening with Tim!"

I grabbed Juliet's arm and we pushed our way into the foyer of the terminal. Once we made it to the shelter of the brick building, the noise of the wind died substantially. "Man—this feels like the Oregon coast!" I said.

"I don't like this one bit!" Juliet replied.

We walked through the terminal doors and found Christine standing next to the giant Christmas tree in the lobby, chatting with one of the Alaska ferry employees. Juliet ran over to the pair and gave Christine a big hug. "Hey, Miss J!" Christine exclaimed. "Fancy meeting you guys here on this fine winter's day!"

"Hi there! I'm sure glad you guys could come help—it's flippin' intense on this side of town!" I said, and nodded a cursory greeting toward the ferry worker. I continued, "Is *your* Jeff out there already? *My* Jeff just went down to see what can be done."

"Yeah, *my* Jeff's trying to help push the fenders back in—I guess they keep popping out every time a new wave shows up. It's deadly down there right now. I didn't bring the right kind of apparel, so I'm staying in here where it's dry and warm."

"Well then, would you mind hanging out with Juliet while I go down to help the guys?" I asked.

"Sure! Miss J and I will keep each other company, won't we?"

Juliet nodded and then said, "Be really careful, Mom. It's not safe out there."

"I will—wait here and I'll be back as soon as I can."

I sensed a sort of dread and *deja vu* as I walked through the terminal doors. My mind replayed a similar incident—one that required me to leave my daughter in someone else's care while I dealt with a dismasting. *Why does it feel like I'm eternally handing off my kids?* An icy blast shook me back to the present crisis as I turned toward *Zodiac*'s gate.

I stared in awe at the scene below me. The ramp was covered in glazed ice and as I followed it to where it met the dock, I was shocked at how the entire structure moved—not merely moved, but undulated... The floating dock actually pitched, yawed and rolled in uneven rhythms. Snow covered over two-thirds of the concrete float, frozen into glacier-like sheets. I could make out four men in foul weather gear; they struggled to keep their balance as the dock threw them about with each swell. There were three other vessels beside the *Zodiac* that were tied alongside; they all lunged and rocked in separate tempos. *Zodiac* had the worst of it, as she was moored on the east side of the dock. The waves seemed to be arriving from a northeasterly direction and smashed her into the dock with each impact. Without her masts to balance her, she had no defenses against the pounding surf. Her deck was covered by a 2x4-framed structure, plastic-wrapped to keep the topsides dry for winter restoration. The weather cover worked against her now—its windage providing more surface area for the gale to assault.

I held onto the rails and carefully picked my way down the slippery ramp. When I set foot on the icy dock, I immediately fell sideways. "We're all going to die out here." I muttered. Searching, I spotted Jeffery alongside the other Jeff—yanking on frozen mooring lines. Further down the pier, I recognized Grant, one of the captains from the large whale watching vessel across from us. His six-foot, four-inch frame was almost completely covered in waves as he pulled on the lines of the *Victoria Star*. The dock surged once more and I grabbed for a piling to steady myself.

I heard the unmistakable sound of *Zodiac*'s 500-horsepower Caterpillar diesel grumble and splutter, then spring to life. I looked over toward the gangway—the only uncovered portion of her deck. Tim leaned out to check the engine's cooling water and then yelled down toward me. "We've got to get off the dock! Are you coming?"

I swallowed hard and paused—unable to reply. A dozen scenarios raced through my mind in a matter of seconds—only to be blotted out by the urgent sound of the captain's voice. "Chris! Now or never—I can't wait!"

I looked over at Jeffery—*my* Jeff—and shouted, "What should I do? What about Juliet?"

He turned toward me and yelled back. "The keys are still in the bus. If you want, I'll go with Tim and you take the kid back to *Kwaietek*—what do you say?"

I hesitated for a second or two longer and then called back. "OK—that's what we'll do!"

The 'other Jeff' helped to untie the lines; cutting several that were under too much strain to undo. I watched Tim slice a make-shift "window" into the plastic covering to be able to stick his head out. As the *Zodiac* began to inch away from her lunging dock, I realized that Juliet would certainly panic if she saw the boat leave—and not know if her parents were on it or not. I decided to return to the cruise terminal and stay with my daughter. It was time to be a mother—not the first mate.

I turned to climb the ramp, leaving the others to wrestle with their respective ships. I hoped that nobody would fall into the roiling water… I prayed that Jeffery and Tim would make it to safety. I fought off feelings of guilt for abandoning the *Z*, yet at the same time, was relieved that I could be with my little girl.

Juliet and Christine stood at the opposite end of the lobby with a small group of spectators next to the large plate glass windows of the cruise terminal. They were glued to the events unfolding on the dock. Christine called me over and I looked out the window—the *Zodiac* was already in trouble.

As dusk approached it became more difficult to make out what happened, but we could see *Zodiac*'s bowsprit heading straight for the 300 foot drydock located parallel to her moorage. The northeasterly winds had taken control of her bow. "Oh my *god!* She's going to collide!" yelled one of the spectators. I held my breath and watched *Zodiac* come within feet of the giant steel hull of the drydock. She corrected herself at the last minute and squeezed by, turning westward toward Post Point buoy. Juliet pressed her face against the glass and watched as the ship disappeared from our view.

Later that evening, we returned to our own dock on the other side of town. I appreciated the tall breakwater and the fact that our home was situated on the north side of the bay. It seemed relatively calm at the marina compared to the turmoil I'd just left behind. The '*other* Jeff and Chris' had offered us a room at their house for the night, but I wanted to be alone with Juliet and do my worrying in solitude.

We stepped aboard *Kwaietek* and immediately noticed how cold she felt. The woodstove had burned out as soon as we'd departed earlier that afternoon. Without her heat source, the entire boat had cooled down rapidly. My breath was visible as I informed Juliet that we were not sleeping on the boat tonight. She grabbed her pajamas and toothbrush and we walked back up to the car. We drove down the road a few miles and spotted a motel. I checked in at the front desk and Juliet ran ahead with the room key. She opened the door for me and I entered our little room; it wasn't fancy, but it was warm.

I lay next to Juliet that night as the winds howled around us. The big window in our room shook continuously. As my daughter slept, I stared out into the darkness. Somewhere out there—who knew where—Jeff and Tim were coping with the storm. I desperately wanted to talk to them and confirm that they were safe. We dialed both numbers all evening—neither phone was answered.

Juliet woke me up the next morning. Rays of sunlight streamed through the window. I blinked several times to confirm what I was seeing, more importantly, to confirm what I was *not* hearing: wind. There was no wind. "Wake up, Mom. The storm's over!"

"Wow. What time is it?" I asked, yawning.

"It's about 9:30. You were sleepy," she said. "Can we go get some breakfast?"

I sat up and rubbed my temples; I had a dull headache. "Yeah, OK. We'll grab our stuff and get something to eat on the way home." I was grateful for the warmth and protection of the motel—but it wasn't really the type of accommodations that made one want to stick around for long.

Juliet and I brought our breakfasts back onboard *Kwaietek*. I threw some logs in the woodstove and lit a fire. We sat together near the grate and dined on cinnamon rolls and cocoa. By the time our little fire had turned to a blaze, my cell rang. Juliet nearly trampled me to answer it first. "Hello… Daddy?" She stood just out of reach so I couldn't grab my phone. "Are you OK? Is *Zodiac* OK?" She nodded and responded with 'mmmhmms' and 'oh no's' until I finally wrested my phone from her. Ignoring her protests, I spoke with my husband.

"Oh my god, how are you?"

Jeff's voice sounded frazzled. "We're both good. The ship is fine too. We're hunkered down here in Teddy Bear Cove—in the lee of Chuckanut Island."

"How'd *Zodiac* ride out the night?"

"A little bouncy, but once we got the anchor down things sorta calmed down. I can't say the ride over here was much fun though. Did you see what happened as we left dock?"

"Yeah—that kind of scared me."

"The wind just took us. I leaned out to check distance and—I kid you not—I coulda touched that drydock. I had to run back to the wheel and help Tim turn her hard to starboard… it took both of us. Right at the end, she responded. Whew, I'm not kidding you."

"I'm glad to hear she's alright."

"Well—she's OK, but she's missing one weather-cover," he said. "It's probably washed up on Eliza Island by now."

"No way! What happened?" I asked. Juliet had pressed her ear up to the cell phone so she could hear our conversation.

Jeff continued his story. "By the time we'd turned west—toward Chuckanut, the state of the bay was pretty dicey. Tim kept sticking his head out of the hole he'd cut in the plastic and I'd lean out the gangway to see where we were headed…we were both trying to locate the buoy. At one point, I leaned out and placed my hand on the frame of the cover for balance… I felt it sort of shudder and then lift. I let go and dropped to the deck just as the entire cover—from the bow aft—just peeled right off the boat, just like when you peel a prawn's shell! Then it sorta hung there, almost vertical in the wind, shimmering for a few seconds—after that, it just tore away and flew straight up in the air!"

"Holy shit."

"Yeah, that's exactly what I said!"

Juliet interrupted, "What happened next?"

"Well, right after it blew away, I thought to myself 'where's Tim—wasn't he looking out through the plastic when all this happened?' And then I panicked—I mean, if Tim had gone overboard there was no getting him back. The best thing he could do at that point would have been to start swallowing water and swim toward the bottom."

Both Juliet and I stopped him and asked, "Was he alright?"

"Yes, he'd drawn his head back inside just before the cover went skyward. We were both pretty lucky in that regard."

"Thank Poseidon for that one," I said.

"Daddy—when are you coming home?"

"We'll be home in a couple days, there's another storm warning in the forecast—but it isn't supposed to be as strong. Once we're sure the bad weather is over, we'll come back to dock."

Satisfied with his answer, Juliet scooted back to the woodstove. I moved into the charthouse and continued our conversation. "Hey, so, I'm feeling pretty bad that you had to leave and I stayed here… I sorta feel like I bailed on my responsibility. Anyway, thanks for stepping in for me."

"What are you talking about? You don't need to feel guilty," Jeff answered. "You're a mom foremost and a mate second. We're done with putting work ahead of our family, right?"

"Yeah—very true. I'm really glad that I stayed with the Bug—for both our sakes."

"Besides," Jeff continued, "Tim and I are holed up here in the salon right now with old black and white war movies—we've got enough chili to last for another two days and half a bottle of

Kracken rum… and when the rum's gone, you'll see us again, I swear."

"Fair enough, fair enough." I chuckled. "Alright then, have a good time watching war movies—and hurry back. We miss you."

I ended my phone call with Jeffery and walked back into the salon. The little stove had done its job well, and our boat was now warm and comfortable once again. Juliet studied her lessons and I pulled out my sketch book. We sat in the salon all morning and fed our little fire, reading and drawing together. It felt just like old times in our new home.

Chapter 33

Rafted Together

The *Zodiac*'s replacement weather cover was almost finished. Once we attached the plastic onto the framing she'd be dry and warm once again. The annual crew Christmas party was scheduled for the upcoming Saturday evening—after the work was over. We expected a large turnout of volunteers for that day and Tim hoped to complete the cover before the celebrating started.

The holiday party was a big event for the ship, when the old-timers and out-of-town volunteers returned for a night and mingled with the new hands and our core crew. The *Zodiac* was appointed in festive attire—even in her mid-restoration state. Her salon glowed with gold and crimson lights strung from the beams, a small sparkling tree stood sentinel underneath the butterfly hatch. Tim strung work lights along the framing of the cover, making her decks luminous under the plastic sheathing.

Jeff and I were on hand to help with preparations. Once the weekend was over, we intended to take our own ship to Seattle and spend the holidays with our kids. Juliet set about baking holiday cookies after she finished her studies each afternoon. By week's end, there were dozens of platters brimming with various cookies laid across the galley mess. This reminded me of my kitchen in Seattle—the kids gathered around the table, squabbling as they decorated their sugar cookies. Juliet and I cleaned the ship from stem to stern so she'd be presentable for the party. Now that we lived aboard *Kwaietek* full-time, the *Zodiac* had begun to slip once again into that lonesome, barren state. The holiday celebration helped to fend off the emptiness for a brief time.

These days we drove from the other side of Bellingham Bay to work on the *Z*. Our winter moorage for *Kwaietek* was in the protected shelter of Gate Five at Squalicum Marina alongside the work boats and fishing vessels. The working docks were our favorite site in the marina. The liveaboards and professional fishermen that we met on these docks matched our personalities. We missed Fairhaven and moorage adjacent to the *Zodiac*, but appreciated the shelter of the marina—especially after the northerly gales of November.

Jeffery woke up earlier than usual on Friday morning and shook my arm. When I rolled over he said, "Let's have some coffee and then fire up *Kwaietek*. We could motor across the bay and raft next to the *Z* for the party.

"And we have to do this right now?" I yawned.

"Well, if you get the coffee going, I can start the engine and let her idle. She hasn't been fired up since we came over here a couple months ago." He sat up in bed and brushed my hair from my face. "I mean, of course, if you want to."

"Ahh, OK. I'm pretty much awake now." I rolled back over and tossed the heavy blankets aside. "Let's have some breakfast first and then get going. Now that I'm up, it actually sounds like a good idea."

I walked into the galley and grabbed the jar of coffee beans. The kettle steamed away on the diesel stove. I poured the boiling water into the French press pot, staring out the portlight at our dock. Frost decorated the edges of the round little window and resembled the sugar crystals on Juliet's cookies. Sunshine glinted off the steel hulls that surrounded us. I opened the port and let the chilly breeze enter the galley. Gull's cries could be heard from the breakwater. I glimpsed a big trawler motoring out the marina entrance; its tall outriggers were the only thing visible from the breakwater wall. This crispy winter morning seemed like the perfect time to go for a ride across the bay.

Pushing the press down on the coffee, I recognized the familiar growl of the Granny Gardner as Jeffery fired up her six cylinders. She whirred and rumbled and then, as each cylinder caught; she settled down into her slow turning *bruhmm, bruhmm, bruhmm…* I walked through the engine room, raising his cup of coffee on my way past. He nodded as he adjusted the heat exchanger. Eventually, he joined me upstairs in the deckhouse.

"By god, I think *Kwaietek* is happy to be going somewhere. She fired right up without a hitch," he said as he accepted his coffee from me.

"That's a good thing, because she's got a much longer voyage ahead of her on Monday when we head south," I said.

We polished off the pot of coffee and rousted a sleepy daughter from her bunk. Jeff went below to check the engine and I hopped onto the dock, ready to release lines when he called for them. Juliet appeared in her pajamas and fleece jacket, her flannel pants tucked into her rubber boots. She walked back to the fender and untied it from the rail. Jeffery leaned out of the deckhouse and asked me for the bowline and the forward-leading spring line. I tossed them aboard. He then called for the stern and stern-spring lines. Juliet moved forward to fend off the pier as I took the first wrap off of the remaining mooring line. The smoke from *Kwaietek's* stack rose into the brisk air in puffy white rings. Jeff leaned out once again and nodded. I undid the aft spring and walked it up to Juliet. She took the line and laid it on the deck so that it wouldn't fall overboard and catch in the propeller. I jumped aboard as *Kwaietek* pulled away from her dock. Jeffery aimed for the mouth of the breakwater and we set off for *Zodiac.*

The bay appeared glassy flat on this sunny, cold morning. *Kwaietek* motored along with Juliet behind the wheel—the old boat seemed downright chipper to go on a morning jaunt. I watched the harbor seals pop their heads above the surface to get a better look at us. Leaning against the deckhouse, I observed the people on the shore from a distance. Couples strolled along Boulevard Park with coffee in hand and cyclists made their way along the boardwalk of Taylor Dock. Above the shore-side activities, I glimpsed the stream of cars nosing along State Street on their way to work or on weekday errands and I offered a silent prayer of thanks for the life that we'd chosen.

As we approached the Fairhaven side of the bay, I noticed Tim and his father Karl on the *Zodiac's* dock. I stepped forward to the bow and waved at them. Skipper Karl returned my gesture with a two handed salute and they walked toward the end of the dock as we motored up. "Hey Chrissy, that's a mighty fine looking boat you have there!" Karl shouted.

"Thanks, we're kinda fond of her!" I called back. How are you this mornin' Skipper? Hey—do you suppose that you guys might catch some dock lines for us if we rafted alongside the *Z*?"

"I'm pretty sure I can talk this guy into helping you out—perhaps I'll just direct traffic," Karl replied.

Tim waved and nodded, then walked back toward *Zodiac*'s gangway and stepped aboard.

Jeff put *Kwaietek* into reverse and shifted her rudder. She backed into position and he began his approach into the narrow slip of water between *Zodiac*'s hull and the overhead dock of the cruise terminal. Juliet and I readied the fenders, hanging them much higher than usual, since she'd be sidled up close to *Z's* topsides. I passed the bowline to Tim as he leaned out the starboard gangway. He walked it aft and secured it to *Zodiac*'s quarterbits. We repeated the process for our bow lines and finally cinched everything up snugly with our spring lines. The two ships nestled side by side with their gangways lined up perfectly. "Well, super! We have an annex now," Tim said.

By the time Saturday's work party commenced, both ships were adorned in their festive best. *Kwaietek* bore a large wreath on her forward mast, directly over the ship's bell. Red and gold ornaments sparkled throughout the greenery. Strands of white Christmas lights ran from her prow to her foremast, across to her mizzen mast and back down to her stern. Megan and Kris Jones, now on their winter break from college, showed up to help us attach swags of garland around her deckhouse. Jeffery twined tiny light strands around the boughs. The ship gleamed from above and below. *Kwaietek* now looked as elegant as our old house in Seattle did for the holidays. Not to be outdone, *Zodiac* sported a long string of lights on both sides of her winter cover. Mistletoe and wreaths dangled from the rafters. She appeared so elegant that one could almost overlook her missing masts and booms.

The multitude of volunteers arrived by mid-morning and set to work, covering the starboard side of the framing with protective plastic. *Kwaietek* turned out to be a handy platform and several crewmembers scrambled back and forth between the ships with tools and materials. Megan constructed a gangplank to connect both ships and Kris fashioned a rope handrail. By late afternoon *Zodiac*'s cover was completed and the final decorations were assembled on deck.

The holiday party started near sunset. The keg of Boundary Bay IPA sat prominently on the salon roof and as Jeffery tapped it, he proclaimed, "Let the festivities begin!"

As the evening wore on, many more crewmembers and invited guests materialized to board the party boats. *Kwaietek* had a steady stream of visitors and Jeff spent a major portion of the night giving tours of her engine room. Juliet and Megan led a raucous game of *Apples to Apples* with the younger crowd up in the main salon.

Onboard the *Zodiac,* the 'tacky ornament exchange' was in full swing and cheers and guffaws echoed across the docks as participants unwrapped their unusual gifts. Captain Karl and his wife stayed for most of the evening. Before he left, he came over and said to me, "You know, it's funny, Chrissy. I used to be the captain on this here ship for almost twenty years—and I don't think I recognize but two or three faces anymore."

"Oh Skipper, you know more than that! But I suppose you're right, times have changed haven't they? I mean, if *I'm* now an old-timer, then there's a lot of new blood on the *Zodiac* these days."

His comment made me think. How many generations of sailors, families and volunteers had passed over these fir decks since she was launched—almost a century ago? So many people, just like us, had labored to take care of her...but in the end, it was the *Zodiac* that actually took care of us all.

As the night drew on, party-goers gathered in groups to converse on deck and down below. Laughter echoed off of the piers. The two ships gently bobbed beside one another as their inhabitants celebrated within.

The next day started leisurely. I managed to get waffles and bacon started around eleven o'clock. The earlier risers on *Zodiac* wandered over to our boat with their coffee for a more sober look at her features. We invited them onboard and had a small crowd in the galley for brunch. The rising tide had elevated our deck to the level of the terminal's upper dock. Sightseers passed by and chatted with some of the volunteers, inquiring about each of the old vessels. Megan sat on the wheelhouse roof, cradling her cup of tea and talking with onlookers. I overheard her telling a visitor, "Yeah, both of these boats were built in the early 1920s."

"Well, well, well, you've developed quite a taste of the sea, for a kid who wanted nothing to do with 'stinky old boats,'" I said as I sat down next to her.

"Oh, Mom. Don't rub it in."

"Are you and Kris planning on cruising down to Seattle with us tomorrow?"

"Yep. We'll run back to the apartment and grab all of our stuff this afternoon. Justine and her friends plan to meet us at the Ballard locks and watch us go through."

"That ought to be fun," I commented. "You guys will want to sleep on board tonight because we're leaving at the crack of dawn."

"No problem."

I stood up and stretched, and went below to clean up the breakfast dishes, leaving Megan to her self-appointed post as our ship's docent for the rest of the morning.

Chapter 34

The Locks

Monday dawned clear and calm. One of the volunteers aboard the *Zodiac* helped us cast off the lines. As Jeff nosed *Kwaietek* carefully away from the bigger ship, the kids stood on her side deck, ready to push off the overhead dock if it got too close. All went smoothly and we glided backward. Jeff raised the throttle and *Kwaietek* cruised out into the bay.

Jeffery and I sat in the wheelhouse and watched the sun rise above Whidbey Island as we steered *Kwaietek* south toward the Swinomish Cut. Megan and Kris napped in the salon—having fulfilled their deckhand duties for present. Juliet climbed back in her bed to curl up and read for the rest of the morning. Jeffery turned to me and said, "Ya know, this doesn't suck, my dear." I smiled and nodded.

I spent most of the day behind the wheel. We motored by Anacortes and through the mouth of the Swinomish Channel. Jeffery pulled the chart table down and checked off the navigation markers as we passed them by. The Swinomish Cut was dredged every so often to keep the depth constant; however it shallowed up rapidly if one veered from mid-channel.

Kwaietek's Gardner engine chugged along and we managed about eight knots of speed. We received waves and whistles from the other vessels as we motored along. There could be no arguing that *Kwaietek* was a sharp looking boat and with her garland and lights she turned a lot of heads. Juliet slipped into her lifejacket and went out to the foredeck to wave at the admirers as we motored south. She pointed at two large bald eagles as they took flight from a tree near the shore.

We arrived in the small town of La Connor around five in the evening and tied up to the marina's guest dock. From our berth we had an excellent view of downtown; the old buildings glittered in multi-hued Christmas lights. We locked up the boat and meandered down the narrow streets to find a place for dinner. Not far from our marina we found a pub where the kids could join us for dinner. Our evening ashore proved to be a relaxing way to cap off a gorgeous day.

Over our morning breakfast, Jeffery computed the distance to Seattle. "If we catch the tide just right, we ought to make it into the locks by around three this afternoon." We started *Kwaietek's* engine and let her warm up for twenty minutes while we stowed the breakfast dishes and woke our drowsy deckhands. "Hey, you guys. Up and at 'em! Let's get going. There's some granola and bagels in the galley for you."

We pulled away from the guest dock and headed down mid-channel. The sun sparkled on the water and the frost lightly dusted the shoreline. Everything appeared crisp and wintery—like a postcard. I headed down to the galley while Jeffery steered *Kwaietek* through the quiescent village. Minutes later I was back with steaming coffee. "Mind if I take the helm again?"

"Not at all, I like watching you at the wheel."

I enjoyed piloting my own vessel—I'd become pretty adept at navigation during my last few years on *Zodiac*, but I didn't get much opportunity to steer. I took the *Z* off and on to her dock and had the helm at certain times when we anchored, but once we were underway, the ship's wheel belonged to our paying passengers. It felt really good as well, to let Jeff advise me and be the skipper. He'd been taking orders from me for so long on the Z, this role reversal was good for both of us.

By lunchtime, we entered Puget Sound proper. *Kwaietek* chugged along steadily. "Boy, does she love to run!" Jeffery said as he emerged from his hourly engine room check. "I haven't had to adjust anything all morning and she's just plowing along clean and clear."

I handed Megan the controls and climbed down below decks to make everyone some lunch. The engine hummed in her deep, *bruhmm, bruhmm bruhmm...* It amazed me that a machine of such enormous size could run so quietly.

The aft scuttle had been latched open and from my vantage point in the galley, I could see right over our stern. *Kwaietek's* wake resembled a narrow, white trough in a field of blue. I assembled all of the sandwiches and opened up a bag of potato chips. As I stepped partially onto the companionway ladder, my gaze lingered on the scenery behind us. Puget Sound opened into an expansive conduit several miles wide. On one bank, rolling green shores alternated with patches of sandy hillsides—the other side offered tree-lined slopes that followed the waterline. The afternoon sun kissed land and sea alike as we forged down the strait.

I heard a rapid series of splashes that differed from the rhythmic pattern of the waves. Suddenly, three charcoal-colored dorsal fins punctured the crest of our wake. "Whoa! Dolphins! ...nope—*porpoises!*" I shouted, pointing toward the fins. It dawned on me that nobody was nearby to hear my announcement. I remained to watch the porpoises frolic in our surf and eventually finished the sandwiches and walked them forward.

"Hey, you guys—lunchtime!" I called out as I slid the platter of sandwiches onto the chart-dash. "Boy, you guys missed a helluva show off of the fantail."

"Nuhuh—look out there!" Juliet said and pointed over my shoulder.

I looked out the doorway to spy four more porpoises matching *Kwaietek*'s pace. "Wow! It looks like we've got ourselves a race!"

By mid-afternoon we were abeam of Shilshole. Juliet scrambled out of the wheelhouse to get a good look at her favorite childhood haunt, Golden Gardens Park. She looked through Jeff's binoculars and called out, "I see the playground—there's the volleyball nets and all of the fire pits!"

Kwaietek motored past the rocky breakwater of Shilshole marina and made the turn into the Ballard Locks entrance. The railroad trestle languished in the raised position, allowing us to continue on our way. Jeffery slowed momentum and called for Megan and Kris to put the fenders over the port rail. We stood off, waiting for the outbound vessels to exit the Locks chamber.

Finally, the last of the procession passed us by and Jeffery throttled up to approach the chamber. I stood beside him and watched as he prepared to maneuver our sixty-three-foot boat into the tight quarters of the Ballard Locks.

The line-handlers that work for the Ballard Locks have always had a well-deserved reputation for surliness. The old saying, *'They do not suffer fools gladly'* might have been coined for these men and women. On multiple occasions, we'd witnessed the ass-chewing of many a boater who fell afoul of the line-handlers. They had the ability to hold the massive doors until they were finished ripping apart an errant skipper or deckhand. To make matters even more unbearable, the Locks were a popular tourist attraction, so the likelihood of having one's incompetence broadcast in front of an audience was pretty high.

Making a mistake in the Locks didn't only cost a skipper his pride, it could result in significant damage to vessels. It was imperative therefore, that boaters behaved professionally and prudently when they transited the Locks. Unfortunately, many recreational operators took the procedure less than seriously and accidents often occurred.

With this knowledge in mind, my nerves were on edge as we pulled into the Locks chamber. I'd continuously drilled *Zodiac's* deckhands on the protocols and we looked like pros every time the *Z* transited through. I knew Captain Tim's skills and could usually predict how he'd react to unforeseen predicaments. However, I hadn't logged much experience with Jeff as a captain or with *Kwaietek's* idiosyncrasies.

The line-handlers stood above us on the rail, watching closely. They waved us into the smaller chamber and it dawned on me that I'd never been through this one; *Zodiac* only transited through the big lock. I vaguely recalled that there was a difference in the way you tended your lines in the two chambers, but as we motored slowly past the gates I couldn't quite place what it was. I stood in the doorway of the wheelhouse, and watched the kids prepare their lines. I resisted the temptation to become the mate.

The kids didn't appreciate their mom pulling rank on them when we weren't on the *Z*. As *Kwaietek* ghosted into the chamber, Kris dropped his stern line onto the passing bollard. Jeffery backed down and *Kwaietek* sidled up closer to the walls. The line-handlers walked toward us. I stepped onto the foredeck just in case something went awry. *Please get this right, Megan.* She deftly draped the line over the bollard and made it fast. The kids stepped away from the cleats and awaited further orders. "Secure your lines and stand by," the line-handler called down and then walked away.

"Hey Kris—Megan!" I yelled. "Excellent job guys—way to go!"

Jeff came out the wheelhouse door as the gates behind us clanged shut. The noisy buzzer announced that the chambers were closed and filling. "Well done, Mister," I said.

"That whole process went beautifully. The kids did well," Jeff said.

We stood on the deck and watched lake water flood into the chamber. Gradually our decks became level with the lock wall and we were face to face with dozens of onlookers. "Hey Mama!" I heard a shout. Justine and several of her friends waved to us from behind the fence.

"Hey, you!" I called back. Juliet scurried over to the starboard rail and they chatted for several minutes until the buzzer signaled that the inland doors were about to swing open. "We'll see you in Lake Union later on—right?" I yelled.

"Yeah, we'll be down later tonight—love you!" Justine shouted back.

"Bye, Sis!" Juliet called from the deckhouse roof. Megan and Kris gave quick waves and then returned to tending their lines.

The steel doors slowly swung open, and a wave cascaded into the chamber, bouncing all of the vessels up and down. The line-handler ambled down the rail and stood next to our boat. He called down to Jeffery, "So, is this a forestry boat?" Jeff poked his head out the door.

"Yeah, headquarters launch for the BC Forestry Service. 1923."

"Nice," he said, nodding as he looked her up and down. As he turned to walk away he remarked nonchalantly, "You guys can release your stern line now. Have a good 'un."

Kris slacked away his line and cast off from the wall. Jeff throttled forward and the line handler motioned to Megan. She undid her bow line and *Kwaietek* pulled gently away from the wall. Increasing speed, Jeffery maneuvered the boat into the middle of the chamber and we passed through the gates. Seattle's familiar skyline welcomed us back home.

Chapter 35

Christmas Ships

The Christmas tree on top of the Space Needle twinkled high above Queen Anne Hill. Juliet, Megan and I stood together on the foredeck as we motored toward the Ballard Bridge. We passed by the bright yellow and blue tugs moored along the canal. The big Alaskan crab boats obstructed our view of Fisherman's Terminal, where *Sugaree* resided for over seven years. "Mom! Can we go visit our old dock?" Juliet asked.

"We'll see," I said. "Remember, we don't have a car on this trip since we came by water."

"Oh yeah, I forgot all about that."

Jeffery sounded the 'prolonged short' blast of *Kwaietek's* horn, it was met with the "proceed ahead" response from the drawbridge operator. We chugged slowly along and repeated the call/response at the smaller Fremont Bridge. Megan steered *Kwaietek* through the canal toward the lake entrance. As we passed underneath the yawning drawbridge, I looked up at the traffic overhead. Headlights shone for several miles down the stretch of Westlake Avenue. Jeffery came alongside and put his arm around my shoulders. "Do you remember that hellish commute?"

"Man, I do *not* miss that, not one little bit." I shook my head and watched the lights of traffic recede astern.

Turning my attention back to our course, I saw Lake Union before us. It made me smile to see all the familiar landmarks. Gas Works Park appeared off our port bow and *Kwaietek* gradually turned away, hugging the west side of the lake. The Naval Armory building sprang into view, bathed in a silver glow from the spotlights at its foundation. Ahead in the distance, we recognized the Center for Wooden Boats. "Head straight for that big white building, Megan," Jeff said.

Before long, we had the boat secure against the west wall of the Armory's park. Kris and Megan had jumped ashore to catch the dock lines. Before Megan secured the last line, her sister bounded off the boat and ran toward the footbridge behind us. She screamed "Dane! Sasha!" at the top of her lungs.

Jeff appeared from the engine room below, "What is she hollering about?" he asked.

"Prepare for impact. The kids are arriving." I said, and then jumped ashore to greet my son and our dog.

Our first night back in Seattle was a whirlwind of reunions. Dane and his girlfriend Kim brought Sasha on board while we sat in the salon and chatted. Dane attempted to get a word in edgewise, but his sisters barely gave him the chance. Sasha dashed around the deckhouse, inspecting every corner and crevice for new smells. Her tail wagged furiously as she made her rounds, and several ornaments met their demise as a result. Eventually Dane corralled the dog long enough to make an announcement: he and Kim were expecting a baby. I gaped at him momentarily while his sisters squealed with delight, throwing themselves on Kim with hugs of congratulations. We cracked open a few beers in the galley to toast the parents-to-be.

Before long, I heard my cell phone ring from the salon and the twins rushed down the companionway to announce that Trent, Jessica and the boys had just checked into the Marriott across the street. They had opted to book a suite at the hotel rather than sleep onboard due to Jessica's uneasiness about boats.

"Trent is here? We have to go over there right now!" Juliet decreed.

The celebrating continued over at the Marriott throughout the evening. Trent bribed the twins into playing with William and Kairen upstairs while the grown-ups adjourned to the lobby bar. Juliet located the hotel swimming pool and begged for a late-night dip; she claimed that a swim that evening would replace her morning shower.

On our way back to the suite, Jessica peeked out the lobby doors. "*That* is your boat?" she exclaimed, "It's so beautiful! I can't wait to see it up close tomorrow!"

"Do you think we could take you all out for a ride on her tomorrow?" Jeffery asked.

"Yeah, the boys would love it," she replied.

I looked at Trent and he winked back at me. I'd worried about whether Jessica would allow the boys go on the water. "OK, everybody to their respective beds!" Trent proclaimed as we cracked open the door to their hotel room. "It's a big day tomorrow!"

We marched Juliet out of the lobby, enduring her complaints about being forced to leave her nephews and big brothers. As we crossed the footbridge, I glanced over at *Kwaietek*. She looked homey. The lights Jeffery had strung from bow to stern reflected off of the dark lake. I was in a fantastic mood; my family was all together once more for Christmas.

We awoke to the unfamiliar sound of heavy traffic. I sat up in bed, wondering briefly where we were. The roar of street congestion and car horns were interspersed by the rumble of construction in the lot across from the Armory. I dressed and climbed up the ladder. The city's commotion encircled us. Juliet joined me in the wheelhouse and looked out at the lake. The Kenmore seaplanes jostled for their take-off position—revving their engines in preparation. Canada geese surrounded our boat in small gaggles, furtively eyeing the lake's new arrival.

"Is it time to go get Trenton and everybody?" Juliet asked.

"Not yet, I haven't had my coffee yet," I replied. Then, seeing the pout emerge on her face, I added. "You may get dressed and go over to the hotel if you want to."

"Yes! Thanks, Mom!"

I followed her below, headed to the galley for my morning caffeine. Eventually Jeffery stumbled into the galley to join me. We enjoyed a half hour of peaceful conversation before the kids descended upon us. William's squeals of excitement heralded their approach. "Wow! Can I drive the boat! I want to blow the horn, Daddy! Whoa—look at those ducks!"

Kwaietek tenderly rolled from side to side as ten family members boarded her. Siblings and significant others traipsed below deck to join us for breakfast. Soon enough, it was time to start the engine. "OK, everybody get ready for some noise!" Jeff said.

I took the youngsters above deck, leaving Trent and Dane to watch Jeffery fire up the engine. We gathered everyone into the salon and passed out the Christmas presents. The entire deckhouse evolved into an enormous party as kids of all ages tore open their packages. Paper and ribbons covered the sole. As the engine rumbled to life, Trent and Dane joined us in the deckhouse. Eventually Jeffery appeared and called for the grandkids to help him steer the boat.

Justine and Megan stood on the deck and their boyfriends tossed them the dock lines, jumping back aboard in the nick of time. I laughed to see William's look of concentration as he sat on Jeffery's lap, turning the wheel. "Here we go!" Trent yelled.

The clouds parted as we motored across Lake Union. Before we reached the University Bridge, the sun had chased the remaining clouds away. Trent and Dane took turns at the wheel and I went on deck to hang out with the other kids. "Mom—this is the *best!*" Justine said. They sat on the galley roof watching the shore as we motored through the Montlake Cut. Jessica came on deck and joined us. I felt relieved that she was comfortable enough on the boat to venture out of the deckhouse. "How do you like it?" I asked.

"This is fantastic! The boys are having a blast—both the little ones and the bigger ones."

"I take it Trent likes being at the wheel then," I laughed.

We spent all afternoon cruising around Lake Washington. Mt. Baker shone iridescently with a new snow cover and from the distant south, Rainier commanded the entire vista. *Kwaietek* motored east and then slowly cruised along the shore side of Kirkland. The kids stared at the mansions that sprawled along the water with their boat-houses and private docks. "What a view those people have," Jessica said.

"Yeah, it's a nice view and all. But they paid a fortune for that privilege... and right now, *we're* the view." Jeff replied.

Kwaietek pulled alongside the west wall at the Armory shortly before dinner. Once the family members had disembarked for their respective abodes, Jeffery and I sank into our seats and cat-napped for a short spell. It had been a fun afternoon, but I failed to remember just how much energy my brood could emit when they were all convened.

Later that evening, the Christmas ships parade lapped the outskirts of Lake Union. Trent's family returned to *Kwaietek* and we gathered on the foredeck to watch forty or more ships troll around the shores, each boat festooned in holiday lights. Several vessels had themes: reindeer pulling Santa, candy cane palm trees and pirate snowmen. The lead ship carried The Seattle Girls' Choir—their speakers broadcast carols for those nearby to hear. It made for a lovely sight on the waterfront. By nine o'clock, Trent and Jessica carried their exhausted kids back to the hotel.

Soon enough it was time for everyone to go their separate ways once again. However, on this occasion, our parting didn't feel as painful or as uncertain as it had when we left our house. It felt normal—*alright*. I said farewell to Dane and Sasha after breakfast and then Justine shortly after. Trent's family piled back into their car to make the journey south before lunchtime. As he buckled his youngest into the car seat, William leaned over and said. "Thank you, Nana Chris! I want to live on a Christmas boat too!"

"Yeah, thanks Mama." Trent said. "You guys made some good memories this weekend. We'll be seeing you this summer I hope."

"You will—I promise," I replied. We waved good bye to their family and walked back to the dock where our home awaited us.

"Let's get things stowed away and I'll fire up the Gardner," Jeff suggested.

Before long, *Kwaietek*'s engine thrummed steadily. Megan and Kris handled the dock-lines and we chugged away from the wall. A seaplane took off directly behind us and soared over our wheelhouse as we made our way back to the Locks.

Chapter 36

Sworn In

Winter did not depart without a fight, but at long last the cold and rain dispersed. April arrived and brought with her sunshine and wispy clouds. I made the most of the dry spell by pulling my kayak off of *Kwaietek*'s deckhouse to refinish it. The mahogany topside had yellowed somewhat over the past two seasons and I didn't like leaving it in that condition. As I applied the third coat of varnish along the grain, a yacht owner paused to compliment me on the workmanship. "That is a beautiful kayak. Did you have it made?" he inquired.

"Thanks, my husband built it for me when I was pregnant with our daughter. I've been using it for over ten years now."

"Lovely, just lovely. I do like looking at these wooden boats—but I'd sure as heck never own one—too much work involved to keep 'em up, if you know what I mean. That's why I own a fiberglass boat."

"Yep, you said it," I replied. He continued down the dock toward his Grand Banks powerboat and I finished the clear coat, musing about our conversation. It was true. Wood required more care and a higher degree of artistry to maintain. But what's wrong with that? These days, too many things are designed to leave people care*less*—devoid of concern. It pleased me to bring faded wood back to life with skill and attention. The character and resilience of wooden vessels—big and small—was what drew me to them. There's something very basic and grounding that happens when I attend to my boats; I keep them alive and they keep me alive. I tried to imagine how dull it would be to just step on board a plastic boat and push the "go button."

I set my brush in the can of turpentine and went below to clean up. I barely had enough time to compile the stacks of application paperwork for my captain's license and then head over to the *Zodiac*. Tim and Jeff were already onboard fine-tuning her new rig. The spring re-fit had taken twice as long as it typically did in order to step the new masts that they'd built for her. The giant fir spars now fit snugly in their resting place with well over twenty gallons of varnish applied to them. The running-rig had been reinstalled and sails bent on last week. The final step was to pass the annual C.O.I.—"Certificate of Inspection" with the Coast Guard. I wanted to be onboard in time to check that all would be ready for our assessment.

I searched around my desk and located the folder that contained all of my merchant mariner's material. It had taken a lot of time and effort, but thanks to my time on the *Zodiac,* I finally had enough sea days to apply for a 200-ton license. During the past winter, I'd spent months attending a captain's class and every evening since studying navigation, stability and the *72 Colregs*. The culminating exam—a two-part assessment— had been intense, but I'd passed it with an impressive score. Now that our upcoming cruise season loomed, I was anxious to submit my application and obtain the official title of "Captain Wallace."

When I arrived onboard *Zodiac*, the volunteers had already laid out all of our orange life jackets. I scrutinized each vest, checking for whistles, reflective tape and proper closures. I rifled through our first aid kits to confirm that we met the current inventory requirements. Tim passed by as I checked the items off my list and called over his shoulder, "Grab the fire extinguisher receipts—they'll want to see every one of 'em."

Before I finished setting out all our necessary documents, I heard the sound of several pairs of boots on the deck above. *Dammit! They're early.* Sure enough, Tim soon appeared in the charthouse companionway followed by four Coasties with clipboards. Hatches were opened and flashlights produced and for the next ninety minutes, I stood nearby to answer questions and fetch documents for Tim upon request. The inspectors pored over her new mast and fittings with great attention. Jeff stood near me, watching the process. He leaned closer to my shoulder and said quietly, "They don't know anything about wooden masts, but that won't stop them from analyzing the hell out of it."

"They don't really have a choice though, do they? I mean, when a ship like *Zodiac* loses her mast and the word gets around… well, they've pretty much got to ensure the new one is up to snuff, right?" I whispered.

"Yeah, they're required to inspect it for sure, but my point is that they never actually see any traditional vessels like this one. They spend all their time dealing with modern steel hulled or fiberglass vessels. They just don't know what to look for when it comes to a classic tall ship like the *Z*."

"Well you and Tim built it—I assume they'll just have to love it."

"I sure as hell hope so—we're out of time if they don't."

After satisfying the Coast Guard inspectors regarding our new mast and paperwork, we took the *Zodiac* out for a short shake-down sail in the bay. They wanted to observe our proficiency at man-overboard rescue and fire scenarios. Several drills later, we were back at dock—our C.O.I. in hand. The officers packed away their clipboards and started to head toward the gangway. I dashed below and grabbed the paperwork for my license. Just before the lieutenant stepped off the gangway, I ran over and said, "Excuse me, could I request a quick favor? Y'see, I'm applying for my Captain's license and there's only one step remaining before I can mail everything to the regional office. Would you mind officially swearing me in with the Coast Guard oath?" I asked.

She looked at me with a puzzled expression. "Huh, I've never had to do this—what exactly does it entail?"

"Well, there's this section here on the first page where I need to repeat after you. It requires a Coast Guard lieutenant-grade-or-higher office to do the oath. Do you have the time?"

"Sure, I guess so. Let me see the application for a 'sec." She perused the paperwork and then said. "OK, I suppose we can do this here. It looks as if you'll need to raise your right hand and repeat after me."

We stepped back to the charthouse and she set down her briefcase. I raised my hand and stiffened my posture—it seemed the appropriate thing to do. The officer read aloud the oath and I repeated it verbatim.

"I do solemnly swear or affirm that I will faithfully and honestly, according to my best skill and judgment, and without concealment and reservation, perform all the duties required of me by the laws of the United States." The officer paused and looked past me, she smiled and winked at something or someone I couldn't see and then continued with the oath. "I will faithfully and honestly carry out the lawful orders of my superior officers aboard a vessel."

After I spoke the last sentence, I glanced over my shoulder to see what had captured the officer's attention. Standing behind me, next to the mast, were Jeffery and Tim. They'd witnessed the whole little ceremony. Their arms were crossed and they smiled like proud parents. Tim said, "Congratulations *Captain*... and you got that last part—the one about faithfully following your superior officer's orders, right?"

"*Yeah* boss, I got it."

Chapter 37

Circumnavigation

The high season months of 2011's summer had been brutal—we'd been running cruises almost back-to-back, with only enough time at dock to clean the ship and re-provision. The volunteers loved the busier schedule, as they had more opportunities to come aboard. However, for the core crew—especially Tim and me, it amounted to an exhausting schedule that offered little time to relax.

By mid-August, my reserves were tapped. I could tell that my patience with the volunteers and some of our passengers had worn thin. I needed some shore leave. After one of our safety meetings, when the crew departed for their ship's details, I held Tim back. "You got a second?" He set down his cup of coffee and looked my way. I continued, "I should probably get off the ship for a few trips before I throw somebody overboard."

He frowned warily. "How many trips exactly?"

"Oh, I dunno. Dane's baby is due any day now. Give me a couple of weeks off and I'll come back fresh as a daisy—promise."

"When do I get *my* two weeks' vacation?"

I smiled. "It sucks to be the boss, huh?"

"Alright, just get Calen up to speed before the next trip and make sure that we're good to go on all of the customs paperwork."

"Thanks a lot, Tim. I appreciate it." As I headed up the companionway, he called after me. "Hey—don't go and get hit by a bus though."

"I'll keep an eye out for it."

The alarm went off at seven o'clock; Jeffery rolled over and swiped it off the counter then fell back into his pillow. I stretched out in our bunk and stared at the butterfly hatch overhead. Clear blue skies. *My first day off!* I blinked away the last of my drowsiness and rolled over to watch Jeffery sleep. He lay on his side with the blankets pulled up to his chin. Sunlight rested on his face, accentuating the angle of his cheekbone. The slightest hint of breeze came through the portlight and played with errant strands of his hair. His breath was slow and even and his eyelids fluttered. I ran my finger gently over his beard stubble and let it rest upon his lips. I watched him stir, eventually his eyes twitched and opened. He stared wide-eyed for a brief moment, and then focused on me. "Hey, you," he said.

"Sorry. Did I disturb you?"

He stretched his arms. "What are you doing awake so early on your first day off?"

"I tried to sleep in, but I guess I'm hard-wired to be up for a safety meeting in about, "oh…" I looked at our clock, "thirteen minutes."

"Wow, what a shame. Well, would a cup of coffee on the foredeck with your husband suffice? We can chat about safety stuff if it would make you feel better."

I yawned and rolled over, tossing my robe over my tank top. "Yup, I think we could probably make that work."

I pushed the lounge chair toward the wheelhouse and leaned back, positioning a pillow behind my neck. Jeffery joined me a few minutes later with a full press pot of coffee. We sat silently for a while and watched the morning sun climb higher in the cloudless sky. The resident mama otter and her three kits played alongside *Kwaietek*'s hull; so cavalier about our presence nowadays, they barely noticed us as they wrestled and chased each other about. Several boisterous gulls swept onto the finger pier in competition for some exposed mussels on the pilings. The faraway sound of a power boat echoed across the marina.

My cup of coffee was almost empty when Juliet walked on deck. Her cheeks were still rosy pink from sleep. She extended her hand with my cell phone and said, "It's for you." Without waiting for a response, she went back into the deckhouse to finish her breakfast.

"Hullo?" I answered.

"Hey, it's me—Calen."

"Mornin', Sweet Pea. I'm technically off the clock, you know."

Ignoring my comment, he continued. "Tim wants the customs paperwork emailed to Sydney as well as Nanaimo. Can you take care of that?"

"Well, I suppose I could, except that you guys have all the original documents onboard. The wireless router's in the charthouse. It's probably better that you do it."

"Well, I can't get my laptop to synch-up with the router. Can you please do it for me?" he asked.

"Jesus Christ, I thought your generation was supposed to be the tech-savvy one!" I said. "Yeah, yeah, I'll do it. Anything else?"

"Uhm, well, other than the fact that one of the volunteers let the topping-lift run through its block, my dad's being a massive butthead and the intern won't do jack shit... we're just super."

"Hah! OK then. Have fun out there—I'll take care of the paperwork." I hung up the phone and smiled. His predicament amused me and it was nice to know that while *Zodiac* could manage, she still needed me around to function smoothly most of the time.

With my obligation to the *Zodiac* completed, I decided to spend some time getting reacquainted with my kayak. I unpacked my wetsuit and spray skirt and Jeffery helped me lift the wooden kayak off of the wheelhouse roof. We placed it gently in the water next to the dock and I slid into the cockpit. The varnished topside sparkled in the sunshine. As I fastened the spray skirt around the combing, Jeff straightened up and watched my efforts. I glanced up as he stood on the dock with his hands on his hips, grinning. He had that whimsical expression on his face that I recognized at once. I asked, "What the hell are you looking at?"

"You."

"Oh yeah, well I'd figured that much. But why, exactly?"

"Because," he said. "I *totally* won." He shook his head from side to side. "Here I am—watching this beautiful woman with hair that glows fire-red in the sun... sitting in the kayak that I made for her—and we're having this conversation in front of a cool old wooden boat that we live on together." Nodding his head, he added, "Yup, I totally won, alright."

I snickered. "You're a hopeless romantic, you know that right?"

"Yeah, maybe. But I sure do build a damn fine kayak."

"That you do, Mister… that you certainly do." I smiled back at him, pushed off the dock with the edge of my paddle, and waved so long.

I spent the majority of my day kayaking in Bellingham Bay. My first few hours consisted of attempts to regain my strokes and disregard the burning ache building between my shoulder blades. My protesting deltoids and triceps drove home the fact that sailing a tall ship utilized a completely different set of muscle groups than those I currently employed. The paddles splashed me with tiny droplets of water as they alternated in and out—and I marveled at how long it had been since I'd been this close to the waves. Onboard *Zodiac,* all of my sea time was spent looking *down* from a deck ten feet above the waterline. Today, I moved merely inches away from the swells.

The *swoosh* of the paddles as they sliced into the waves accompanied my steady breathing. It felt good to be back in the seat of my cockpit. As I neared Post Point, I slowed my pace to allow a group of small sailboats to tack past me. They breezed alongside of me and suddenly, with a series of short commands, they came about in unison. It resembled a school of herring switching direction en masse. Within a matter of seconds they were gone.

I resumed paddling and gained a great deal of satisfaction from the monotonous dip and arc of the blades. The stinging muscle-burn had receded and in its place was a warm, elastic sensation. My thoughts focused on the sounds and sights directly surrounding me. I hadn't experienced this singularity of purpose for a very long time. The demand for constant multi-tasking wafted away. I concentrated on my paddle's rhythm and the rising and falling swells of the bay. I fell into a trance of just *being*.

As the afternoon wore on and the temperature climbed, I turned the boat toward Fairhaven again. The noises on shore increased as I approached our dock. Easing out of my paddling-Zen, I transitioned back to my connection with the land. *Kwaietek* rested alongside the pier and I noticed my daughter's new kitten "Lucky Jack" sitting in our charthouse window. Jeff's sawhorses and tool bench were situated at the bottom of the ramp with Juliet's bike and skateboard piled nearby. My little planter of herbs sat next to our mooring lines. *This is our neighborhood now. No garden to plant, no fences to mend or weeds to pull—we'll take our home with us when we leave.*

The familiar hum of a power tool emanated from inside the forepeak. I found Jeffery fitting teak trim pieces around the shower stall he'd recently built. The grout had almost dried and the one-inch glass tiles gleamed in the tiny space. I sat down on the bunk and handed him a glass of lemonade. The cross-breeze from the open ports was refreshing.

"So, what do you think about finally having a shower in your very own boat?" he asked as he sat back on his haunches and took a long drink.

"Well frankly I think it is pretty cool—and only a *few* months behind schedule," I said.

"OK, let's just focus on how nice it looks—not how long it took to finish."

"I tipped my glass toward him and said, "Fair enough. It looks beautiful and you did a first-rate job. I remain awestruck at your abilities, yet again."

"Thanks, my dear."

"… and it's about *eff*ing time."

Later that night, we grilled salmon steaks on deck and opened a bottle of Pinot Noir, the last of what we'd moved up from Seattle. Juliet, Jeffery and I sat together on the foredeck and watched the harvest moon rise above Mount Baker, illuminating Bellingham's skyline. "It's been a lovely day," I said. "I got to do nothing at all—except for what I wanted to do."

"And you didn't have to shout orders at anybody either," Juliet chimed in.

"Yes, well there's that too."

We picked up our blankets and glasses and headed below. *Kwaietek* cooled down rapidly, so we closed the ports in the galley and staterooms. "Man, I am wiped out with all of that paddling today," I announced. "I don't know about you guys, but I'm all for calling it a day."

"I'm right behind you on that," Jeff replied.

Kwaietek rolled lazily from side to side as a swell from a passing tugboat reached our dock. I overheard the muffled conversation from Juliet's stateroom as Jeffery gave his goodnights. I pulled back the covers of our bunk and made ready to crawl into bed when Jeff leaned in through the doorway.

"Hey, it's your youngest son on the phone. He'd like to speak with you."

"Ooh, it must be getting close to Kim's due date," I said and reached for the phone. "Hey there Dude, what's up?"

"Hey, *Madre*, I just wanted to let you know that Kim's contractions are like, about five minutes apart. We're on our way to the hospital now."

"Cool—right on! So, how's she doing? How are *you* doing—you nervous?"

"Oh, you know, we're both doin' pretty good… So, are you planning on coming down?"

"You better believe it! We'll keep the phone right next to the bunk so we can hear the call. It's only an hour-and-a-half to get there. Just call me when they're about two minutes apart, OK?"

"OK. Two minutes apart. Got it. Well, we better go now I guess. We'll be seein' you pretty soon."

"Hey. Congrats, you. Tell Kim good luck—and to remember to breathe! And don't forget—*two* minutes apart, OK?"

"Got it. Love ya *Madre*."

"And I love you, too."

Juliet called out from her stateroom, "Mom, is Kim having her baby now?"

"Yeah, well, she's starting to have her baby," I replied. "Remember, she's a first-time mom, so it might take a little while. But I bet that you'll be an auntie once more by tomorrow sometime."

Part of me wanted to drive down to Seattle right then for the entire labor, but I resisted the temptation. I remembered from my days as a doula how too many family and friends could disrupt the process. I wasn't Kimberly's mom, or even her mother-in-law, yet. From what Dane had told us, Kim had an extensive network of women from her Peruvian family that were attending. I imagined what it might look like in that small birth suite, with five or six Latina women chatting in Spanish

344

throughout the labor—and Dane the only non-Spanish-speaker and male in the room.

I thought about the birth of another grandchild—this one at Ballard's childbirth center. *My old stomping grounds.* I couldn't deny my ambivalent reluctance to revisit that part of my life again. I pushed those memories out of my head and climbed into bed, setting the phone next to my pillow.

The much-anticipated call arrived around seven-thirty the next morning. An exhausted-sounding Dane reported that Kim's contractions were occurring every one to two minutes apart. I discerned the apprehension in his voice. "You doing OK?"

"Oh, yeah," he answered. "It's crazy around here, but I'm doin' good. I gotta go though. I'll see you soon probably—right?"

"I'm getting dressed now. We'll head out right away and be in Seattle as soon as we can. Hang in there, dude," I said. "Tell Kim we're pulling for her—and remind her to take some deep relaxing breaths."

Dane signed off and I put the phone on top of the quilt. Jeff mumbled from underneath the blankets, "I take it we're heading down to Seattle now."

"Yup, the dude sounds like he could use some reinforcements," I replied. "I'm not sure if this is exactly Dane's cuppa tea."

"Well, he did go to all of the childbirth classes and even took a dad's class, didn't he?" Jeff asked.

"Uh huh, he's done great—but I think he's reached his *Waterloo.* Let's get dressed." I strolled into Juliet's room and shook her awake. "Pssst, wake up. Do you want to head down to Seattle and see your new niece?"

"Oh boy, yes!" She bounced out of her covers. I returned to our stateroom, bumping into Jeffery as he struggled to get into his Levi's. He balanced on one leg as he yanked on the jeans. "Man, you're not much good at that first thing in the morning, are you?" I quipped. "Good thing the boat's not sinking."

"I prefer to have a cup or two of coffee in my system before I negotiate this process," he stated.

"Well, I'll see to it that you're well caffeinated before we place you behind the wheel of the car."

"Yeah, I'd greatly appreciate that," he said as he buttoned his fly.

By the time we pulled into the parking lot of Swedish Ballard Medical Center it promised to be another stunning August day in the Northwest. I wondered what my crew would be up to at nine o'clock in the morning. I figured they'd be raising sails about now, and if I remembered their itinerary correctly, they'd be in Reid Harbor. I wondered if Calen had whipped the wayward intern into shape. I pictured Tim at the wheel, eyeballing the mainsail as it climbed its way up the mast, biting back the urge to correct Calen once the peak got too high… I smiled, and then returned my thoughts to my own son and the event at hand.

As Jeffery came around the car and opened my door for me, Juliet popped out of the back seat and yelled, "I'm going in first!"

"Hold on!" I stopped her before she tore through the parking lot. "Don't you think it would be nice to run over to the florist and pick out some flowers for Kim?"

"Oh yeah—can I pick out which ones to give her?"

"We'll see."

We strolled across the street and found some pink roses in a small vase. Juliet picked out a card and we all signed it. The florist wrapped a yellow bow around the box and handed it to Juliet. "Is this for you?" the woman asked.

"My brother and his girlfriend are having their baby!" Juliet exclaimed.

"Oh, well then, we should put some of these in with the flowers, don't you think?" She placed several branches of baby's breath in the bouquet and handed one to Juliet.

Once the floral arrangement was to my daughter's satisfaction, we headed over to the hospital. Juliet began to recount the times she'd been by its familiar landmarks—and they numbered many. I could feel my pulse accelerate as we drew closer to the lobby entrance. I had not been back to this setting since I'd closed Gracewinds.

I paused at the familiar statue of a mother lifting her baby overhead and recalled how often I'd rushed by those figures on my way to a birth. Suddenly, too many memories from those days elbowed their way back into my thoughts. Jeffery stopped in his tracks and turned toward me. "You alright?"

"Yeah. But… it's been a long time, huh? Seems like a different universe," I said. "It's sort of weird for me to come back here again."

"I imagine so." He walked over to where I stood, gazing at the granite sculpture. He gestured toward it and said, "Y'know, I never really liked that thing; it's way too '70s style for my taste." He waited for me to reply and when I didn't, he asked, "Anything I can do for you?"

I inhaled quickly and replied, "Nah, I'm OK." I nodded at the statue of the Madonna and child, "I've actually always kind of liked it—she's uncomplicated."

Jeff shrugged and said, "OK. Let's go and see this baby."

We walked along the sidewalk and it struck me, "Hey—y'know, you're a granddad two times over now, *old* man."

"Oh no, I am definitely not; it doesn't count if it belongs to one of the step-kids. You're the grandparent again, not me. I have at least another decade and a half before I get labeled with that title."

Juliet held the door for us. "Come *on*, you guys! I want to go see Dane and Kim!"

Jeff and I hastened our pace. As the glass door slid closed behind us, I glanced around the hospital entryway. Nothing had changed. There was a new coffee cart in the cafeteria entrance, but other than that it looked as it did the day I'd left for good. The senior volunteers at the information desk—still wearing the same burgundy vests emblazoned with "Swedish Hospital, Ballard Campus"—greeted us warmly, and then we made our way to the lobby elevators.

Juliet rushed to be the one to punch the *Up* button and turned to us, asking, "What do you think they're going to name her?"

Jeff responded. "I dunno, but I guess you're about to find out, huh?"

The digital screen announced that we had arrived at the fifth floor. My heart started to pound harder inside my chest. I didn't really know for sure if I wanted to step foot though those Family Childbirth Center doors. That world was long gone for me. I doubted that the nurses, midwives and obstetricians would even recognize me any longer—and maybe I didn't want them to; they'd just remember me as the woman who was once top in her field who'd lost the big prize… that aspiring CEO with such promise whose business collapsed around her. Intense feelings of failure flooded back into my brain. I balked at having to walk through those doors once again.

The elevator came to an abrupt stop and its metal door glided open. I was met with the unforgettable, visceral scent of childbirth. I marveled at how this combination of iodine, blood and some sort of vital *Chi* could produce such deep emotions within me.

Juliet grabbed my elbow and pointed at the wall. "Look, Mom! They still have all of their babies on the wall! Remember all of the Gracewinds babies that were up there?"

"I certainly do, Juliet."

"I wonder if any of them are still there," she said. "I want to see if I recognize any of them."

"Sheesh, Juliet, it's been over three years since Gracewinds was around. The hospital has to change those boards every six or eight months because of how many babies are born here. I don't think there's been a Gracewinds baby up there for several years."

"Do you s'pose they keep all the pictures?" she asked.

"I'm sure they store them somewhere. I don't think the nurses would throw away any photos of babies that were born here." I knew exactly where this conversation was leading.

"So, do you think they still have *my* baby picture then?"

"Oh, most definitely. Especially yours, dear."

"Well, that's good." Satisfied, she bolted ahead toward the nurse's desk.

I took another deep breath and squared my shoulders, and then followed Juliet through the big doors.

The Family Childbirth Center consisted of eight rooms that surrounded the nurse's station like spokes of a ship's wheel. The central space had wood-paneled cabinets and a kitchenette for laboring couples to use. Between the rooms, fanciful posters of newborns nestled amidst fruit, seashells or flowers hung on each wall. I recognized every single detail; it was as if I'd only been absent for a day.

As we approached the desk to check in, I spotted three of the nurses with whom I'd worked closely three years ago. An obstetrician stood near the counter, reviewing a patient's chart. She looked up briefly as we entered and a look of recognition crossed her face. She smiled and nodded politely. But when the unit's receptionist looked up, she exclaimed, "Oh my gosh! Chris! What are you doing here?"

"Hi, Noreen. It's nice to see you—you look really good," I replied. "I'm here to see my youngest son and his girlfriend; they just had their first baby today."

"Wow! You are? That's great! Gee, I hardly recognize you! Hey everybody, remember this lady? It's Gracewinds! Holy smokes, you're so tan and, and well… so blonde! Where have you been?"

At Noreen's greeting, the nurses all turned to face us. One of the labor suite doors opened and my old friend Rose walked toward the station, pushing a bassinet with a newborn baby sleeping inside. She glanced our way and said, "Chris? Wow! You're back!"

The nurses gathered around us to welcome me. Jeffery and Juliet stepped back a few paces and watched as I caught up and exchanged hugs with my former colleagues. Finally, Noreen said, "So, I expect you guys want to know which room your family members are in."

Before we could respond, the door behind us opened and a very sleepy looking Dane walked out into the central area. It didn't register with him that we were standing right in front of him; he walked right past us looking at the screen of his cell phone.

"*Dane!* It's us! We're *here!*" Juliet called out.

Dane startled and looked up. His little sister ran toward him and squeezed him around his waist. He smiled and said, "Hey, little Bug! What's up?"

"I'm good. How's Kim? Where's your new baby?" she asked.

"Good, good—we're all good. She's sleeping with Kim right now. Go on in and see her—I'll be right back in soon, sis."

"OK, bye Dane!" Juliet rushed off in the direction he'd just come from. I watched her pull open the door and slip inside the dimly lit room. Then it hit me: Room 204. *Sara and Charles' room.* The vivid images of that birth came rushing back to me for a brief moment.

I briefly studied Dane, his appearance seemed pretty good overall. In his typical style, he wore a white muscle-tee and baggy jeans. The ever-present silver chain hung around his neck and his Seattle Mariners baseball cap sat askew on his head. There was a decent three-day's growth of beard stubble on his chin. I smiled and gave him a bear hug.

"So, how does it feel to be a papa?" I asked him.

"Whoa. Intense, Mom. It was real intense," he answered, shaking his head.

Jeffery stepped forward and offered Dane his hand. "Congratulations, Mister."

Dane dismissed the handshake and grabbed Jeffery around his shoulders, giving him a long embrace. "Thanks, man. I'm glad you came down... it means a lot."

I smiled to see them together. "So, did she have a good labor?" I asked.

Dane took his cap off briefly and brushed his hand over his closely shorn hair. "Wow. Yeah, she was great. She did a great job. Man... Mom, it was like, *crazy*. I like, stood at the head of the bed—up by her face, y'know. They kept sayin' 'Don't you want to come down here and watch her push?' but I just said, 'Nah man, I'm here for support.'" He shook his head again. "Yeah. Crazy."

At that moment the elevator opened down the hallway and Justine stepped out. She saw us and screamed, "Dane Wallace! Momma! Jeffery! *Aaaaghh!*" She rushed through the big doors and gave us all a bear hug. "I took the bus up from Olympia when I got your text last night."

"Hey, sis," Dane said and buried his head in her neck as he squeezed her tightly. They rocked back and forth for several minutes.

Finally, Jeffery said, "Let's go check out this mini-Dane before Juliet adopts her."

Dane led the way. "Oh hey—you guys just missed Megan. She was here for about an hour before she had to catch the bus.

She's heading over to sail on that tall ship I guess—what's it called—the Chief?"

"The *Hawaiian Chieftain*," Jeff replied.

"Aw, I'd hoped to see her and say goodbye before she left," I said wistfully. "My little sailor girl, heading out to sea all on her own now."

We all walked into the quiet room together, carefully closing the door behind us so as not to disturb the sleeping Kim. I glanced around the familiar suite and that old *deja vu* feeling swept over me—days and nights of attending countless labors in rooms just like this one were etched into my memories.

Kim stirred. She lay back against several pillows and sleepily chatted with Juliet. Her mother sat on the sofa holding the bundled-up newborn baby. She looked up at us and smiled. I returned the smile and whispered, "Hi there, new Grandma."

Justine stepped closer and let out a big sigh. "*Ooh*, she's so pretty!" She sat down next to Kim's mom and gazed upon her new niece. Kim looked over at Justine and said, "That's my mom, Justine. *Madre, ella es la hermana de Dane, Justine.*"

"*Hola*," said Justine

"It's nice to meet you," Kim's mom replied. She placed the baby gently in Justine's arms. "Here is Bri*ella*."

"Cool! So tiny!" Justine said, smiling widely.

I went over to the bed and gave Kim a hug. "Good job, *Mamacita*. What's her full name?"

"Briella Claire Wallace," she said.

I smiled; touched that they'd given her my middle name.

Kim said, "Dane was pretty great. He didn't like the pushing phase very much, but he hung in there."

Dane walked over and stood across the bed from me. He chuckled and added, "Man, there were so many people in here, you couldn't believe it. Kim's mom and her sister and all these cousins…. They all had their phones out and were taking pictures while Kim's pushing and I was like, *Whoa*—she's gonna want to edit those pictures, man."

Kim laughed. "He was standing here and gripping onto the bed—his knuckles were so white, I worried that we'd have to get a nurse for *him* if he passed out on the floor."

Soon enough, several more of Kim's relatives came into the room to see little Briella and there were no more places for people to sit. As the relatives chatted away in Spanish, I took out my phone and snapped some photos. Dane had pushed a chair over to the bed and was resting his head against Kim's arm. They dozed peacefully as all of the respective family members held the baby. Jeff got up and stretched his arms. "Do you want to grab something to eat while they have their turn with the baby?" he asked.

"Yeah. I'll check with Dane to see if he wants us to bring back anything."

When I nudged Dane he jumped. "Huh? Whew, I was really out!"

"Funny how staying up for thirty-some hours can knock you out, huh?"

"Shit, how'd you do it for so many years I wonder?"

"Practice, boy. A lot of practice," I said. "Hey, can I get a picture with you and *Grandpa* Jeff before we go grab some food?"

Dane yawned widely and nodded. "Yeah, sure. Who's holding Briella now?"

"Juliet is hogging her... *again,*" said Justine.

I relieved Auntie Juliet of her new niece and placed the baby in Jeffery's arms. He held her gently, almost awkwardly. "Whatsa matter there, Pops... forgot how to do it?" I joked.

Dane stood beside his stepfather and pulled the receiving blanket away from his daughter's face. The two of them looked down at the baby and smiled. Jeffery said, "Ya done real good, Mister."

I snapped several photos and then just watched the two of them in that moment. My troubled son had matured into a true adult—a father, with a child of his own to worry and care about. I felt the tears well up and wiped my eyes.

"Let's go get something to eat!" Juliet said.

Our dinner at the Ballard *Hi-Life* had mutated into an over-the-top reunion between Justine and her little sister. They teased one another, stole food off each other's plates and switched their desserts back and forth. They entertained us with their arguments and jokes and eventually broke out in a duet rendition of "Bohemian Rhapsody"—so comically that even the waiter joined in the laughter.

Several hours later as we walked back to the hospital, Jeffery and Juliet strolled ahead, kicking a rock back and forth. Justine hung back with me and chatted. "I can't believe how much Dane has grown up lately," she said. "He was definitely making some bad choices for a bunch of years."

"Yep. He's come a long way. I'm pretty darn proud of him," I agreed.

"Ya know, I can't believe how much you've changed too, Mom… In all honesty? I think that losing Gracewinds might have been the best thing for you."

I glanced over at Justine, my eyebrow raised. There she stood beside me, barely an inch of height difference between us. Her hipster glasses coupled with her asymmetric hairstyle gave her a sophisticated appearance. She looked, and now acted, much older than her nineteen years.

She continued her commentary as we strolled along. "It's like an age-reversal thing or something. I used to think you were so uptight and boring. We sort of… y'know, didn't really see eye-to-eye much for about five or six years. Remember? But now, you're like one of the coolest people I know. I tell my friends about how awesome my mom is and how she's kickin' ass on this big boat and everything. Seriously, Mom, they all get really tired of hearing about you."

I laughed. "Well, I'm glad to know that you've finally figured out how ludicrously awesome your mother is!" Before we caught up with Juliet and Jeff, I threw my arm around her shoulder and pulled her closer. "I'm pretty damn pleased with how life has turned out, and how my kids have grown up. You each took different paths to get to where you are now—and some of 'em weren't the roads I'd have chosen… but you've all arrived exactly the way you should be. I'm a really lucky mom—to be able to see it happen."

Before we left Dane and his family that evening, I sat down next to him to chat. I massaged his neck and congratulated him for attending the childbirth and fathering classes. "You've really come a long way. I'm very impressed."

Dane rested his elbows on his knees and folded his hands together underneath his chin. He stared at the floor as I spoke and nodded occasionally. Finally, he turned to face me and said, "You know Mom, I want to do the right thing here. This whole thing's really helped me... kinda see what's important in life, y'know?" He cleared his throat and shook his head. "I really love you, *Madre*. I've learned a lot from you. I'm gonna try and be a good dad to little Briella." I didn't say anything, but sat next to him and kept my arm around his shoulder.

"Anyways, thanks a lot, Mom."

We packed up around eight-thirty that evening. As we pulled the door open to leave, I caught one last glimpse of the new family. Dane was stretched out on the sofa with Briella lying on his chest—both soundly asleep. Kim had propped herself up against a bank of pillows and chatted quietly with her mother, they both waved goodbye as we left the room. I smiled at them and returned a wave before I shut the door behind me.

The nurses at the desk made me promise to visit again. I gave them my email and *Zodiac*'s website information so they could follow our adventures from their desks at work. "Hey— keep some sunscreen on that nose of yours!" Noreen called after me. "You're looking like Rudolf the red nosed reindeer!"

"You got it! I promise!" I laughed, waved goodbye, and caught up with Jeff and Juliet who were holding the elevator for me.

"See. Aren't you glad we came?" Jeff asked.

"I'm *so* glad—I really am."

Chapter 38

The Course Made Good

We spent the next few days off from the *Zodiac* at Trent's farm in Oregon. His son William, had turned four years old earlier that summer. We parked our VW bus in their backyard and popped the canopy-top—William immediately climbed into the top bunk with the windows unzipped; Juliet read him stories and they played 'wilderness explorers' together for hours at a time. Trent piled stacks of wood in their fire pit one evening and I taught my grandson how to make s'mores over the blazing embers. With an actual yard to run around in once again, Juliet romped in their sprinkler until mosquitoes drove her back inside.

On our last evening, we sat outside with Trent and Jessica while the kids played in the house. The late summer heat had baked the fields of corn and sugar beets that surrounded their farm and lent a sweet, earthy quality to the air. The stereo played John Prine and we listened to music as we talked. I sat back in my chair and watched the fire crackle.

It pleased me to see the good life Trenton had made for himself and his family here on their farm. Even though I no longer wished for permanent ties to land, it made me happy that he had created just that—a big yard where the dogs could run, a home where his kids could grow up and good friends nearby with whom to share it.

Late the next morning we said farewell to Trent and family. William ran up to his 'Auntie Juliet' and squeezed her long and hard. "We'll see you all for the holidays!" I called out as Jeffery backed the bus out of their drive. "Take care!"

The bus made good time northbound on I-5 and soon enough we crossed the I-205 bridge that separated Oregon from Washington. I dozed in the passenger seat with one bare foot propped on the dash and the other resting on the side-view mirror outside—*Hippie* cruising, as Jeffery called it. My cell rang and roused me from my nap. It was Megan.

"Hey there, sailor! How's the *Hawaiian Chieftain*?" I asked.

"Hi Momma! I'm having such a blast out here!" Megan launched into her story. "We left three days ago from Coos Bay and got into San Francisco early this morning. There were, like, fifteen-foot waves on the open ocean—and everyone was puking. I didn't puke, but I felt really queasy. Then, I thought I'd probably feel better if I made myself throw up, so I leaned over the rail and stuck my finger in my mouth—and I threw up just when this beautiful dolphin came up out of the waves…and it had all this phosphorescence all over—it was actually *sparkling!* So, I like, threw up all over this glittery dolphin—but it didn't care, I think. Anyways, it was the most magical thing ever!"

"Wow," I said. "That *is* pretty incredible, I guess, for you and for the dolphin."

"Yeah. It's so awesome here, 'cept I'm pretty sunburnt."

"Where are you guys going after San Francisco?"

"Uhm, we head up river and then we're spending two months or so in Sacramento. Hey—I've got more 'near coastal' sea days than you do now. How 'bout that?!"

"Good on ya. You'll be getting your captain's license before you know it."

"I might just do that," she said. "Hey, we've gotta day-sail in a few minutes, so I have to go. I just wanted to call and say I love you guys lots and wish I'd been able to see you when Dane's baby was born—tell Jeff and Juliet I love 'em… Bye!"

"So long, ya little *yarrbeedar!*"

Jeff glanced over and smiled. "I guess she's having a good time on the high seas?"

"Oh, most definitely."

Back in Bellingham, we made the most of my remaining shore-leave. Some of our friends came over to *Kwaietek* and we grilled oysters on the BBQ. Jeffery took a break from cabinetry work and the three of us sailed *Sugaree* to Pleasant Bay for an overnight trip. I managed to spend a few more hours in my kayak and gave Juliet some paddling pointers as well. One evening she surprised us both and said, "I'm going to watch a movie on my computer while you and Dad go out to dinner—happy anniversary!"

Jeffery and I put on our date night clothes and left Juliet alone with Lucky Jack. We drove along the winding road called Chuckanut Drive to our favorite restaurant. Sitting outside on the deck that overlooked Samish Bay, we drank our wine and quietly watched the sun sink behind Lummi Island. The fading crimson sky reflected across the water—so peculiar to observe from land.

The San Juan Islands' dotted the horizon, their silhouettes fluctuating between hues of blue and green. Jeffery leaned over and placed his hand on my leg. "I'd totally do it all again—all of it. After sixteen years, I'm still crazy about you, my dear."

My vacation time drew to an end. On my first day back, I woke in time to shower and grab a quick breakfast before heading to the Z. I stuffed my sailing gear back inside the duffle bag and yanked my jacket off its peg in the passageway. Jeff pressed a pot of coffee and we climbed on-deck to enjoy a few more minutes together. *Kwaietek*'s fantail was already in full sun and our teak deckchairs had absorbed the morning heat. "It's gonna turn into a scorcher today... it'll be one of those 'bob and bake' kind of sails before you anchor tonight," Jeff predicted.

"Yup, the jellyfish may very well beat us to Echo Bay if this keeps up."

Juliet came out of the galley to join us carrying Lucky Jack under one arm and balancing a bowl of strawberries in the other. "Mom, may I borrow the kayak while you're on the next cruise? I won't take it past the breakwater unless dad says it's OK."

Jeffery chuckled. "It's a boat-kid's version of asking to borrow the car keys!"

"Yeah, I reckon you're good enough now that you can go by yourself—but stay around Gate Five and only paddle when your dad's around here. Cool?"

"Thanks, Mom. I swear I won't wreck the kayak."

My cell buzzed, vibrating itself right off the table—it was a text from Calen, informing me that there weren't enough bunks for all the crew. His message ended with a plaintive, "Come back!"

"Sounds like it's work time. The natives are growing restless."

"Well, it sure was fun having you to myself for a couple of weeks," Jeff said.

I polished off my cup of java and leaned over to give him a kiss. "Just four days this time, and I'm home."

I climbed aboard the *Zodiac* and waved a quick hello to the deckhands. Everyone had finished their pre-voyage duties and now occupied themselves with extra projects from the bosun's list. I ducked into the charthouse and saw Calen at the chart-table, filling out forms. He gave me the bunk chart and we sorted out crew assignments. Afterward, Calen pushed the log book toward me and said, "Here ya go doll, it's all yours again—oh, and I didn't get around to filling in the watch schedule yet." He went below for more coffee and turned back to face me at the bottom step. "It's good to have you back, by the way."

Before long, our enthusiastic passengers were brought onboard. They were guided to their seats on the salon-house and my crew lined up next to the main mast. I came back on deck to do the orientation.

"Hey everybody, welcome aboard! We're glad to have you out sailing with us this weekend. My name is Chris and I'm the first mate on the schooner *Zodiac*. Lemme give you a quick run-down on the ship and some safety tips. First off, does anyone know what this is called? Well—it's a 'rope' on land, but when we're on a boat, it becomes a 'line.' Now, we have these lines that run through these things called 'blocks'—on land they're called 'pulleys.' The lines are meant to run through the blocks, but your fingers aren't. So try and remember to keep your hands at least twelve inches away when you're working on-deck. Got it? Now, there are four sails on this ship: far up forward, we've got the jib..."

When Tim arrived, the *Z* was prepped and ready to leave the dock. The passengers had disappeared below to find their berths and some were roaming about the ship, acquainting themselves with her details. After Tim had stowed his gear in his stateroom and stopped in the charthouse to check the log book, he walked aft and found me on the quarterdeck. "OK, so you're fresh as a daisy now, right?" he asked.

"Fresh as the morning dew, Boss."

"What's our wind and current doing?"

I stepped over to the caprail and looked at the water. It seemed slack and clear. Glancing up in the rig, I looked for the telltales. They fluttered softly with a southward breeze.

"There's no current to mention and a light southerly from our stern," I said.

"Alright then. What's your plan?"

"Cast off the number one line and then call for two and four. After that, I'm springing off number three and we're outta here."

"OK. Let's go for a ride."

I fired up the engine and called for deckhands. *Zodiac* sprang away from the dock and slid out into the bay. Tim invited one of the older passengers who'd been eying the helm-station to take the wheel, and then asked him to give "three spokes to port." The *Z* turned westward and the elderly man was directed to "steady up." His face beamed as he followed the captain's orders.

Once we were on a course for Vendovi Island, I asked Tim, "Shall we call them all together?"

"Yep, let's raise 'em and play out here for a while,"

With little effort, the crew and passengers raised the sails and *Zodiac* fell off the wind by a few degrees. "Let's tack and then we'll set 'em," Tim said.

"You got it." I stepped forward of the scuttle and cupped my hands near my mouth. "All hands to sailing stations—prepare to come about!" I then called "Helm's a*lee*!" and the ship turned into the eye of the wind. As she came about, her sails moved in unison, drawing fully. "Set your sails!"

The *Zodiac* glided forward toward Rosario Strait.

Christine Wallace is the author of two books including *The Pocket Doula* and *Prepare to Come About*. Her work has appeared in the literary journal *Clover* (vol. 3, 2012 and vol. 6, 2014). Christine was founder and CEO of "Gracewinds Perinatal Inc." She is a mother of five children and a grandmother of six. Christine holds a USCG 200-ton captain's license and currently resides in the Pacific Northwest onboard an ex-forestry boat with her husband, youngest daughter and a seaworthy tabby named Lucky Jack.

Christine can be contacted through Windline Press.

windlinepress@gmail.com   windlinepress.com

Made in the USA
San Bernardino, CA
06 November 2014